North of El Norte

North of El Norte

Illegalized Mexican Migrants in Canada

PALOMA E. VILLEGAS

UBCPress · Vancouver · Toronto

Chapters 3 and 4 originally published in a slightly different form in Paloma E. Villegas, 2013, "Assembling a Visa Requirement against the Mexican 'Wave': Migrant Illegalization, Policy and Affective 'Crisis' in Canada," *Ethnic and Racial Studies* 36 (12): 2200–19; and Paloma E. Villegas, 2015, "Moments of Humiliation, Intimidation and Implied 'Illegality': Encounters with Immigration Officials at the Border and the Performance of Sovereignty," *Journal of Ethnic and Migration Studies* 41 (14): 2357–75. Reprinted by permission of the publisher (Taylor and Francis Ltd.).

29 28 27 26 25 24 23 22 21 20 5 4 3 2 1

Printed in Canada on FSC-certified ancient-forest-free paper (100% post-consumer recycled) that is processed chlorine- and acid-free.

Library and Archives Canada Cataloguing in Publication

Title: North of el norte : illegalized Mexican migrants in Canada / Paloma E. Villegas.
Names: Villegas, Paloma E., author.
Description: Includes bibliographical references and index.
Identifiers: Canadiana (print) 20200259466 | Canadiana (ebook) 20200259628 | ISBN 9780774863377 (hardcover) | ISBN 9780774863391 (PDF) | ISBN 9780774863407 (EPUB) | ISBN 9780774863414 (Kindle)
Subjects: LCSH: Mexicans—Government policy—Canada. | LCSH: Mexicans—Canada—Social conditions. | LCSH: Immigrants—Canada. | LCSH: Canada—Emigration and immigration—Government policy. | LCSH: Mexico—Emigration and immigration.
Classification: LCC FC106.M5 V55 2020 | DDC 305.8/6872071—dc23

Canadä

UBC Press gratefully acknowledges the financial support for our publishing program of the Government of Canada (through the Canada Book Fund), the Canada Council for the Arts, and the British Columbia Arts Council.

This book has been published with the help of a grant from the Canadian Federation for the Humanities and Social Sciences, through the Awards to Scholarly Publications Program, using funds provided by the Social Sciences and Humanities Research Council of Canada.

UBC Press
The University of British Columbia
2029 West Mall
Vancouver, BC V6T 1Z2
www.ubcpress.ca

Para Chuy, Carmen, y Pancho, mi familia de sangre y del alma.

Contents

Acknowledgments

I want to thank the research participants who shared their experiences with me. In writing this book, my goal is to illustrate the complicated ways in which migrants navigate, endure (*aguantan*), and resist oppressive structures and construct meaningful lives.

This book was difficult to write. And it could not have been done without my family. I therefore want to begin by thanking my husband Jesus Maya for his support throughout this process. *Eres la persona mas generosa que conozco. Me inspiras todos los dias. Tu mente, tu corazon, tu alma, y tus palabras. Tu trajiste el arte a mi vida, la musica, los colores.*

A mi mama, una migrante luchona, feminista quien me enseño la importancia de la educación, no solo en la escuela sino también en como tratar a la gente con respeto. Es mi campiona numero uno.

For my brother and colleague, Francisco Villegas, I could not have chosen a better person with whom to make my academic journey. He is truly the only person that can understand the experiences of pain and joy that are involved with my personal and academic engagement with migration.

I would also like to thank my mentors in Toronto: Patricia Landolt and Luin Goldring. They took me under their wings. They embody important aspects of the academic I hope to become: generous, interested in social justice, and committed to their work and students. I also want to thank Kari Dehli and Roland Sintos Coloma who cultivated my love of theory.

Finally, I want to thank my colleagues and friends in Toronto and California who supported me throughout the writing of the book with their feedback, smiles, and presence.

North of El Norte

Introduction

Leonel arrived in Canada at the end of 2001. International security concerns were high at the time, but he found it relatively easy to enter the country because there was no visa requirement for Mexican nationals. He arrived as a tourist and then lost his status. Years later he applied for refugee status on the advice of a friend. The claim was denied. Leonel received a removal order and became enveloped in a surveillance web that made him vigilant as he worked and moved around the city, knowing that immigration authorities and the police could be looking for him at any moment.

Zyanya arrived in Canada in 2006 as a tourist after deciding that she wanted to "see the world." Her visa expired as she worked in a series of factories, where managers and co-workers made life difficult because of her immigration status, race, and gender. She eventually found a decent job that promised an employment-sponsored work visa and began to hope for a more secure future, only to find out that the company had been sold and that the new management was not interested in sponsoring her. Zyanya's and Leonel's creative projects helped the two to keep their hopes up throughout their uncertain time and legal statuses in Canada.

Libertad arrived in the mid-2000s, fleeing persecution after exposing corruption in her workplace. She applied for refugee status. While awaiting a response, she became pregnant. However, the child's father was physically, financially, and emotionally abusive. At one point, she had to juggle her immigration case, a child custody case, and a criminal case against him. When her refugee claim was refused, she became deportable and had to rethink her participation in the criminal case.

In the fall of 2006, I made my own journey to Canada. I did not know it at the time, but like Leonel, Zyanya, and Libertad I was part of a growing number of Mexicans travelling to Canada to study, live, work, and/or seek protection. I arrived as an international PhD student after living undocumented in the United States for almost fifteen years. I expected Canada to be very different spatially, culturally, and in terms of its immigration regime. My first impressions were that, though the houses and roads looked very similar, there was a striking absence of Spanish speakers as I walked around Toronto. Coming from California, this was new to me. Were there not many Latinxs in the city? Was I not looking in the right places? I eventually found a Latinx and Mexican presence with varying degrees of immigration status. One of the lessons that I learned, which informs the trajectory of this book, is that the ways in which Mexicans become "undocumented" or experience periods of less than full immigration status are not the same as those in the United States, though there are definite parallels. Navigating the intricacies of immigration status in Canada reveals how the boundaries of citizenship and belonging are becoming increasingly cemented, extended, as well as resisted and blurred.

Each year Mexican migrants who travel to Canada with insecure or precarious immigration status add to these stories. Precarious status is an umbrella categorization for various types of vulnerable immigration status (i.e., not permanent residence or citizenship) (Goldring, Berinstein, and Bernhard 2009). It includes temporary foreign workers, refugees, refugee claimants, refused refugee claimants, international students, visitors, spouses being sponsored for permanent residence, and anyone with an expired study or work visa. Many people who experience precarious status also experience violence. A recurring theme in their stories is the idea of *aguantar,* tolerating injustice, violence, and dehumanization at the border or in the workplace and/or community as well as a lack of access to social entitlements. However, stories also demonstrate the piecing together of meaningful and dignified lives, waiting for the right moment to act despite the forces that seek to exclude them.

This book has two interlayered objectives. The first is to provide a snapshot of the context of Mexican migration to Canada, particularly for those arriving without permanent residence in the mid-2000s and 2010s. Much of the research about Mexican migrants, particularly those who do not have secure immigration status, focuses on migration to the United States. However, the transformation of social, political, and economic structures at the end of the twentieth century and the beginning of the twenty-first century have led to a diversification of migration strategies and points of destination, making Mexican migration to Canada important.

During this time, immigration policies and practices were transformed globally, some of which influenced local experiences of precarious status in Canada. For example, post-9/11 discourses of national security circulated widely, aligning with increasingly punitive immigration policies that intensified border, detention, and deportation regimes globally (Ashutosh and Mountz 2011; Coutin 2015; De Genova and Peutz 2010; Flynn 2015; Gibney 2006). Activist responses also became more visible, including mobilizations against US House Resolution 4437 in 2006 (Gonzales 2008) and later the development of the DREAMer and Undocumented and Unafraid movements (Nicholls 2013), the Sans Papiers in France (Hong 2014), as well as the building of immigrant rights coalitions such as No One Is Illegal in Canada. At the same time, increasing *insecuritization* in the Global South, as well as the global recession in the late 2000s, led more people to evaluate cross-border movement as an option.

For Mexicans travelling to Canada without permanent residence, this period had both ups and downs, including relatively easy entry because of the lack of a visa requirement (until 2009 and after 2016), a high possibility of entering precarious labour markets in Canada, various ways to attempt to stay and "regularize" (including through refugee claims), and the vilification of those deemed "bogus refugees." These interrelated processes provide a context for examining the changing landscape of immigration policy and practice, the categorization of non-citizens, and their experiences navigating these structures. These are not easy narratives or binary understandings of exploitation and resistance. Instead, they are complicated examples of immigration regimes' attempts at capturing, categorizing, and banishing migrants and the practices employed to navigate and challenge these processes.

They also inform my second objective, to build on existing theoretical frameworks to understand migration, the production of migrant illegalization, and the concept of assemblage. Overall, the book will help to clarify the different processes that influence public understandings and experiences of migration and migrant illegalization and how these processes affect social, economic, and political life.

Contextualizing Mexican Migration to Canada

Canada as a Settler Colonial State

Canada is a white settler colonial society whose history is intertwined with the genocide of Indigenous peoples, the exclusion or differential inclusion of non-white subjects, and the exaltation of white citizens (Thobani 2007; Walia 2013). Until the 1960s, these ideologies were manifested through explicitly racist immigration policies and limited access to citizenship and self-determination for racialized and Indigenous nations (Bohaker and Iacovetta 2009; Dua 2007; Mongia 2003; Oikawa 2000). After the Second World War, unmet labour demands and the decline of European immigration prompted changes to these explicitly racist policies. One example was the entrenchment of a liberal multicultural project in Canadian nation building and its effects on immigration policy and practice. Although seemingly open and welcoming, multiculturalism essentialized racialized groups to their "exotic" foods and festivals, making them palatable for "mainstream" Canadian audiences and a global neoliberal cosmopolitan project while continuing their invisibilization and neutralizing their equity demands (Bannerji 2000; Sharma 2011; Thobani 2007).

In terms of immigration policy changes, the postwar period saw the development and prioritization of economic immigration streams (Simmons 2010). These streams promote class-based exclusions while implicitly continuing a racialized nation-building project (Chatterjee 2015). For example, the implementation of the Skilled Worker Program in the 1960s focused on importing workers permanently to fill labour needs. Immigrants were hand-selected for their qualifications: language skills, work experience, "Canadian experience," amount of savings/income, and educational attainment. The government has amended the program through the years, most recently with the implementation of the Express Entry system in 2015 (Bhuyan et al. 2017; Citizenship and Immigration Canada 2017).

Alongside a skilled migration agenda, the 1973 Non-Immigrant Employment Authorization Program (NIEAP) specifically recruited "guest" workers for "low-skill" work (Sharma 2002). Initially, it sought agricultural workers (Basok 2003), but now temporary migrant workers participate in a number of both low-wage and "skilled" sectors. Temporary migration streams have grown significantly since the 1970s (Basok 2003; Nakache and Kinoshita 2010). Currently, migrant workers coming into Canada each year outnumber new permanent residents, signalling a shift away from permanent "settlement" – a term used to refer to the process of immigrating permanently into Canada whose link to colonialist ideas about settlers is not accidental – as a nation-building strategy to fill labour needs and toward precarious conditions and deportability (Nakache 2013).

In addition to economic streams, immigrants can enter Canada through family reunification, which entails being sponsored by a spouse or close family member. However, policies in the late 2000s and early 2010s implemented barriers to family reunification, including long application periods as well as the limiting of sponsorship streams. For spousal sponsorship, the government implemented a two-step process in which spouses received conditional permanent residence for two years before receiving the full benefits of permanent residence (Citizenship and Immigration Canada 2012a). This policy (revoked in 2017) limited divorce during the conditional period, making a spouse dependent on her or his partner, and was influenced by the perception of a growth in "fraudulent marriages" (see Chapter 5). The focus on "fraud" and dishonesty was a recurring trend during that period, illustrating a lack of trust of non-citizens who sought to achieve secure status (Gaucher 2014). The sponsorship of parents and grandparents was also curtailed, mostly because of concerns that they would create an "undue" expense, particularly for the health-care system (Root et al. 2014).

Refugee determination is also structured through a racial logic (Razack 1998). The system underwent a number of changes in the late 2000s and early 2010s, including the designation of two streams for inland applications: applicants from "safe" and from "unsafe" countries (Silverman 2014). The former, which included Mexican nationals beginning in 2013, are subjected to a more stringent process, in terms of both evaluation and the period to submit supporting documents. Like the changes to family reunification, these changes drew on entrenched discourses of fraudulent claimants or bogus refugees (Pratt 2005; Pratt and Valverde 2002).

Finally, though there has been little public discussion of the "undocumented" or non-status population, its presence has been documented in policy and academic texts. Citing a 1982 report from the Canada Employment and Immigration Advisory Council, Robinson (1984) estimated the undocumented population in Canada at 200,000, a figure that he argued was similar to estimates in the 1970s but nonetheless led to public anxiety. More recently, it has been estimated that between 20,000 and 500,000 migrants live without status in the country, leading to similar manifestations of anxiety, though those numbers have not been corroborated and might actually be much higher if we include a broader definition of precarious status (City of Toronto 2015; Jimenez 2003; Standing Committee on Citizenship and Immigration 2009). Non-status and other precarious status migrants face the ever-present possibility of deportation, a process that augments their exploitation. Therefore, non-status workers fill gaps in the Canadian labour market while receiving limited benefits and experiencing long-term temporariness (Bailey et al. 2002; Vosko, Preston, and Latham 2014).

Toronto: The Land of "Diversity"

Although situated within the national landscape of immigration policy, much of my research occurred in Toronto. It is an important immigrant gateway and a major destination for im/migrants to Canada, particularly Mexicans (Lujan 2017). Its motto has been "Diversity, Our Strength" since 1998, and through this branding the city draws on existing discourses of multiculturalism that have shaped the Canadian imaginary since the 1970s and 1980s (City of Toronto 2018; Wood and Gilbert 2005). In recent years, the city has emphasized equity measures related to undocumented migrants, anti-black racism, reconciliation with Indigenous peoples, and poverty reduction (City of Toronto 2015, 2018). However, these policies have come short because of jurisdictional tensions related to service provision, the power of policing authorities and their continuation of racial profiling, the spatial organization of poverty, health-care disparities, and neoliberal erosions to social entitlements (Hulchanski 2010; Meng 2017; Noble 2009; No One Is Illegal Toronto 2015; United Way 2011). In short, City of Toronto policies can be tasked with what Ahmed (2004b) calls non-performatives: declarations that "do not do what they say" and instead maintain the status quo.

"Counting" Mexicans

Given this context, why did Mexicans travel to Canada, and what types of "reception" did they experience when they arrived in the late 2000s and early 2010s? Canada is a top migration destination for Mexicans after the United States and Europe (mainly Spain) (Instituto de los Mexicanos en el Exterior 2016). From 2006 to 2011, individuals from Latin America and the Caribbean made up 12.3 percent of the foreign-born immigrant population in Canada (Statistics Canada 2013). Mexico is a top-three country of immigration from that region (Latin America) and a top-ten source country overall (Statistics Canada 2013). However, official numbers do not tell the full story, for not everyone registers or is counted by the Instituto de los Mexicanos en el Exterior (Institute for Mexicans Abroad), which measures out-migration, or the Canadian government, which measures in-migration.

Mexican migrants arrive in Canada in various ways: as landed immigrants (permanent residents), refugee claimants, tourists, or on work or student visas. The migration of Mexicans under these streams has been increasing since the 1990s for several reasons (Escalante 2004; George and Young 2006; Lujan 2017; Mueller 2005). First is the relative proximity between the two countries, not only in terms of distance but also in political and trade relationships, particularly after the North American Free Trade Agreement was implemented in 1994. Second is that, until 2009 and after December 2016, Mexican migrants did not need a visa to enter Canada (see Chapter 3). Third is the level of migration through temporary migrant worker programs (Basok 2003; Preibisch and Hermoso Santamaria 2006). Since 1974, Mexico and Canada have had a bilateral agreement to export Mexican workers for temporary periods to work in the Canadian agricultural sector through the Seasonal Agricultural Worker Program (SAWP). Although workers are documented and have work permits for set periods, they have insecure immigration status and are subject to the ongoing possibility of deportation. Because they are considered low skilled, these workers cannot apply for permanent residence as workers.

Table 1.1 lists the numbers of Mexicans who entered Canada from 2003 to 2015. As illustrated, the rate of permanent residence has risen through the years, but it is low compared with migrant workers and students, whose rates have steadily increased. Refugee claimants increased sharply until

TABLE 1.1
Mexican im/migrants to Canada by category

Year	Permanent residents	Temporary migrant workers	International students	Refugee claimants
2003	1,738			
2004	2,245	11,153	5,582	2,827
2005	2,851	12,266	5,871	3,461
2006	2,830	13,901	6,291	4,946
2007	3,224	16,967	6,481	7,248
2008	2,831	20,745	6,458	9,491
2009	3,092	18,180	6,733	7,614
2010	3,865	18,152	7,108	1,200
2011	3,947	19,115	7,606	653
2012	4,227	21,056	8,094	322
2013	3,996	21,842	8,429	84
2014	4,478	22,521	8,367	80
2015	3,231	22,966	8,241	111
2016	3,400	25,918	9,066	260

Sources: Citizenship and Immigration Canada 2014, 2015; Government of Canada 2015a, 2015b, 2018a, 2018b.

2008, given the widespread insecuritization in Mexico. They then decreased after the visa requirement in 2009 as well as the designation of Mexico as a "safe country" in 2013. Finally, rates increased again when the government rescinded the visa requirement in late 2016.

In addition, in 2008 Mexicans made 257,000 trips to Canada and spent a total of $364 million Canadian, ranking Mexican tourists fifth in terms of spending and sixth in number of trips to Canada (Statistics Canada 2009). This revenue decreased after the 2009 visa requirement but remained significant: in 2015, 190,000 Mexicans travelled to Canada, spending $330 million Canadian (Statistics Canada 2016). After the travel visa requirement was lifted in 2016, tourism again increased steadily (Statistics Canada 2018). Importantly, a tourist visa is a common pathway to precarious status (see Chapter 2). In terms of return migration, because of the high numbers of temporary migrants and refugee claimants in Canada, Mexicans have also been subject to high rates of removal orders (and by extension deportations; see Chapter 3).

These statistics provide a background for the stories shared here. They illustrate the opening and closing of borders as well as the Canadian state's push and pull between a desire for in-migration, workers, and consumers, on the one hand, and a focus on national security and border management, on the other. The statistics also signal the numerous untold stories of violence, resilience, and triumph.

Theorizing Assemblage, Migration, and Migrant Illegalization

Assemblage

Global migration flows, patterns, and regimes have been reorganized over the past few decades (Sassen 2010). Examples include increased border and immigration controls, an extension of borders beyond and within the nation-state (Frelick, Kysel, and Podkul 2016; Gibney 2006), reformulations of citizenship (Rygiel 2011), and increased emphasis on both free trade and national security. These reorganizations illustrate how migration processes are interconnected to other social, political, and geographic events and actors. Given this reorganization, migration involves a multifarious set of practices that includes the movement of people across different types of borders, facilitated or made difficult by technologies of documentation, surveillance, and detention as well as discourses about the viability and desirability of such movements. These practices are affected by political, social, emotional, and ethical relationships. Therefore, though migration cannot be reduced to, or explained in its entirety by, factors such as neoliberal restructuring, unfettered capitalism, organized crime, heteropatriarchy, white supremacy, borders, migrant illegalization, and insecuritization, it can become *assembled* with these factors in contextually situated ways. As an analytical tool, assemblage is useful for framing, disentangling, and understanding such social phenomena.

Daniel (2013, 7) tracks one root of the term "assemblage" to the French *assemblance* and links the term to "arrangement," as in physical bodies made up of component parts and the coming together of people, as "an assembly, a crowd, a gathering of distinct bodies." Alternatively, according to Deleuze and Guattari (1987, 23), who use the French *agencement,* "an assemblage establishes connections between certain multiplicities" and operates along two axes. The first axis includes "bodies, of actions and passions," as well as "expression" – "a collective assemblage of enunciation, of acts and statements, of incorporeal transformations attributed to bodies" (88). This axis can reveal relationships among "things" in the physical landscape (bodies, places, states, territories, machines, actions), language (discourse), and emotions. The second axis includes spatial and temporal components (de/territorialization). It can clarify the relationships among bodies, language, and emotions from the first axis as they occur in space and time as well as the possibility that such relationships become unstable and reorganized or de/territorialized (88).

Three aspects of assemblages are particularly relevant to my analysis. First, assemblages are *fluid* yet available for examination and inquiry (Ong and Collier 2005; Puar 2005). They can be imagined as having frayed or textured edges that change over time. However, this definition does not mean that assemblages are constantly being rearranged and therefore are unexaminable. An assemblage "brings together disparate elements – social actors, relations of power, regulations, discursive frames, bureaucracies, sectors, etc. – in patterned and changing ways" (Landolt and Goldring 2015, 854). The specificity of elements and how they are situated within space and time provide fruitful avenues for social analysis: we can track their temporal and spatial shifts and relationships to other phenomena.

Second, assemblages are *relational* (Anderson, Kearnes, and McFarlane 2012; DeLanda 2006; Dittmer 2014; Olds and Thrift 2005): they are determined by the relationships among elements or their "agreements of convenience" (Olds and Thrift 2005, 271). These agreements are important to map the relationships among processes that might not, at first glance, be connected. Relationality also means that an assemblage should be considered a "process of becoming" instead of a concrete event (Anderson, Kearnes, and McFarlane 2012; Marcus and Saka 2006, 102).

Third, assemblages are *productive*. They can create newly articulated spaces or forms. These outputs reveal how value is organized in society. Ong (2005, 338) argues that assemblages "not only create their own spaces, but also give diverse values to the practices and actors thus connected to each other." This linking involves power, or what Mezzadra and Neilson (2013) refer to as "assemblages of power," which circulates across and through assemblage elements given the specific spatiotemporal context (Dittmer

2014). I use assemblage to examine such power relations and their connections to insecuritization, precarity, borders, and migrant illegalization, thinking through the often fragile interconnections and entanglements among elements.

My analysis emphasizes five interrelated elements. The first is *ways of knowing* and focuses on knowledge production and how understandings and interpretations of social phenomena are produced in different contexts. This involves the formal production of policy (immigration, labour, health care), academic scholarship, personal experience, and other informational outputs. Such knowledge is produced by and about different *actors* (the second element). Actors include migrants, politicians, non-migrants, reporters, and border and immigration agents. Knowledge production takes work and operates in different contexts or sites, organized under the third element: *institutions* or *organizations*. Included in this element are academia and schooling, the law and criminal justice system, the media, the family, social services, faith-based organizations, and economic institutions. Sometimes these actors and institutions utilize the fourth element – *technologies* – including databases, biometrics, forms of identification, to store and disseminate *ways of knowing*. Therefore, assemblages produce, affect, and are affected by relations among people, institutions, governments, and the types of information that circulate among them. They also produce and mobilize affect or socially circulated *ways of feeling* about migration and its associated processes. Each of these elements exists within a *spatiotemporal* context: changes in time and space can rearticulate elements or make them unnecessary.

Citizenship, Migrant Illegalization, and Precarity

A growing body of literature employs the framework of assemblage to understand the fluid, relational, and productive aspects of migration, bordering, and non-citizenship (Bailey 2013; Landolt and Goldring 2015; Leitner and Strunk 2014; Lindquist 2018; Mezzadra and Neilson 2013; Ong and Collier 2005; Puar 2007; Villegas 2015a). My analysis of Mexican migration to Canada contributes to these conversations in several ways.

First, I draw on theories of citizenship to understand how precarious status migrants enact claims to membership despite formal legal status. Citizenship involves "*both* a set of practices (cultural, symbolic and economic) and a bundle of rights and duties (civil, political and social) that define an individual's membership in a polity" (Isin and Wood 1999, 4). The "bundle of rights and duties" is often contingent on a citizen/non-citizen binary. Foundational to this relationship is sovereignty, the idea that nation-states have the right to control what occurs within and across their borders and to define and delimit membership. Furthermore, citizenship rights are not always allocated equitably to the nation-state's members and rely on the construction of boundaries and hierarchies, often based on individuals' social locations. In North America, such hierarchies are organized under the pillars of white supremacy, patriarchy, heteronormativity, and compulsory able-bodiedness (McRuer 2006; Smith 2006) despite, or perhaps because of, liberal ideologies of equality and multiculturalism (Bannerji 2000; Sharma 2011; Thobani 2007).

Citizenship is *practised* through cultural, political, and other acts (Isin and Nielsen 2008). Those identified as non-citizens often practise citizenship in ways similar to citizens, engaging in political acts such as public demonstrations, voting in municipal elections whenever possible, and otherwise participating in the communities in which they are embedded (Coll 2010). These practices disrupt normative understandings of citizenship/membership given that some non-citizens might never achieve access to legal citizenship status yet continue to engage in and make specific claims to membership (see Chapters 4 and 5). Another example is the creative practices in which migrants engage (see Chapter 8). These examples illustrate both a yearning for formal citizenship and a contestation of normative citizenship

Second, I further understandings of migrant illegalization, a process that ascribes "illegalities" as inherent conditions of migrant/non-citizen subjects. Despite a shifting understanding of citizenship as practised and inclusive of non-citizens, the reverse is also possible: we are seeing a deepening entrenchment of hierarchies of status, from citizen to non-citizen, that identify non-citizens as illegal, bogus, and illegitimate. By positioning illegalization as a socially constructed and contingent process that incorporates differently situated subjects (Coutin 2003; De Genova 2005; Inda 2006; Ngai 2004; Willen 2007), it is possible to problematize taken-for-granted understandings of migration and immigration status trajectories in Canada.

One way to explore migrant illegalization is through the lens of *multiplication*. This involves problematizing the binary relationships that dominate understandings of immigration status: documented/undocumented, legal/illegal, citizen/non-citizen. As I demonstrate in this book using the Canadian context, the experiences of undocumented, illegalized, and/or non-citizens vary depending on the personal, geographic, political, and historical situation. As immigration regulations change, the border can shift (become reassembled) to encompass new, or expanded, forms of illegalization (Goldring, Berinstein, and Bernhard 2009). For example, new categories of precarity can emerge, as in the case of temporary workers or temporarily protected non-citizens (Marsden 2012; Menjívar 2006; Nakache and Kinoshita 2010). Citizen subjects and permanent residents can also become illegalized, as evident in shifting understandings and rewritings of immigration law in relation to the "war on terror," "war on drugs," and "war on gangs" (Burman 2010; Coutin 2007; Henry and Tator 2002). The result is multiple legalities and illegalities within an immigration system that allocates value to individuals categorized through them. To signify this multiplication, I use the term "precarious status" (Goldring, Berinstein, and Bernhard 2009).

Migrant illegalization is also productive. One key example is deportability, the constant possibility of deportation (De Genova 2002). Deportability operates through the spectacle of deportation, produced and disseminated through immigration authorities, media reports, threats from employers, service providers, family members, friends, and rumours. It thus works to place precarious status migrants into marginalized jobs and to receive little access to social services. Deportability is an embodied experience and affects how migrants move around and understand their spatiotemporal contexts (Willen 2007).

Third, extending this analysis, I focus on how migrant illegalization operates across temporal and spatial scales. This process involves the compressing and stretching of time and space across various scales of social analysis (Andersson 2014; Harvey 1989). In terms of space, I examine migrant illegalization both locally and transnationally through the imposition of precarity and borders and their effects on migrants' mobility. For example, I examine how the risk produced pre-migration can affect individuals' experiences during transit and post-migration transnationally. This occurs when immigration applications are refused or visas expire and in particular contexts: the workplace, the street, the immigration hearing, and even creative spaces. Risky spaces inside the nation have been referred to as *internal borders*. Although not always physical, like a wall, they exist through *everyday* encounters with specific actors – police officers, service providers – and through processes of accessing social goods, decent work, and security (Leerkes, Bachmeier, and Leach 2013; Mutsaers 2014; Francisco Villegas 2016).

Temporal scales also affect illegalization and interlock with the production of space and place. For example, Willen (2007) examines the "temporality of everyday risk" that illegalized migrants experience. This temporality operates through specific time scales, including the production of institutional, biographical, and everyday time (Robertson 2018) and state versus subjective time (Andersson 2014). State time involves processes of coercion, control, and usurpation (Andersson 2014; Robertson 2018). Temporality also involves the wait times that migrants experience at borders, through immigration applications, and how they prove their length of stay in a country, in sum, the continuities and ruptures of their presence and subjectivities (Coutin 2003; Dow 2007; Gutierrez Garza 2018; Mattingly 1997; Villegas 2014). Wait times can be conceptualized as "wasted time" (Andersson 2014, 796), a "long, slowing time of waiting (sticky time), one that can decelerate into complete stagnation (suspended time), a fast time rushing out of control (frenzied time) and tears in people's imagined time frames (temporal ruptures)" (Griffiths 2014, 1994). These temporalities produce material and emotional effects for precarious status migrants, particularly as they await the resolution of applications or endure waiting for the right moment to apply for status. In terms of immigration applications, Goldring and Landolt (2012) refer to a "chutes and ladders" process whereby migrants can move across statuses in an upward and downward manner across time, where some statuses provide increased access to social entitlements whereas others refuse them. These experiences, described in Part II of this book, complicate assumed teleologies from no status to status – the idea that someone will eventually become documented or gain citizenship. They can also act as "time capital" (Andersson 2014) providing migrants with ways to strategize for future or alternative steps (Villegas 2014) and engage in "strategies of defiance" (Khosravi 2014).

While migrants experience these temporal negotiations, they are not frozen in space and often engage in creative work. Thus, fourth, I illustrate the creative work (Grant and Buckwold 2013) in which precarious status migrants engage (Menjívar 2006). I examine how this process generates experiences similar to those of other internal borders (the workplace, health care and other public goods, public spaces). For example, though "passing" as an artist can become a protective mechanism for "uncomfortable questions" regarding immigration status (Bernhard et al. 2007), there are limits to its protection.

Fifth, I focus on affect, which migration scholars are increasingly taking up as a conceptual tool. Although related to emotions, affect goes beyond them. It circulates across and through bodies. Vukov (2003, 339) explains that, "whereas emotions tend to refer to discrete states that are experienced as subjective moments of interiority, affect refers to a less subjective, signifying set of resonances, sensations and intensities that circulate socially between bodies and among bodies and populations; it is a process that cements the feel of everyday life." Similarly, Ahmed (2004a, 117) argues that "emotions play a crucial role in the 'surfacing' of individual and collective bodies through the way in which emotions circulate between bodies and signs. Such an argument clearly challenges any assumption that emotions are a private matter, that they simply belong to individuals." Finally, Richard and Rudnyckyj (2009) describe affect as a productive and relational "medium" through which subjects are produced and circulate. In other words, affect can be considered a transitive verb – *affecting* subjects.

I explore three interrelated affective processes: the production of anti-migrant sentiments, the maintenance of nationalist ideas about protecting Canada from migrants, and the effects of such discourses/affects on precarious status migrants, particularly through the concepts of yearning (Burman 2002) and aguantar. Burman (2002, 50, 52) describes yearning as a "future-oriented and galvanizing mode of desire," as in yearning for a better life, or better conditions, stating that "yearning moves subjects to change the seemingly fated conditions of their involvement in a globalized socio-economic setting, whether by seeking out the possibilities for physical and social mobility opened up by the technologies of globalization or by articulating new subject positions artistically and culturally."

Related to yearning, aguantar is a recurring theme in my analysis. It refers to bearing, tolerating, and enduring, as in injustices and violence in the workplace or community and a lack of access to social entitlements. Aguantar can also refer to being resourceful, resilient, and strategic: *waiting* for the right time. Thus, it can be considered a future-oriented process of imagining better conditions while tolerating present ones.

Puerto Rican hip hop duo Calle 13, in their song "El Aguante" (Cabra and Pérez 2014), list examples of the things that humans and societies endure: war, oppression, hunger, pain, etc. In a newspaper article, one member of the duo, Residente, explained the song as a list of "events, circumstances and themes that 'encompass the different ways in which humanity endures, permits, molds itself, fights and superimposes itself in light of the diversity of factors we all have to face: from resistance to survival; from tolerance to adaptation; from permissiveness to what becomes unacceptable'" (*El Espectador* 2014). The song specifically refers to the body as a site of endurance as well as the power relations that circulate to make that endurance necessary: racial capitalism and associated precarious employment arrangements, enduring systems of governance and lawmaking, and enactment of borders. As my analysis illustrates, precarious status migrants' use of aguantar is a strategic form of waiting and tolerating these assembled forces as well as *yearning* and working for a better future. However, this process is not a romantic "overcoming"; aguantar can be a humiliating experience of tolerating negative treatment from employers, peers, and strangers. It can also illustrate an anxiety-producing process of waiting for secure status.

Gathering and Analyzing the Stories

Drawing on my theorization of assemblage, I bring together different sources of data that narrate Mexican migration and precarity in Canada: interviews, media accounts, policy documents, and creative works. I seek to understand how migrant illegalization is produced, experienced, and resisted in relation to and by Mexican migrants in Canada. Specifically, I am interested in examining how notions of space and time have influenced accounts of migration, borders, deportability, and in/security.

I conducted semi-structured interviews between 2009–10 and 2014–15 with twenty-one Mexican migrants in Toronto. The Appendix includes a summary of participant information. Interviews ranged from one hour to three hours. The first project was part of my dissertation research and focused on understanding how Mexican migrants navigated their precarious status in Toronto. I undertook the second project to examine the effects of deportability on Mexican migrants given the 2009 visa requirement and continued immigration enforcement (see Chapter 3).

All of the participants were born in Mexico and came from several states (Monterrey, Aguascalientes, Chiapas, Guerrero), though many (fourteen) lived in Mexico City and its outskirts before travelling to Canada. Only one participant, Sergio, lived in a rural area (Chiapas). Of the twenty-one participants, eleven were men and ten women. All had participated, at some point in their lives, in precarious work in Canada, mostly in the service and construction industries and mostly without work authorization (no social insurance number). At the times of the interviews, all participants had been in Canada more than one year. All had arrived before the 2009 visa requirement imposed on Mexican nationals. The names included here are pseudonyms that were chosen by the participants and sometimes reflected their lived experiences, creativity, and political ideologies (e.g., Emiliana Zapata and Libertad). In fact, the participants shared two distinctive characteristics. First, many had an interest in artistic or creative expression, including visual, literary, and performance arts. Second, they shared a critical understanding of their insecuritization and illegalization, with many engaging in activism, broadly defined. Some of this activism began in Mexico, but some participants described experiencing a critical formation in Toronto because of their immigration status, racialization, and/or sexual orientation.

During interviews, I situated myself by relating my undocumented experience in the United States. I saw this as a way to create a bridge or point of departure and to demonstrate that my interest in the project was personal, political, and intellectual. However, I also recognized that my experience was very different from those of the participants and that experience is contingent and socially constructed (Scott 1992). Although participant narratives cannot be celebrated uncritically, in this book I attempt to make visible experiences often invisibilized to paint a picture of the interlockings of migration, citizenship, illegalization, and precarity. This follows De Genova's (2005, 422) proposal of not studying migrants themselves, as objects or units to count, but focusing on the conditions that led to their illegalization and deportability.

In addition to interviews, I participated in meetings, social events, and informal sessions with participants, other Mexicans with precarious status, and social justice activists. I also regularly volunteered at a health clinic that provides services for uninsured clients, mainly precarious status migrants. These encounters influenced my analysis and corroborated the trends that I saw during participant interviews. However, I avoided noting names and descriptions of meetings and places to protect participants and the community at large, given that the Mexican community is small and that some participants had public personas.

I also utilized media accounts, government documents, grey literatures, and creative work that addressed Mexican migration in Canada, particularly precarious status migration. Newspaper sources were primarily Canadian, though I also used sources from the United States, Europe, and Mexico. Canadian government documents came primarily from Citizenship and Immigration Canada (now Immigration, Refugees, and Citizenship Canada), Statistics Canada, and the Immigration and Refugee Board. Grey literatures came from local social service organizations: health clinics, community centres, and workers' centres. Finally, I also drew from creative work, particularly the poetry of Jesús Maya (2012), a Mexican migrant living in Toronto whose work speaks about insecuritization in Mexico, difficulties during migration, and precarity in Canada. His poetry frames my conception of the three sections of this book: immigration trajectories, immigration status trajectories, and internal borders. It also influences my analysis in Chapter 8.

In the data analysis, I paid attention to the elements outlined above: ways of knowing, actors, institutions/organizations, technologies, and ways of feeling. This analysis centred on discourse and power relations, examining how "specific views or accounts are constructed as real or truthful or natural through particular regimes of truth" (Rose 2001, 140). Such regimes include the belief that nation-states have the sovereign power to dictate which bodies can cross national boundaries (Torpey 2000), the belief that illegality is a condition ascribed to individuals instead of being socially produced, as well as the belief that the law and its associated discretionary practices are fair instruments to differentiate between citizens and non-citizens and the benefits to which they are entitled. Finally, the analysis involved examining sources as interrelated components of a patchworked and contingent story given that precarious status migrants do not live in and embody fixed conditions or subject positions. Instead, discourses of illegalization and deportability, among others, have significant effects on their lives. Therefore, I analyzed migrant illegalization as an event or practice, "as an active 'occurring,' . . . that implements power and action, and that also is power and action" (Hook 2001, 20).

Organization of the Book

The book is organized into three sections. In the first section, I discuss the insecuritization that influences migration decisions as well as the im/mobility produced through transnational border practices. I examine how this occurs through violence and impunity in Mexico, border policing through transit, and affective and discursive manifestations of anti-immigrant and bogus refugee sentiments. In the second section, I focus on migrants' immigration status trajectories and discuss the options that exist to achieve secure status as well as the barriers in place to prevent it. Given those barriers, in the third section I explore internal borders by examining how they relate to social exclusion and inequality, with a specific focus on work, health care, and creative practices. Throughout the book, I highlight the ways in which migrants, despite the conditions that situate them as abject, exploitable subjects, engage in creative practices and resourceful processes that negotiate their status and work to counter feelings, discourses, and practices of illegalization.

PART I

Immigration Trajectories

Soñaba que ya no estamos en México
Y no éramos Ninguno de los 72
asesinados, asesinadas En Tamau-
lipas.
Que nos tocábamos nuestras carnes
No éramos parte de los 72, Ni de
los 400 que caen todos los años, Ni
de los miles que son puntos en el
mar, Arizona es sólo una noticia.

Soñé que tú y yo cabíamos aquí Que
no fuimos plantados en Toronto

I dreamed that we were no longer
in Mexico and that we were not
among the 72 murdered men and
women in Tamaulipas.
We searched our bodies for any
wounds, relieved That we were not
part of those 72 Or the 400 that
collapse on the way every year
Nor those thousands who are
now just specks on the sea. Ari-
zona is only a news story.

I dreamed that you and I might actu-
ally fit in here, That we weren't just
plopped down in Toronto

– Excerpt from "Toronto," by Jesús Maya (2012, 53),
translated by Jeannine Pitas

Immigration trajectories are transnational. Basch et al. (1994, 7) define migrant transnationalism as "the processes by which immigrants forge and sustain multi-stranded social relations that link together their societies of origin and settlement." This does not just mean that migration transgresses national boundaries through the movement of bodies across borders. Migration is constituted transnationally by factors that occur within the edges of nation-states, in spaces that exist across and beyond formal boundaries. Maya's (2012) poem alludes to this process. The narrator, a migrant in Toronto, describes a dream about a real-life event: the assassination of seventy-two migrants in the northern state of Tamaulipas by the Zetas cartel (Pérez Salazar 2015). He also refers to those who perish trying to cross the US-Mexico border or large bodies of water such as the Mediterranean Sea, two border regions that have become increasingly policed and rigid in recent years. Thus, he points to the factors that lead migrants to leave their country of origin and their conditions during transit.

An understanding of migration as transnational involves going beyond the "push" and "pull" factors traditionally understood to frame cross-border movements. According to Gonzalez and Fernandez (2003, 32), the problem with push-pull theories is the disconnect between the push and the pull. Because of globalization and the transnational assemblage of economic, political, and social processes, push and pull factors do not occur in isolation from each other. One example is migrant illegalization. Migrants and non-migrants are also subjected to a transnational system of unequal distribution of resources, capital, and opportunities, leading to insecuritization, which in turn influences migration decisions as well as how potential migrants will be treated in the country of migration. Therefore, individuals in their contexts of departure might have experiences of precarity and insecurity that then extend, in similar or new manifestations, to the country of migration. For example, people fleeing persecution can become refugee claimants subjected to state processes of legitimation (of their refugeeness) that do not guarantee full status. Similarly, people unable to migrate through state-accepted (read "legal") channels – such as applications that require certain work experience, education, and capital – might also be channelled into precarious status.

However, transnationalism does not always signify mobility. Espiritu (2003, 2) argues that "immigrants – in this age of transnational flow of labor, capital, and cultural forms – are *both spatially mobile and spatially bounded*" (emphasis added). Migrant illegalization is often accompanied by a diminished freedom to move across national borders, in effect "locking" precarious status migrants in place post-migration. Migrants often cannot return to their "homes" or travel elsewhere for fear of being denied entry, or they might not want to travel if they have fled persecution. Being "locked" into place makes them (physically) absent in their country of departure, which can be especially frustrating when they are needed for family celebrations, births, deaths, or legal matters. Thus, migrant illegalization shapes the transnational practices in which migrants engage.

In the following chapters, I map some of the factors that affected immigration trajectories for Mexicans travelling to Canada in the 2000s and 2010s. These factors include the Mexican context of heightened insecuritization in the 2000s and 2010s, the process of transit, and policy responses to increased Mexican migration to Canada. In Chapter 1, I provide an understanding of push factors: economic insecuritization given the growth of transnational corporations, neoliberal restructuring, low wages, and underemployment; the criminalization of dissent to maintain the political order; and the interlocking processes of racism, class-based exploitation, sexism, and homophobia. The examples of insecurity discussed in this chapter parallel the examples of deportability in Canada that I discuss in Part III.

Chapter 2 follows with a discussion of cross-border travel, the mechanisms in place to control it, and the resourcefulness of migrants. Returning to Maya's (2012) poem, I relate the experience of transit to conditions of security/insecurity. Because of increased border enforcement at the US-Mexico border, Mexicans found themselves making their way farther north, to Canada. I outline participants' plans to migrate, their experiences with border officials, and the techniques used to enter Canada.

In Chapter 3, I examine Canada's 2009 visa requirement for Mexican migrants (and its revocation in 2016). The policy was implemented as a response to a growth in refugee applications from Mexico. It led to the construction of a de facto border that contributed to the criminalization of Mexicans in Canada. The visa was lifted in 2016 after changes to refugee policy made it more difficult for Mexicans to apply for and receive refugee protection.

1

Assembling Insecuritization in Mexico

Güero and I met in my Toronto apartment in early 2015. At the time, he worked as a landscaper and participated in creative community projects in music and theatre. Given his busy schedule, winter was a good time for the interview to take place, for his work was slow. Born and raised in Mexico City, Güero felt that his life was going nowhere in the late 2000s. Although he was involved in creative work in Mexico, particularly theatre, it was badly remunerated, and he felt pressure to provide for his young son. He described his decision to travel to Canada as a strategy to create some distance between himself and the insecuritization that life in Mexico City offered working-class persons. He made his decision after experiencing a lightbulb moment one day:

> I wanted to leave Mexico City . . . Through a series of events, I realized that I was trapped in the city. I realized that, that, I had a son that was about to start elementary school and that I had nothing. Right? I did not have a future, I did not have a career, I did not have a stable job, and I was very into, into . . . the streets, the city. Drugs, all those things, and I had, it was one of those five minutes of clarity, first time in my life.

Leonel experienced a similar process. He lived in Estado de Mexico on the outskirts of Mexico City and worked as a street vendor until 2001, when he accepted an invitation from his sister to migrate to Canada. When I asked him why he agreed, he stated, "I'm going to try to be objective, but I feel it was a lot of things." Leonel's reference to objectivity was an attempt to create a coherent narrative from diverse experiences of insecurity. However, as the conversation continued, Leonel became more specific: "The fucking police. My inability to accept, to not resign myself to having to live that life. The need to have a bit of security, perhaps not for myself. I now think that I refused to accept that my daughters would grow up there." Although his business was not thriving, he had survived for some time until he had to pay for an impromptu surgery and was forced to borrow money. His decision to migrate meant leaving his daughters behind, with the hope that they would be reunited in the future.

Güero's and Leonel's experiences are a point of departure to examine and problematize why Mexican migrants travelled to Canada in the 2000s, particularly binary framings that identify reasons for migration either as economic or because of violence. Instead, I examine how insecuritization influenced participants' emigration decisions, a process that included economic instability because of poverty, underemployment, lack of opportunities, and threats to their well-being ranging from physical harm to more generalized feelings of fear.

Cruz (2009, 2) explains insecuritization in the following way:

> Economic security, institutional performance, ecological conditions and individual characteristics may affect levels of public insecurity. All these conditions interact with crime and violence to generate more uncertainty and, in some cases, social unrest . . . Fear of crime is a result not only of threats and vulnerabilities but also, and more important, of the representations people have about their social situation and their satisfaction with it. Mass media and processes of social communication, as well as perceptions of economic uncertainties, play an important role in boosting public insecurity.

Insecuritization is assembled. Ways of knowing, including government policies, media accounts, and civil society reports about the labour market, corruption, and organized crime, influence its manifestation. The actors and institutions that become the protagonists in this assemblage are policy makers, the police, perpetrators of violence, and everyday people who contemplate emigration. Technologies play a role by facilitating the surveillance and persecution of citizens. Finally, insecuritization demonstrates the affective circulations of fear and uncertainty that have permeated Mexican society in recent years.

Cruz (2009) also draws our attention to the role of time and place in insecuritization. Economic restructuring, the effects of globalization, and insecuritization operate at local, national, international, and transnational scales. Specific places also figured prominently in participants' narratives of economic precarity and dislocation: the workplace, the streets, the home, and the police station. Proximity to insecurity, what I describe as *insecurity by association,* also affects this process. Finally, insecurity was described as an everyday, normalized experience: the belief that violence *could happen at any moment* and the lack of confidence in policing authorities.

Mexico's Neoliberalization, Precarious Livelihoods, and Economic Insecurity

Economic insecurity is one strand of insecuritization. It involves unemployment, underemployment, and the lack of a safety net for a population that faces a continuous erosion of social entitlements, forcing some to seek alternative income-generating strategies. Much has been written about the economic situation in Mexico as a reason for emigration, particularly to the United States (Massey et al. 1987). These processes have also influenced the precarious status migration of Mexicans to Canada.

Beginning in the 1980s, the Mexican government imposed a series of policy and economic adjustments that followed the logic of neoliberal restructuring. For instance, in 1985, Mexico signed the General Agreement on Tariffs and Trade (GATT), the predecessor of the World Trade Organization. In 1988, the United States and Canada implemented a bilateral free-trade agreement, prompting the Mexican government to lobby for inclusion. While talks among the three governments took place, Mexico began internal preparations, including a revision of its constitution. For example, in 1992, changes to Article 27 virtually ended the *ejido* system of communal land ownership in place (at least in theory) since the 1930s to protect the lands and livelihoods of *campesinxs* from large agribusiness operations. The revision allowed the selling of *ejidos* in general as well as the selling of Mexican land to foreigners and corporations (French and Manzanárez 2004, 25; Pastor and Wise 1998, 65).

The United States, Canada, and Mexico signed the North American Free Trade Agreement (NAFTA) in 1993 and implemented it in 1994. NAFTA's objectives included integrating the three countries' economies and facilitating trade, but its effects on the working-class Mexican population were widespread and mostly negative (Carlsen 2008; French and Manzanárez 2004; Gomez Cruz and Schwentesius Rindermann 2009; Hing 2010; NACLA 2005; Rivera, Whiteford, and Chávez Márquez 2009). This neoliberalization intersected with the devaluation of the Mexican peso in the mid-1990s. International loans provided to "offset" the crisis included conditions that Mexico move to increase exports, reduce spending, and increase interest rates (Drachman and Shank 2003, 124). These national and transnational policies led to a growing gap between the rich and the poor that disproportionately affected rural *campesinxs* and the urban working class. NAFTA renegotiations began in 2017 and, by March 2020, all three countries had ratified the new US–Mexico–Canada Agreement (USMCA) (Ljunggren 2020). Changes are poised to impose more critical erosions of Mexican sovereignty and the country's agricultural and labour sectors, further affecting Mexicans' well-being (Cypher and Crossa 2019).

Temporal Reflections of Escalating Precarity and Displacement

> I come from places evacuated by emigrants
> Where agriculture is an expensive reality
> And a distant memory for many
> Places built through remittances, those who stayed behind, those who returned and those who were forcibly returned (Villegas 2019c, 87)

Participants framed their experiences of living in the economic context and generalized insecurity outlined above using references to time. For instance, Eduardo and his wife, Rebeca, lived in Mexico City with their two children (a third was born in Canada). Like Leonel and Güero, Eduardo left his family behind when he travelled to Canada, and during our interview he referred to the insecuritization that they faced in Mexico as "el pan nuestro de cada día," literally "our daily bread." Echoing this sentiment, Lencho, a musician from Estado de Mexico who worked in a neighbourhood market, stated that

> Oftentimes you don't have another point of view. Because a lot of people in Mexico, including myself, sometimes don't get out . . . So they don't have another perspective, they don't know how the world is outside their neighbourhood. Perhaps it's the crime we experience that ends up being an everyday thing. You see it every day. It's the norm. I don't know if you get accustomed to it because it's an everyday thing. It's normal. When I was in Mexico, I saw it as normal. I wasn't shocked at what happens there until I came here.

I asked Lencho if he thought that people adapted to such normalized violence, and he was adamant that one did not have to become accustomed because it was always present, ordinary, and intricately woven into the social fabric. By referring to the social fabric, my goal is not to identify Mexico and Mexicans as inherently violent, as has been done through references to the violent practices of Aztecs and other essentialist depictions. Lencho was adamant in making this statement despite knowing that he was implicated in it. My goal is to examine how local and transnational practices lead to the enactment of generalized and constant violence in Mexico, particularly for working-class families. Given this *cotidianidad* (everydayness or routineness), a literal or figurative distance allowed many participants to re-evaluate their experiences of insecurity.

One example involved how neoliberalizing practices displaced Mexicans from their lands and initiated a whittling away of rights and access to economic opportunities. Although I interviewed only one person who lived in a rural setting in Mexico, his experience is a good contrast to the narratives of urban participants. Sergio, an Indigenous *campesino* from the state of Chiapas, found it increasingly difficult to sell his crops for a decent price in the mid-2000s, so he decided to emigrate after he was invited to Canada by friends and relatives:

> The harvest over there is cheap . . . The city people pay us a low price for our products. That is, what they pay us is very little. I'll give you an example, pineapples. If I sell pineapples, they pay me a low price. Then, if I buy their pineapples, they charge me a high price. So there is quite a difference . . . It's the same thing for soap, salt, sugar, they are also very expensive. Everything that comes . . . from the city is very expensive, and for us the

> rate paid for production is very cheap. It is cheaper every day. So . . . that is the reason why I'm here in Canada, because we couldn't afford to live working every day without a, a salary, a way to support my family or to have a way to generate more money. We couldn't do it because, even though we work a lot, they paid us very little, so I had to come here to get ahead.

Sergio compared two spaces: the community farm in which he participated based on cooperation, not competition, given its association with the Ejercito Zapatista de Liberación Nacional (Zapatista National Liberation Army) and the space of the city, where capitalist exchange occurred. NAFTA separated a number of agricultural products from the tariffs that had protected them in the past, making it difficult for Mexican products to compete with US. products flooding the markets (Pastor and Wise 1998). Although US farmers often receive government subsidies to remain in business, Mexican support was discontinued after NAFTA, leading *campesinxs* to fend for themselves (Gomez Cruz and Schwentesius Rindermann 2009, 5). One effect was that the number of agricultural jobs fell from over 8 million before NAFTA to 6 million in 2006 (Hing 2010, 14).

The community experienced fluctuating crop prices and rising costs of "city products" that could not be produced by its members. They felt forced to participate in additional capitalist forms of exchange to make ends meet. Sergio elected migration and marked his decision to migrate through space and time, explaining it as *salir adelante*, meaning to get ahead. *Salir* also refers to leaving, or exiting, inadvertently pointing to the fact that Sergio felt that he had to leave Mexico to pursue his dream of getting ahead. The decision, however, implied leaving his wife and children behind and experiencing a transnational household that had emotional costs (Abrego 2014).

In urban centres, participants' economic difficulties involved the ability to have secure, long-term work and adequate housing. Informal, contingent work increased in Mexico after NAFTA (Delgado Wise 2015). In 2005, when a number of participants were leaving or getting ready to leave Mexico, almost 25 percent of all employment was self-employment, whereas the informal economy generally accounted for one-third of jobs (Carlsen 2008; Oliver 2007, 91). And the few jobs to be had did not provide a reprieve from precarious conditions: "Of all the jobs created between mid-2000 and mid-2004, 65% came with no benefits whatsoever, and frequently without a written contract" (NACLA 2005). Furthermore, since NAFTA, Mexican wages have declined, while the cost of living, inflation, and poverty rates have increased, the latter being above 50 percent (Alba 2010; UNICEF 2010).

Urban participants also described this insecuritization as a process of *increasing* precarity regardless of profession. For instance, Lencho's family business in their Estado de Mexico neighbourhood market faced deteriorating conditions:

> The economic situation at the business my parents owned, or still own, was not very good. We work at a market, and the market began to lose business after two stores opened nearby. One is a Walmart, and the other is a Bodega Aurrera. So the market lost its business. Sales decreased, and I didn't have enough money just working at the family business.

Time exacerbated Lencho's feelings of insecurity. He hoped to attend music school, but he could not pay his tuition by continuing to work in the family business. The arrival of big-box stores meant a big decline for specialized vendors, and the losses were significant at a time when a global recession was in full force, particularly since small businesses are often sites where multiple family members find employment.

Similarly, Leonel's work as a street vendor meant that his economic situation in Mexico became worse in the years preceding his emigration in 2001. Leonel described the neighbourhood context and situation for himself and his colleagues:

> My neighbour sold chickens and lived in his parents' house. The person who sold music . . . also lived in his parents' house. The vendor in front, and his children, all of them lived in his mother's house. They divided the property and built up, but it was still his mother's house. Another vendor in front of me did not own a house . . . Perhaps they did not live full of debt, and neither did I, but we lived *al dia* (hand to mouth).

Leonel identified different strands of economic insecurity over time. Neither he nor his colleagues could own land in the city because of cost and overpopulation. In addition, he worked on a sidewalk, in front of the marketplace, which he took over from pedestrians since he could not afford to pay rent for a state-recognized business. He also thought that it was more profitable to have a visible business, at the entrance to the marketplace, than one hidden inside it.

Despite his approach to business, Leonel and vendors like him could only make ends meet. While living *al dia* is common, particularly in working-class communities, as soon as a job is lost, the economy goes into recession, or an unexpected expense arises it becomes unsustainable. Therefore, living *al dia* implies an inability to save or invest. For someone like Leonel, paying for merchandise at the point of purchase was the norm, meaning that he always had to have surplus money to restock his inventory. And, like Sergio, he was at the whim of vendors who could raise prices at any time and discount stores that sold the same goods for less money to his customers. Although Leonel did not normally have much debt, before he left Mexico he had surgery and owed $2,000 US, a significant amount given Mexican wages. He explained this temporal shift: "There were better times for me. But before I came here, the situation for me was not very good financially."

Eduardo had a good job in the 1990s and became accustomed to living comfortably. When he lost his job, however, he could not find something similarly remunerated:

> I was never able to find a job with the same salary . . . I was no longer able to pay for everything that we were used to, credit cards, with outstanding debt, the car . . . That was when my wife [Rebeca] began to take care of everything. At that time, I paid 3,300 pesos, maybe 3,400, for the house. I had to pay about 2,200 per month for the car, along with all our other expenses. Food, clothes, etc., etc. And my wages were about 3,000 [pesos], 4,000 if I worked overtime . . . So every passing month we were accumulating debt, especially with the house.

Like other participants, Eduardo identified *escalating* economic insecurity, referring to the growing amount of debt for his family each passing month. Monthly payments are timely reminders of potentially losing those things (e.g., a house) from which we create our conceptions of stability and wealth.

After losing his job, Eduardo found employment in a series of precarious jobs with flexible hours and low pay. Ironically, some of those insecure jobs were in the security industry, working for wealthier Mexicans. Thus, his job experience straddled in/security, providing security for others while becoming less and less secure himself economically.

Eduardo's description of his economic insecurity was also gendered. When Eduardo lost his job, the family began to depend on his wife's income to pay the bills. Yet, in his description of the family's inability to make ends meet, he discussed his earnings and not Rebeca's, effectively invisibilizing her contribution. He used *yo* (I) instead of *nosotros* (we/us), portraying himself as the principal earner. Therefore, in addition to having had better times in the past because of economic security, his stable job afforded him a sense of masculinized privilege in the home. Seeing himself as the primary provider for his family allowed him gendered privileges that he did not suspend when he lost his economic status.

Participants with university training were not protected from increasing insecurity. For instance, Liz had a good job before the economic recession hit in 2007, accumulating material goods that led to a comfortable quality of life:

> I worked in an import-export company. It was really good; I worked there for almost three years. However, during and a bit before the recession, companies were going under. We didn't have as many clients, and even though we tried to increase business the companies were not in a good state . . . Little by little, it happened, and my company went under. I was left with a lot of debt. I had a mortgage for an apartment that I had in Mexico, . . . a car that I was paying little by little, and credit debt. I looked for work, I did find some, I found work that paid very little . . . I remember that they hired me for 6,000 pesos, . . . and based on my debt and lifestyle I needed 18,000.

The reference to companies going under "little by little" parallels Lencho's description of big-box stores taking over the business of small marketplaces. It indicates a creeping of economic insecurity across time through a reorganization of economic processes leading to lower earnings and fewer benefits for workers.

To supplement a decrease in earnings, some participants opened small businesses. Armando was studying architecture in Puebla before he emigrated to Canada. He opened a retail store using a loan from what he later found were fraudulent lenders:

> I opened a business when I was nineteen years old and signed a promissory note, . . . and I was paying it off little by little, . . . but I never asked for the promissory note back. So, after about three years, I got a summons saying that . . . I owed like 35,000 pesos, from an 8,000-peso loan! So, ugh, it was very difficult, and my mom helped me [to pay for the legal fight] . . . So I came here [to Canada], and that was part of my goal, to pay my mom back.

Armando's business experience and legal costs affected his ability to pay his university tuition despite also working at an architectural firm. His experience is an example of how corruption influences economic precarity, augmenting the effects of globalization and neoliberal restructuring. His solution was to ask his company for short-term leave so that Armando could travel to Canada and raise the money that he owed.

Maria Pérez held a business degree. Like Armando, she sought to supplement her income by starting a small business; however, her debt was compounded by the insecurity produced through property crime:

> Another reason that made me come [to Canada] was that I was in debt. I had a business there. I had an internet café. It was going well, but they robbed us, and afterward business suffered. The woman who rented the space did not want to help us improve security, . . . and I had a lot of expenses. Obviously, I incurred a loss of merchandise. And I decided, that was the reason I said, "I want to leave here." . . . So I ended up owing the bank and the credit card [company].

In her description of the events, Maria Pérez recounted, "casi casi salí, me salí corriendo," which translates into "as I left, it was almost running." This rushed exit demonstrates the urgency created by economic insecurity. She also discussed the ways in which technologies of surveillance can help to improve security, but they involved a cost too high for Maria Pérez to afford.

Finally, several participants discussed their families' economic situations as *one* reason for their emigration. Aquetzalli held an education degree and worked in the south of Mexico for some time after finishing university in Mexico City. Upon returning to the capital, she was unable to find work in her profession. Furthermore, her father became unemployed, and she stressed over seeing him increasingly depressed. Similarly, Emiliana Zapata, whose pseudonym came from Emiliano Zapata, a leader of the Mexican revolution in the early twentieth century who fought for land reform and redistribution, was involved in cultural rescue projects in Mexico, particularly related to Indigenous beliefs and traditions. She was politically active in her university and began to feel increasingly threatened by the police because of her politics. Emiliana Zapata also experienced economic precarity after graduating, describing the situation thus: "At home . . . we had less and less money. It was getting uglier [*cada vez más fea*]. We were starting to experience hunger, well, we had before, but now it was stronger." Her family's deteriorating situation led her to look for opportunities abroad. The fact that Emiliana Zapata and Aquetzalli, both single women, and not their male relatives, migrated also points to the reconfiguration of gendered migration trajectories in recent decades (Abrego 2014; Hondagneu-Sotelo 1994; Pessar and Mahler 2003).

Tener y Hacer Algo (To Have and Do Something)

Another way to describe economic insecuritization is in relation to planning for the future. The general term that participants used to describe this was the desire to *tener algo* (have something). *Tener algo* can imply the ownership of commodities; however, for participants, the desire to *tener algo* also related to their stability. For instance, for Eduardo and Rebeca, owning a house implied having a more stable livelihood than renting. This belief influenced Eduardo's decision to emigrate in order to send money so they could keep their house. The same idea of stability influenced Sergio's view of communal land ownership and the yearning for a profitable business in Leonel's and Lencho's families.

In addition, for some participants, it was not only about *having* something but also about *doing* something, having the stability to pursue something of interest, to create or learn. After university, Emiliana Zapata received job offers as a linguistics expert in the south of Mexico. However, she discovered that the jobs entailed working for the government and aligning herself ideologically with it. She referred to this as "selling out" and declined the jobs. Her decision, however, led to few employment opportunities. She was interested in continuing to learn about the rescue and maintenance of Indigenous knowledges, and she thought that she could do this in Canada while also contributing to her family's decreasing income.

Similarly, because of the displacement experienced in the family business, through the imposition of a Walmart nearby, Lencho did not have enough income to attend music school. Although he did not plan to work in the family business as a long-term option, his declining family income affected his short-term goals. As he related, "I no longer had enough for my expenses, and I wanted to do other things, I wanted to study other things. So I saw the opportunity to come here to Canada and work for a while and then go back, get some money." Lencho had toured with his rock band in Mexico and internationally, travelling to Canada for a few concerts. He also had family members in Canada. Both processes facilitated his migration decision.

Threats to Bodily Integrity: State Violence, Organized Crime, and Homophobia

State Violence

Another strand of insecuritization that participants identified involved violence. One example was institutional violence, which manifested itself in participants' workplaces and/or through a lack of police protection. This type of violence sought to discipline individuals and produce "docile bodies" (Foucault 1995). It was also systemic. Although participants' narratives were particularized, the violence was part of a system that allows the erosion of rights and entitlements of individuals, explicitly seeks to remove them when they have opposing views, or fails to protect them when they experience violence.

Libertad, a journalist who worked at a Mexico City university and whose pseudonym means freedom, explained this type of systemic violence succinctly: "In Mexico there is no freedom of expression, in Mexico there is no freedom of association, in Mexico there is no freedom of movement, you are stopped only because of how you are dressed, what you look like, or the colour of your skin." Libertad pointed to a racial hierarchy ingrained in Mexican society. Therefore, while the freedoms that she discussed are often used to define democratic societies, which the Mexican state has tried to impersonate, participants' narratives depict some of the cracks in the mirage.

Leonel provided several examples, referring to police corruption and regular instances of extortion as people go about their day-to-day activities. He described how certain social spaces in Mexico City, including rock music concert halls, denied him entry because of the colour of his skin. He also faced harassment from the police because of his taste in music, which influenced how he dressed and styled his hair. In terms of his work, he regularly travelled to Mexico City, from its outskirts in Estado de Mexico, to purchase the goods that he sold in his business. He discussed the daily struggle of having to negotiate with the police: "When people go to wholesale markets to buy products, it is very common that the police stop you and extort money from you, for any reason." This action, commonly referred to as *la mordida* (a bribe, literally a bite) affected his freedom of movement. Leonel's experience also points to the relationship between insecuritization initiated by the police and economic insecurity: people often account for the money paid to the police for protection or through extortion in their already restricted budgets.

After Eduardo emigrated to Canada, Rebeca experienced harassment from a neighbour who accused her of flirting with her husband. Although she went to the police station, she did not obtain protection because there was no evidence of the violence: "There [in Mexico] the law has no value. Not until you are killed . . . You can press charges if you have been assaulted, but you can't press charges if you are not injured . . . It wasn't until she hit me that I was able to press charges." Rebeca's referral to the "value" of the law demonstrates how the legal system is constitutive of insecuritization in Mexico. Although protections exist for citizens, they are not executed in practice, what Ahmed (2004b) describes as non-performatives: declarations that "do not do what they say" and instead maintain the status quo. Rebeca made a formal complaint when her neighbour physically assaulted her, but the police only sent the neighbour a court summons. Rebeca continued: "I had to pay for a police car only so she saw that I had protection." In fact, Rebeca paid for a daily *performance* of protection in which the police were the actors and her neighbour the audience. And, similar to Leonel's experience of having to pay the police so he could transport the goods that he sold, it illustrates the intersection among insecurity, time, and money.

Other participants experienced police violence more directly. Manolo, a man in his thirties, worked as a political cartoonist and bartender in Mexico City. He was also active in neighbourhood improvement projects. That work involved producing and disseminating flyers explaining the political platforms of candidates vying for local office. Furthermore, he attended meetings with the local government to advocate for safety measures, including increasing the number of street and traffic lights to prevent crime and vehicular accidents. This type of work angered one local official who worked for the Partido Acción Nacional (PAN) as a campaign organizer. Because of illegal polling, Manolo explained, the PAN official found out that his party was not doing well in Manolo's district and held Manolo responsible. Initially, he called Manolo out during community meetings, using offensive names for cartoonists such as *pintamonos*. Manolo explained that cartoonists in Mexico are often called *moneros*. *Pintamonos* translates into someone who paints monkeys. *Mono* means monkeys, and both words begin with *mon,* thus a play on words. When Manolo responded by calling him a *politiquito* (little politician), the man became more enraged. Manolo explained the process whereby the violence escalated:

> One day he attacked me along with some *madrinas*. What are *madrinas?* This is very important. *Madrinas* are people who work with the police in Mexico City – but actually the Mexican states also have their own *madrinas* ... They are the people who follow orders. They are the soldiers. They go, trap someone, kill them, or anything else. They do all the dirty work ... They do not have police plates, or names, or anything ... They drive police cars without plates. They don't carry any identification. That's how they operate. They kidnap, rob.

Madrina, Manolo told me, comes from the word *madriza,* which refers to being beat up. A report by the Immigration and Refugee Board of Canada (IRB) compiled research about *madrinas:*

> *Madrinas* [are] persons who work "in the shadows" (*a la sombra*) of the Procuraduria General de la Republica (PGR . . .) [Attorney General], doing groundwork such as drug purchases . . . A 1999 report states that the *estibadores* or *madrinas* who assist PGR officers can be a small "mafia" that operates independent of changes in the PGR, adding that the networks of *madrinas* remain in place and simply await new officers to deal with them . . . *Madrinas* have also been reported to have dressed as soldiers and manned highway checkpoints to extort drivers . . . and in the State of Morelos worked closely with judicial policemen who carried out a majority of the kidnappings for ransom in the state. (Immigration and Refugee Board of Canada 2001)

Madrina also means godmother. One could argue that persons who work in the background, granting the wishes or desires of those to whom they are responsible (in this case those who pay for them) can be seen as godmothers. The use of this gendered term for a task largely masculinized complicates how violence is narrated and imagined in Mexico.

Another example of this gendered narration occurred the last time that Manolo was attacked: "He told me that, if he saw me again, he would kill me. That they were tired of me. They hit me, they assaulted me, one of them punched my testicles, grabbed my testicles from behind hard." While Manolo discussed the encounter as one of physical violence, the focus on his testicles can also be understood as a form of emasculation by his attackers.

Manolo was afraid that, even if he went into hiding, his attackers would easily discover him. In fact, both Manolo and Libertad commented that it was common for the police, or government officials, or anyone with enough money to buy citizens' personal information kept by the Instituto Federal Electoral (Federal Electoral Institute, IFE), now Instituto Nacional Electoral (National Electoral Institute, INE), the federal agency that deals with elections and issues electoral cards for the purposes of voting and identification. Information could also be bought regarding other government databases and banks. A 2010 investigative report by the Mexican newspaper *El Universal* found that one could buy a set of three external memory drives, 160 gigabytes each, in Tepito, a neighbourhood in Mexico City known for the selling of extralegal material (Gonzalez 2010). The drives included "the country's electoral register, the registry of all the cars and driver's licenses among other 'products.' The information has been acquired by organized crime groups as well as police officers who use it to work, since in their sectors that information is not available" (Gonzalez 2010). A *New York Times* story in 2017 also noted that "human rights lawyers, journalists, and anti-corruption activists have been targeted by advanced spyware sold to the Mexican government" (Ahmed and Perlroth 2017). These practices exemplify how technologies to produce docile bodies include not only verbal threats and physical violence, which create emotional and physical marks, but also an extensive "surveillant assemblage" of tracking marked bodies across national, and even international, spaces (Haggerty and Ericson 2000).

Like Manolo, Johann also experienced persecution because of his political work. Born in Veracruz, Johann lived undocumented in the United States as a child before returning to Mexico to attend university in the northern city of Monterrey. He hoped to become a lawyer and contribute to social change in the country. He became associated with the communist community and interested in the work of the Ejercito Zapatista de Liberación Nacional (EZLN, Zapatista National Liberation Army). Through his involvement in the latter, Johann travelled with a caravan organized in 2006 to support La Otra Campaña (The Other Campaign), a campaign designed to operate alongside the presidential elections that year but whose goal was the creation of grassroots social change (Marcos and Ejército Zapatista de Liberación Nacional 2006). During this time, flower vendors in San Salvador Atenco in Estado de Mexico were denied access to sell their products and brutalized. They previously had their land expropriated by the government to build an airport and successfully resisted it. To support them, the EZLN suspended the caravan, and Johann returned to Monterrey. By that time, the local Monterrey activist organizations to which he belonged were facing increasing repression from the police. When the EZLN announced that it was renewing the caravan and travelling to Monterrey, the organizations became more visible, and the repression intensified.

Johann's involvement in actively questioning the government's legitimacy led to a variety of attacks. Like Manolo, Johann identified the last attack as an important factor in his decision to emigrate:

> The last time they picked me up was after a May 1st parade [International Workers' Day], . . . and that day, when they picked me up, I thought I would not return home. Fortunately, nothing happened. They didn't kill me. They beat me up and whatever, but they didn't kill me . . . I feel my life is in danger though. Even though I feel supported by a group, just like during the dirty war, you never know when you won't return home or when they are going to do what they are threatening to do. So, due to all that, I decide, you know what? I'm going to escape for some time.

Johann's use of *la ultima vez* (the last time) draws our attention to the experience of a series of attacks and the continuous repression experienced by activists. His narrative also points to a normalization of violence. Furthermore, the unmarked aggressors who beat Johann could have been police officers, disrupting the assumed identity of the "criminal," a process to which Johann alluded through his reference to dirty war strategies and infiltration. Documenting violence becomes important after migration, particularly in refugee applications, but it is difficult to do this if the aggressors are not identifiable.

A similar example of the interlocking of different forms of persecution came from Arne Saknussemm, who chose his pseudonym after a character in Jules Verne's (2005) *Journey to the Center of the Earth*. A musician, activist, and journalist, Arne Saknussemm ran for local office in Mexico City in the early 2000s as part of a political party created to mirror the nineteenth-century party of Benito Juarez, the first Indigenous Mexican president. He participated because he was part of an ethnic minority, the *Gitanxs* or Roma. Although a number of Roma have identified the term "gypsy" as derogative and offensive, Arne Saknussemm did not share that belief and identified himself as a *Gitano*. Although he lost the election, his party performed very well in his district, attracting attention from the left-leaning Partido de la Revolución Democrática (PRD), which won the election.

PRD officials sought revenge, affecting the livelihood of Arne Saknussemm in two ways. First, they conspired to terminate a contract that he had to produce music events across the country. Second, a PRD official in Mexico City publicly vowed to close his businesses, including a café that had become a general meeting place for the *Gitanx* community in the area.

The official succeeded. Despite these attacks, Arne Saknussemm found it difficult to believe that he was facing persecution: "People would tell me, 'Don't you think you're facing persecution?' And I would respond, 'No, of course not.' My lawyer regularly told me, 'Listen, I've never seen them be so fixated on a person. You don't get out of something when you're already involved in something else.' And I got used to fighting."

Arne Saknussemm also worked as an investigative journalist for several newspapers and magazines. He covered stories ranging from organ trafficking to political extortion. Some stories implicated government officials, including those from the PRD. As a result, he was detained and questioned by the police. His car and computer were also stolen. Mexico is a dangerous country for journalists. According to the Committee to Protect Journalists (2020), since 1994 ninety-five journalists and media workers have been murdered in Mexico, with the bulk coming after 2004. For instance, in 2010, thirteen were murdered, "targeted by drug traffickers, police and members of the army" often with impunity (Canada Newswire 2010). The violence has led a number of Mexican journalists to seek protection in the United States and Canada (Law 2012; Méndez Pineda 2017). In 2011, the United Nations Office of the High Commissioner for Human Rights urged Mexico to investigate the deaths, which it argued demonstrate the growth of general insecurity (Terra Networks 2011).

Immediately before leaving Mexico, Arne Saknussemm and his partner, also involved in activist work against the PRD, were beaten. At the police department where they went to file a complaint, they discovered "that the same people who had beaten us up arrived at the police station greeting the police officers with whom we were making the complaint." This meant that unmarked police officers (perhaps *madrinas*) had enacted the violence, making a complaint ineffective.

Libertad, also a journalist, worked at a university in Mexico City looking to expand from three to four campuses. She explained that the building of another campus would bring the university more prestige, particularly to administrators, commenting that it was common knowledge that top administrators, for instance university presidents, often moved on to hold government posts. However, the university was facing a serious deficit that led to the implementation of cuts. Because Libertad was active in her labour union, particularly in relation to gender-based labour discrimination, she participated in events to resist the cuts.

Despite its deficit, the university bought the land to build the campus. Surprised by this move, Libertad discovered that the land was covered under environmental protection, so very little of it could be used. She also found out that the university had overpaid for the land. She made the information public among students and outside the university, prompting her colleagues and supervisors to recommend that she stop "agitating." One day her employer sent her to cover a story at an isolated place, where three men were waiting for her, planning to sexually assault her. As feminist scholars have argued, the threat of sexual violence is a tool to silence women who engage in activist practices (Kaufman and Williams 2010). And, since there is a general problem with impunity in Mexico, a large number of cases go unpunished (Godoy 2011).

Libertad escaped from her potential attackers and decided to leave her job. However, the threat of violence led to a complicated escape from the city: "I lose my job, they [look] for me at my house, I move to other places within the city, I move to the neighbouring town, Cuernavaca, but then decide to go to Acapulco. They go to Acapulco and look for me at my [mother's] house." When "they," unmarked men, arrived at her mother's house, Libertad was not present. However, they spoke to her brother: "My brother . . . gets mad and hits me. Then, as he is hitting me, he gives me some fragmented details: 'You are a communist, you have always had those types of problems. Now you come here, you're putting us in danger.'" The reaction added another layer of gender-based violence, to which the rest of the family contributed by dissuading Libertad from pressing charges. At that point, her sister invited her to travel to Canada.

When I first interviewed Libertad in 2009, it was five years after she had left her university job. Yet her university email address remained valid. Curious, Libertad checked it from time to time and reported that she sometimes received "friendly" emails asking her how she was and where she was living, demonstrating the operation of a "surveillant assemblage" (Haggerty and Ericson 2000).

Organized Crime

Another aspect of insecuritization involved the drug trade and organized crime associated with it. Although the trafficking of drugs to and from Mexico can be traced to at least 1910 (Recio 2002), its policing intensified in recent decades. During the Calderon presidency (2006–12), Mexico saw an increased emphasis on national security and the intensification of a "war on drugs" that continued with his successor, Enrique Peña Nieto.

Calderon's strategies of increased militarization marked a shift in how Mexico engaged with narcotrafficking. From 2006 to 2010, 45,000 troops and 5,000 federal police were deployed to eighteen states in support of the "war" (Jimenez 2010). Although some leaders of organized crime organizations have been arrested, the cost, in both capital and lives, has been tremendous. Between 2007 and 2014, the death toll was 164,000 (Breslow 2015). Furthermore, from 2006 to 2010, almost 4,000 human rights abuses were committed by the army as evidenced by complaints submitted to the Mexican government (Jimenez 2010). In addition, 30,000 Mexicans were forcibly "disappeared" (Pastrana 2016). Thus, though the war on drugs was proposed as a way to stop drug trafficking, the violence has disproportionately affected a large number of non-military and non-narco civilians in urban and rural areas (Joynes-Burgess 2009). In addition to murders and forced disappearances, the Comisión de Defensa y Promoción de los Derechos Humanos (Commission for the Defence and Promotion of Human Rights) identified over 280,000 instances of forced displacement between 2011 and 2015 (Pastrana 2016).

The war on drugs has always operated transnationally. In the 1970s, US President Richard Nixon "launched the original 'war on drugs' ... This policy contained both domestic and very prominent international components, explicitly targeting Mexico as a key site for the eradication of opium crops and marijuana" (González 2009, 72). In the 1990s, in preparation for NAFTA, Carlos Salinas de Gortari allowed US Drug Enforcement Administration agents to operate in Mexico, demonstrating the links between economic neoliberal policies and those focusing on "national security" (González 2009). Transnational "collaboration" to combat the drug trade continued. For instance, in 2007, the United States sponsored the Merida Initiative, a $700 million assistance package to Mexico that included "$5m funding for human rights training for Mexican police, and $1m to support human rights monitoring by the UN High Commissioner for Human Rights Office" (United Kingdom Foreign and Commonwealth Office 2010, para 17). Canadian officers have also participated in training Mexican police. In 2010, Canada sent "eight Spanish-speaking RCMP [Royal Canadian Mounted Police] officers to train Mexican police" along with $4 million "to help Mexico strengthen its judicial system" (Jimenez 2010, para 18).

The war on drugs and approaches to "managing" it led a number of Mexicans to relocate abroad in search of security. For instance, in recent decades, the number of asylum claims by Mexican nationals in the United States and Canada because of narcotrafficking increased (Hansen 2009). During my interviews with participants, Teresa, a photographer from the north of Mexico, was the only one who explicitly discussed narcotrafficking as a reason for emigrating. In doing so, she was reluctant given the potential for identification. In Mexico, Teresa had worked at a photography shop with close relations to organized crime. Although she never participated in illicit activities, she felt implicated in them:

> I think that I carried a bit of insecurity with me, in an indirect way, even when I did not have anything to do with the situation ... The connection to those people is so strong . . . In some way, they have the power to observe you anywhere you go such that you don't have the option of simply changing jobs and pretending you have other things to do. In some way, you are still . . . connected to them. Your name never comes off a list of people there.

Teresa spoke of indirect insecuritization or what I call *insecurity by association*. Broadly, this refers to an exposure to increased insecurity because of loose or tight social relations. In Teresa's case, the insecurity by association involved being part of a web of people loosely associated with organized crime. Teresa thought that the police could not protect her from the wide lens of surveillance of the narcotraffickers, which as I described above, can draw on easily bought and sold police and government data. According to Teresa, narcos kept a "list of people" loosely associated with them, and once your name makes that list *nunca sales* (you never leave). Thus, relocation can be counteracted by a person's inability to leave the association, which Teresa was aware of, even in Canada.

Homophobia

Experiences of homophobia and the insecuritization that it produced also affected participants' lives and influenced their decisions to migrate.

We can think through these experiences using the work of queer migration theorists (Cantú, Naples, and Vidal-Ortiz 2009; Luibhéid 2004; Luibhéid and Cantú 2005; Somerville 2005). Cantú, Naples, and Vidal-Ortiz (2009, 37) argue that "sexual identities . . . are linked to capitalist development and urban migration," which migration scholars have not addressed adequately. They also emphasize sexual identities as part of an interlocking system of social relations.

The accounts of queer participants therefore not only diversify the experiences and subjectivities of participants pre-migration but also complicate my use of insecuritization. As Cantú, Naples, and Vidal-Ortiz (2009, 161) state, we need to "[examine] homophobia and sexism as structural issues, as are poverty and racism." Thus, ways of knowing related to homophobia are part of an assemblage of general insecuritization that participants experienced in Mexico, and like other forms discussed above homophobia is affected by the general impunity, lack of police protection, and police violence that exist in the country. A 2010 poll on discrimination in Mexico found that 42.8 percent of lesbians, homosexuals, and bisexuals surveyed saw the police as the "most intolerant sector of society" (Nicaragua Solidarity Network of Greater New York 2011). The police have also been implicated in perpetuating violence against queer Mexicans, leading to increased distrust (Ortiz-Hernández and Granados-Cosme 2006, 134). This is in contrast to recent efforts to improve the rights of queer Mexicans, at least on paper, through the passage of same-sex marriage in Mexico City in 2010 (civil unions since 2007) and the right of transgender individuals to change their names legally since 2004 (Arce 2010; Outright Action International 2004).

For Teresa, the everyday insecurity by association of working in a business tied to narcotrafficking interlocked with experiences of homophobia at work and at home. She was cognizant of the lack of protection available for queer Mexicans:

> In terms of homophobia, even though Mexico supposedly has some tolerance, it is something that is quite invisible because the reality is that people who marry and/or have relationships with people of the same sex are not protected. It is subjective to say that as human beings we have rights that can't be infringed in terms of our security because they don't

> really exist. There rights are disregarded in terms of security, personal integrity, and no institution exists to really protect us. There are lots of [institutions] that claim to protect us, in fact, I don't know all of them [laughs] . . . But in reality they can't legally do anything to protect us. That means that one has to reach something like Amnesty International, after having experienced a number of atrocities, in order for them to call it an act of violence, aggression, homophobia . . . And, on the other hand, narcotrafficking is the same thing. You can supposedly go to the police, but unfortunately in Mexico they are all part of the same business. So there are no options on either side . . . Unfortunately, Mexico is not a safe country; in my opinion, it is a country that is about to explode. In terms of security, we are walking around with our lives hanging by a thread. And you had better not be part of a vulnerable group: gay or a woman. Because being part of either group means you end up losing.

Teresa discussed a contradiction between the mirage of tolerance, which the Mexican government tries to mobilize to seem "democratic," and continued homophobic violence. Therefore, though citizens in theory can access bundles of rights, Teresa identified her distrust of the institutions meant to implement them (the law, the police, the government, and international NGOs). Put differently, a disconnect exists between laws, marked on paper, and their non-performativity (Ahmed 2004b), which leads to precarity or living, as Teresa described it, *con el alma en un hilo* (with one's life, literally soul, hanging by a thread).

Teresa also referred to a hierarchy of citizenship that privileges heterosexuality to the detriment of "vulnerable groups" such as queer Mexicans and women. Mexicano en Acción (Mexican in Action), who had lived undocumented in the United States as a child, before returning to Aguascalientes, where he attended university, also described this hierarchical citizenship: "There is no support when even heterosexual citizens don't have rights. Less so being a homosexual, they treat you worse. They even laugh at you, they almost throw eggs on your face." His comment refers to a lack of respect from the general population that interlocks with other systems of oppression.

A case in point is Berenice's experience. When Berenice was a newly graduated lawyer in her twenties, and living in the state of Guanajuato, she worked at a government agency that provided subsidized housing loans to Mexican workers. After some time, Berenice discovered that some of her colleagues were asking their clients for bribes (*mordidas*). Concerned, she made it known to her supervisors. The first consequence was that she became more visible to a supervisor in the Mexico City branch who began to harass her sexually and from whom she narrowly avoided sexual assault. Therefore, like Libertad, Berenice experienced the threat of sexual assault as a way to silence and control her questioning of corrupt institutional practices.

Berenice's supervisor became increasingly violent when he noticed a picture of her and her partner on her computer screen. His response was to write, in English, "welcome to Lesbos" on the monitor and to attempt to sexually assault her again. He also outed her to her co-workers, something that she had not done in order to prevent homophobic violence. This interlocking of gender-based sexual and homophobic violence led Berenice to quit her job.

In addition to the workplace violence, along with her partner, Berenice experienced gender-based and homophobic violence at home. Although they did not publicize their relationship, Berenice thought that neighbours knew because of how her gay friends performed their sexual orientation through their mode of dress when they visited the couple: "[Our neighbours] knew that we were lesbians, and they did different things to us. They cut our water, they cut our electricity, they wrote graffiti on our house. One time we had to paint the whole house; I even have pictures and everything ... They painted *machorras,* which is a pejorative way to say lesbian."

This violence demonstrates how place is used to regulate sexuality and enforce heteronormativity (Brown and Larry 2003). The actions marked the neighbourhood as heterosexual and punished, through the cutting of utilities and graffiti on the walls, anyone who deviated from the norm. Berenice and her partner became increasingly visible to other neighbours and passersby and potentially vulnerable to more attacks. We can return to the concept of insecurity by association here. The association of Berenice's home as a "deviant" space extended the violence (Valentine 1998).

Berenice faced an additional source of violence: her partner's brother. This was another example of family members disciplining women for their actions (similar to Libertad). One night he arrived at their home and began to shout at them. This was a somewhat common event for the couple, who endured the violence whenever he was in town (he worked as a *coyote* or cross-border migration facilitator and had US permanent residence). This example also demonstrates how violence can move transnationally: if Berenice and her partner had decided to migrate to the United States instead of Canada, they might have had to encounter the brother's violence again. However, that night Berenice decided to put an end to the situation:

> So I open the door to put a stop to it. We were stupid! We exposed ourselves too much [laughs] by opening the door. He came in, and the first thing he did was to punch me, bam! And I fell to the floor. My partner came out and began to fight with him, and he also hit her ... Then he took out a gun and put it on my head and began to tell us a bunch of things ... Then suddenly my ... partner stood up, he was very drunk, almost falling, and my partner hit him with a, it was like a figurine that we had, made of metal, and she hit him, but she only made him budge. Then he stumbled, and my ... partner pushed him, and he fell. I stood up, and we pushed him. I swear I don't know how we did it ... We closed the door.

The police augmented the violence by failing to protect the couple when they reported the incident:

> I arrived with my partner, [and the police asked us], "What is this about?"
>
> "Well," my ... partner said, "my brother hit us."
>
> "Why did he hit you? What happened?" etc.
>
> "Because she's my partner." [Berenice claps] They changed like that.
>
> "Ahhh," like that. With an attitude you would not believe. "Oh, that's why he hit you?"
>
> My partner says, "Yes, because he doesn't agree with our relationship."
>
> They begin to tell [her] "Well, don't you agree? You have to understand how he feels." ... Those type of stupid comments.
>
> So of course I got angry and said, "You know what? You shouldn't give your opinion. You should do your job and take her statement."

At that moment, the police asked Berenice to leave the room. Given her legal expertise, she tried to act as her partner's representative, but she did not have the proper identification to work criminal cases. Therefore, she had to wait outside. The police continued to listen to Berenice's partner's story while repeatedly telling her partner that she was too pretty to be a lesbian. However, they did not follow up, demonstrating again impunity for perpetrators and sending a tacit message that the violence was warranted and could be repeated in the future. This failure to protect them enforced heteronormativity and illustrates why queer folks distrust the police.

Mexicano en Acción experienced a more dispersed type of violence. He felt the pressure of hegemonic masculinity (Connell and Connell 2000) as homophobic comments circulated constantly around him: "'Men don't cry, suck it up like a macho,' and 'Go play soccer,' and 'Go to the street and get dirty' [literally, drag yourself on the floor or dirt] . . . They always made humiliating comments . . . I don't know if maybe it was because I was young and perhaps they thought I acted effeminately." As a gay man, he found it increasingly difficult to bear such comments from his family, schoolmates, and the media, knowing that verbal abuse could always escalate to physical abuse.

Mexicano en Acción also experienced instances of homophobia at school, resulting in depression and leading him to contemplate suicide. He recounted leading a "double life," trying to hide his encounters with gay and lesbian friends from his family and school friends. This double life made it difficult for him to reach out when he experienced abuse:

> Then I met a guy, but he was older than I was . . . He saw I was naive, stupid, or whatever you want, and some unpleasant incidents took place, and how was I to ask my parents for help? . . . How and where could I find help? My own family did not support me . . . That was when I said, "Enough is enough. What am I doing in this country?" They treat me almost as bad as a stray dog.

Lack of family support and state violence are important push factors for queer migrants who often look abroad to places like Canada for protection (Murray 2015; White 2014). However, this strategy is not always successful.

Returning to the Transnational Production of Insecurity

Although participants focused on localized experiences of insecuritization, some also scaled up and discussed international processes, including imperialism and trade relations. US imperialism in Mexico is well documented (Gonzalez and Fernandez 2003; Johnson 2001; Ngai 2004). In the 1930s, President Lazaro Cardenas acted to nationalize a number of industries as a way to sever ties with international interests in Mexico (French and Manzanárez 2004, 26). He also distributed more land to *campesinxs* than his predecessors through the communal land ownership *ejido* system (French and Manzanárez 2004, 25). However, the rupture was short lived, and the Mexican economy again showed ties to foreign interests, particularly those of the United States, in the mid-twentieth century.

Canadian imposition in Mexico historically has been less visible. However, it has had important effects: "After Cardenas, much Mexican capital operated in increasingly close partnership with U.S. and Canadian corporations" (Bacon 2008, 55). There are several examples of Mexico's growing ties with Canada (Gutiérrez-Haces 2015), including via NAFTA. Some theorists argue that "NAFTA ushered in political and economic dependency to a degree not seen since Spanish colonialism, with more than 85 percent of exports and the majority of imports oriented to the U.S. market" (Carlsen 2008). Although the emphasis is often on Mexico's immediate neighbour to the north, when measuring such dependency, "Canada's merchandise trade with Mexico has nearly quintupled since NAFTA came into effect," and "Canada and Mexico are now among each other's largest trading partners, while Canada has become a major foreign investor in Mexico" (Foreign Affairs and International Trade Canada 2011).

Of particular importance is resource extraction: "Mexican statistics rank Canada as the fourth largest investor in Mexico, with mining and oil extraction being the largest sector attracting Canadian investment" (Foreign Affairs and International Trade Canada 2011). Canadian mining and oil extraction accounted for 42.5 percent of direct Canadian investment between 1999 and 2009 (Foreign Affairs and International Trade Canada 2011). Furthermore,

> of 1800 mining projects up and running . . . 813 are transnationally owned, an astounding 87% of them Canadian, according to the Camimex,

> the Mexican national mining chamber that oversees the industry. The Canadians are armed with revisions to Article 27 of the Mexican Constitution . . . that give them carte blanche to 'buy, rent, or enter into association' with the nation's 2800 ejidos or farmers' rural collective production units. (Ross 2009)

Canadian mining companies foment violence and environmental degradation (Hoffman and Galloway 2009). In fact, a report by the Canadian Centre for the Study of Resource Conflict found that the percentage of environmental, human rights, and other abuses by Canadian mining companies around the world exceeded those from other companies (Whittington 2010).

Another example is labour importation through the Seasonal Agricultural Worker Program (SAWP), in which Mexico became a participant in 1974 (Service Canada 2004). The program sought to alleviate the demand for agricultural workers in Canada. However, it was also imagined as a sort of charity for Mexico. In sum, it was depicted as "a good foreign policy gesture, being a form of foreign aid and a safety valve for masses of frustrated unemployed agricultural workers, as well as a deterrent for illegal migration" (Basok 2000, 218). If we conceptualize Canadian imposition in Mexico as an imperialist process, then we can see that the effects of this insecuritization become exported to Canada through the SAWP and other migration flows.

Finally, imperialist relations play out through the imposition of an "American dream narrative" (Chavez 2001, 116). The hope of *arreglar papeles,* literally to fix one's papers or to regularize one's status, is powerful. That hope often arises from what *arreglar papeles* represents for individuals: security, economic stability, and/or an end to persecution. Yet, as the southern United States border has become increasingly militarized, migration patterns have diversified. In that process, the "American dream" has also undergone a reassemblage in which those who migrated to Canada, or had ties with migrants to Canada, could imagine a "Canadian dream."

Although participants did not mention Canadian imperialism specifically as a reason for emigrating, some did articulate imperialism as a cause. Johann's historicizing of the displacement of *campesinxs* by NAFTA is a case in point. His activism linked questions of class struggle and the transnational dispossession of land. One facet of his political work involved local *ejidatarios* who lost their lands because of changes to Section 27 of the Mexican constitution:

> Due to the free-trade agreement, where they started importing products that we used to consume locally, the land began to be destroyed, the people became impoverished, and the government wanted to buy their land, so the people had to sell huge tracts of land for very little. But it so happens that some time went by, I don't remember what the time period was, I think it was five or ten years. If during that period the land was not used by the government for the reason it had bought it, the land returns to the people. So the people begin to reclaim it . . . And the government doesn't want to give it up. Why? Because there's rumours that there's natural resources there.

Similarly, Manolo linked localized violence to other transnational relations:

> You're seeing that the police are colluding, that those who don't cheat don't get ahead in Mexico, that if you have money you can pay for anything in Mexico. That's because there's no jobs, the people live in an illegal manner. It's anarchy, its chaos, but ultimately this is all sponsored by the United States and other countries. It's sponsored by them because you can have a country, divide it, instigate chaos, and whoever brings peace gets the most out of it.

Manolo asserted that those who do not participate in "illegal" activities cannot get ahead in life, describing this process as *avanzar,* advancing (through time and space but also progressing in life or seeking a more livable life). In fact, he argued that people negotiate or make do with being unemployed or underemployed by resorting to extralegal means. This does not mean only engaging in criminal acts such as theft. For instance, as I stated above, street vendors such as Leonel took up sections of the sidewalk to make makeshift businesses and paid the police regular bribes (*mordidas*). Such practices are caused in part by a systemic and institutionalized corruption in which the police and bureaucrats participate and that are supported by international interests.

***

Focusing on migrant narratives and the social, economic, and political contexts in Mexico, in this chapter I have proposed a view of insecuritization in Mexico as economic instability because of poverty, underemployment, and lack of opportunities as well as the generalized threat to one's well-being. More specifically, I have outlined insecuritization through interrelated elements: the economic and political contexts in Mexico from which participants emigrated, the role of transnational imperialist practices in dislocating Mexicans, and specific narratives of insecuritization. Insecuritization is revealed as an assembled process that includes the production of knowledge about security and economic "development," often through the law, academic scholarship, and reports from nongovernmental organizations. They promote or resist ideas related to criminality, the punishment of dissent, gender-based violence, and homophobia. Knowledge is also produced by individuals who experience and enact insecurity: family and community members, the police, and *madrinas*. Organizations and institutions include workplaces, the police, the criminal justice system, and the family. These processes are facilitated by technologies that produce knowledge about those deemed in need of surveillance and capture. Finally, they also produce affective responses, including uncertainty and fear, which, given the extent of insecuritization, permeate Mexican society.

I have paid particular attention to how participants narrated their experiences through time. For instance, they used metaphors of time to describe their current conditions – living day to day or hand to mouth – as well as to describe their hopes for a better future. They also used time to historicize experience, for example by noting the opening of a superstore that displaced small business owners or the length of time that they experienced violence and the eroding of security. Such a process was something to withstand, aguantar, until enough was enough, and the opportunity or need to migrate ensued.

The implication is that illegalization is not a nation-state-bound process. In fact, experiences of insecuritization can mark and follow emigrants and continue to affect them post-migration. Thus, markers that affected participants in Mexico, such as socio-economic status, sexual orientation, and gender, continued to affect their migration and status trajectories. In the following chapter, I extend that analysis by discussing participants' experiences during transit.

2

Transit and Encountering Borders

I interviewed Armando in his Toronto apartment in 2015. After a bad business venture in the late 2000s, he travelled to Montreal to learn French and earn money to repay a debt. He eventually made his way to eastern Ontario and then Toronto after a refused refugee claim. During the interview, he described his experience arriving in Montreal:

> [It was] horrible, horrible. The first person [a border official] was very unpleasant. The second was nicer . . . I was coming from Mexico, right? . . . I knew it was summer, but I didn't know how things were [weather-wise in Canada]. I arrived with a jacket that would be somewhat warm in Mexico, . . . and the first woman asked me what I planned to do and what I did in Mexico.
>
> She asked, "Do you know that it's summer?"
>
> I said, "Yes."
>
> She said, "So why do you need that jacket you have on?"

Armando alluded to several factors that motivate this chapter. First, he described the border official's demeanour as hostile, a demeanour that other participants also identified. Second, he described officials' scrutiny of his belongings and clothing choices as a strategy to identify potential "overstayers."

Mexican migrants experienced such practices during their transit to Canada. Transit encompasses more than the act of physically crossing the border between two nation-states. It begins pre-migration, extends post-arrival, and involves complex travel that disrupts normative ideas about migration being a quick unidirectional process (Bailey 2001; Collyer 2007; Sladkova 2016). Two elements informed participants' transit experiences. The first element involves the amount of planning that goes into the act of migration. Participants compiled pre-migration information from different types of networks: the internet, family members, and migration facilitators (individuals who assist in migration, both directly and indirectly). However, some migrants do not have time to make plans, their quick departures making them less likely to investigate conditions in their countries of destination. The second element involves what happens once migrants embark on a trip and encounter borders, as in the case of Armando's interaction with airport officials. Participant experiences support the argument that borders are not just geographic divisions between territories, notably nation-states. They are *practised, negotiated,* and *contested* (Godenau 2014; Kolossov and Scott 2013; Kyle 2000). In fact, we can think of *bordering* as a verb, a process that involves the management of migration, categorization of bodies, requirements for transparency (Hall 2015), and exclusion of those identified as undeserving of entry (Van Houtum 2010, 959).

Transit should be understood as a space where and a time when migrant illegalization operates. This assembled process involves *ways of knowing, actors, institutions/organizations, technologies,* and *ways of feeling.* Border enforcement organizes formal ways of determining entry eligibility that are then enforced by individual actors. To do this, enforcement agencies capture, archive, and share information about potential travellers and their migration histories through databases, biometrics, and other technologies. Alternatively, migrants put together "paperealities," information stored on paper that produces a particular travel narrative: tickets, accommodation plans, tourism plans, letters of invitation, et cetera (White 2014). To do this, they rely on technologies to seek out information about the best places, times, and modes of migration. They also draw on networks: family members, other migrants, and migration facilitators. However, the evidence that they compile might not fully convince immigration officials, and migrants might have to be resourceful during immigration interviews. As a result, the process of crossing borders produces affective responses. Potential entrants can experience fear and uncertainty, a process that can be prolonged (Dow 2007; Griffiths 2014).

For participants, encounters with immigration officials and surveillance practices were sometimes straightforward. However, having the ability to travel to Canada without an entry visa (which they did until 2009) did not preclude them from experiencing moments when their race, gender, and class status became markers for potential illegality.

Planned Departures and Learning to Emigrate

Although planning is always partial and incomplete, it provides potential migrants with a bit of control over their mobility. Planning can include deciding what to do with one's possessions, saying goodbye to family members, saving money for the trip, and researching information about the destination. The last one illustrates a process of compiling knowledge (ways of knowing) by migrants, demonstrating agency in a structured migration process. For instance, Eduardo's lifestyle in Mexico City changed significantly after he lost a well-paying job. He eventually patched together several precarious jobs, including providing security to wealthier Mexicans. One of those jobs was at the airport, where a co-worker shared that he was planning to migrate to Canada. Eduardo asked to join him, hoping to find stable work abroad. The two planned the trip together, researching facts about Canada on the internet.

The internet is an important starting point for researching migration information. Although much research on migrants' internet use focuses on incorporation techniques, political activities, and transnational practices of communication (Chadwick and Howard 2009, 278; Staeheli et al. 2002), potential migrants also use the internet to learn to migrate. Researching information therefore involves appraising the value and accuracy of each source and/or comparing different sources to find possible trends, particularly when potential migrants are not versed in the immigration and labour laws of the country of migration.

In the case of Canada, official migration information is available through government websites, including Citizenship and Immigration Canada (CIC), now Immigration, Refugees and Citizenship Canada (IRCC). However, most of that information is available only in English or French and targets permanent immigrants or those who seek information about specific temporary means to travel to Canada to visit, work, or study. There are also several blogs and forums. For instance, an online article entitled "Trabajar de ilegal en Canada" [Working Illegally in Canada] described the process of falling out of status in Canada as well as its associated benefits and detriments (Consejos Gratis 2011). Although some information was useful, such as the outlining of precarious status migrants' entitlement to social goods and the possibility of deportation, the article included misinformation. A stated "benefit" of not having status was not paying taxes, which precarious status migrants pay via sales taxes and paycheque deductions.

Another example involves social media groups to which potential migrants post questions to learn about Canada. A 2017 news story by Aristegui Noticias (2017) recounted that "dozens of Mexicans [in the United States] try to continue north with their 'American Dream' and social media references to 'Mexicanos en Canada' [Mexicans in Canada] have become a first step to remigration, because they provide information about work permits, employment and rental prices." Similar examples exist for those in Mexico who yearn to travel to Canada. However, in my experience, social media group members often berated those asking questions for their intention to become "illegal" and for making their legal co-nationals look bad. This process of illegalization can affect migrants detrimentally both during transit and in the context of migration. They can also be provided with partial or wrong information. Of course, the opposite is also true; pre-migration information can facilitate or lessen impending illegalization.

Despite the difficulty in evaluating information, the search yielded some benefits for Eduardo and his friend. They discovered that the best time to arrive in Canada was during the summer because of the weather and job opportunities. Construction and cleaning, the types of work more readily available to migrants without work permits, were rumoured to be more abundant during that season.

For sources beyond the internet, Eduardo found an ad in a local Mexico City newspaper that asked "Piensas inmigrar a Canadá? Nosotros te ayudamos" (Are you planning to migrate to Canada? We can help you). He called the number and paid the 100-peso fee to attend a meeting. At the meeting, organizers briefed attendees on information about Canada, including job opportunities. Again, though such information can be useful, it is difficult to know its accuracy. During the meeting, the organizers offered to take

Eduardo and his friend to Canada for a fee: "He charged, I think, one thousand dollars per person, which included a month of accommodation and a job . . . Well, supposedly, I don't know. And he said he would advise us and train us so that we could pass the interview with the immigration official without any problems."

Eduardo declined the offer to be transported to Canada, yet his experience points to the existence of an industry to facilitate migration, what Kyle (2000, 67) refers to as "migration merchants": that is, "anyone profiting legally or illegally from the commodification of the international migration process." Although the predominant images of immigration facilitators are *coyotes* or smugglers working across the US-Mexico border, diversity exists in both the industry and the destination sites. As Kyle (2000, 203) comments, migration merchants can include moneylenders and transit facilitators. Such practices help migrants to reach their destinations, making it less likely that they will experience deportation and precarious conditions *during* transit. However, uncertainty plays a big role in using such services. And, once migrants/clients arrive at their destinations, illegalization can manifest itself through the taking of travel documents, extortion, and threat of deportation. Finally, fees are also major roadblocks, as Eduardo commented. Migration facilitators can charge exorbitant fees that many cannot afford, forcing potential migrants to attempt the process without help.

Like Eduardo, Liz faced a similar prospect of downward mobility after she lost her job at an import-export company in Mexico City. To gather information, she opted to send an email to the Secretaria de Relaciones Exteriores (SRE) (the Ministry of Foreign Affairs), asking about travelling to Toronto. When she did not hear back, she forwarded her email to the SRE representative's superiors and immediately received a response:

> [They] told me the weight and measurement requirements of my luggage, they recommended I not carry liquids, they recommended I speak English or French. If I could not or was nervous, they gave them the number to call for, what do you call it, a translator which they also had, and they told me my rights as a traveller . . . [and defined] the types of discrimination.

Liz's strategy demonstrated how potential migrants access knowledge about migration processes by interacting with state institutions. Her experience working at a transnational company influenced her sense of entitlement to go above the SRE representative, given that, as she stated, they "worked for the people." She felt more confident after the interaction, understanding her rights and responsibilities as a traveller, despite planning to work in Canada without a work permit. And her confidence might have influenced her border experience.

Friends and Family Members as Facilitators

In addition to migration merchants, some participants drew from friends, family members, and existing networks in Canada to facilitate their migration trajectories. Scholarship on migrant networks is extensive (Boyd 1989; Kyle 2000; Massey et al. 1993; Menjívar 2000). Networks demonstrate the workings of global assemblages, bringing together social actors, the circulation of capital (e.g., loans to facilitate migration), the recruitment of labour, the role of immigration policy in the context of reception, and the complexity of affective ties.

Access to social networks in the country of migration can provide personalized information and have the added potential of coming from seemingly trustworthy sources. However, though friends and family members are often important sources of support during transit, this is not always the case (Mahler 1995; Menjívar 2000; Zlolniski 2006). In fact, such networks can also maintain or produce forms of exploitation. Knowing someone in Canada can also be useful during the immigration interview at the point of entry because potential entrants can provide a friend's or family member's contact information to facilitate entry if that person has secure legal status.

Migration facilitators within their personal networks helped some participants with the financial costs of emigrating. For instance, Emiliana Zapata had recently graduated from university and had few job prospects in her field of linguistics and Indigenous language recovery. Her family was also facing an increasingly difficult economic situation. Unsure about how to proceed, she considered emigrating after she spoke to a friend living in Canada: "So I had the opportunity to have a friend here, whom I had visited before, and she told me 'Come here, I'll give you a hand. You can come and pay me [back for] the plane ticket and whatever else here.' I said, 'Let's go!'" In addition to the financial offer, Emiliana Zapata's friend offered a place to stay and help finding employment. Such opportunities mean that migrants do not have to worry about looking for housing right away, especially given the high cost of short-term accommodations (hotels, motels, and hostels) and renting in Toronto. The promise of employment assistance also facilitates transit because it provides an income potential. Finally, Emiliana Zapata's account demonstrates the benefit of having migration "experience." Because Emiliana Zapata had travelled to Canada in the past, to visit her friend and work temporarily, she could already foresee, to a certain extent, what it would involve to do so again.

For Leonel, a street vendor from Estado de Mexico, the decision to migrate to Canada involved a work opportunity facilitated by a family member:

> My sister had never invited me before. She had never invited me to come. She did that time. And I accepted . . . Perhaps my sister knew that I was having problems and decided to help me, I thought . . . I came because my sister told me there was a job where I would be paid twelve dollars an hour, that's what she told me. And, if I worked hard in Canada, they paid more. That's what she said.

His sister also helped him to pay for his plane ticket. During our interview, Leonel emphasized that he had made his decision because the invitation included a job and the opportunity to pursue the American or Canadian dream. However, familial help is not always straightforward. Zlolniski (2006, 10) notes that "the household can be both a bastion of resistance against hostile external forces and an arena of inequality and exploitation at the hands of family and other kin." When Leonel's sister invited Leonel, she was living in Canada with precarious status. In retrospect, Leonel thought that she had painted a picture of Canada as a place that rewards hard work but had not disclosed the day-to-day hardships associated with a lack of status and proficiency in English – as he reflected to me, "I was very naive." Once in Canada, Leonel faced hostility and exploitation in the job that his sister had arranged for him.

Another example involved Rebeca and Eduardo. She worked in sales and supported the family while he was underemployed in Mexico and Canada. Rebeca wanted to be with Eduardo but thought that he imposed her emigration, and she was resentful because she had to quit her job. While I was interviewing them, Rebeca turned to her husband and stated, "Well, I emigrated for you, I had a job [in Mexico]." Her comment pointed to her discomfort at not having equal say in deciding in which country their family should live.

Finally, some participants benefited from additional information. Berenice left for Canada with her partner because of persecution from her supervisor, family members, and community members for her sexual orientation. Berenice recalled a conversation that she'd had with a friend, who had invited her to travel to Canada: "He told me, 'Why don't you come here? Look, you can stay with me, I can help you . . . You can even apply for refugee status because of all you've been through, because of your sexual orientation, everything.'" Their conversation is an example of how potential migrants strategize to prevent migrant illegalization *before* emigrating, including compiling the necessary documents to apply for protection. Berenice was the only participant who mentioned gathering such documents before her departure.

Measuring Departures through Time

Participants who faced persecution or dire economic prospects hoped to emigrate quickly. Two interrelated factors affected quick departures: the procurement of travel documents, which took time, and the reasons that participants chose to migrate to Canada. Leaving one's life and place of residence can be difficult, and doing so in the span of days means prioritizing. For participants, this included immediate decisions such as what and how much to pack, negotiating their need to pack essential long-term items with the possibility that immigration agents would deny their entry if they were identified as potential "overstayers." Rushed decisions also involved coming up with enough money for travel costs and starting a new life.

Johann left Mexico after experiencing violence by the police and unmarked attackers in Monterrey for his activist work. Given the imminent threat, he had to perform several tasks in a limited time:

> The decision took around a month, twenty-nine days, well, the decision took three or four days, but the following two to three weeks I had to

> empty my house and, you know, the normal procedures. So I went and took my things to a friend's house and stayed there for a few days because I didn't want to return to my house, because we had used it as the main office for our organization.

The bureaucratic process of applying for a passport slowed Johann's plans, extending his insecurity and controlling his interactions in risky places, such as his home, where potential attackers could find him. Like other participants, Johann experienced two different time periods: the time that it took to decide to leave and the time that it took to carry out the decision.

For other participants, such as Berenice, financial need attenuated the urgency to leave the country: "It was about fifteen days, less than fifteen days, . . . and I even wanted to leave that same week, but we didn't go because we didn't have enough money. We had to get money from here and there to pay for the flight." Her comment points to another factor mediating quick departures: last-minute flights are expensive, especially if they are non-stop. Flights to Canada often stop in the United States, but if travellers do not have visas to stop there (and they are difficult to obtain for many Mexicans) they have to take a direct flight. During this dead or sticky time (Dow 2007; Griffiths 2014), Berenice compiled information for her refugee case, a process facilitated by her legal background.

"Choosing" Canada

One reason that participants chose to travel to Canada was that, until 2009, they were not required to apply for a visa to enter the country. Applying for an entry visa adds layers of work and time in addition to applying for or renewing passports. Furthermore, participants saw Canada as a good option because they could arrive via plane, whereas entering the United States without a visa, a traditional trajectory for undocumented Mexican migrants, meant potentially risking their lives crossing the desert. This is an example of how migrants negotiate, to a certain extent, migrant illegalization across different nation-states.

However, the fact that Canada did not require an entry visa did not make it the automatic choice for participants. Arne Saknussemm recounted how choosing Canada was a question of chance for him. After seeing his attackers arrive at the police station where he was making a complaint because of persecution for his journalistic work and his Roma or *Gitano* identity, he decided to leave Mexico. He "left the police station around ten at night. Among the group of friends and colleagues emerged the idea of leaving the country. One of them took the phone and called a travel agent, where he was told the countries for which it was easier to get a flight without a visa." When booking his flight, his only requirement was that the country of destination did not require an entry visa. At that time, two countries satisfied that requirement and seemed to be agreeable: Spain and Canada. The travel agent advised him that the next available flight was to Canada and would depart in twenty-four hours.

Participants also identified choosing Canada because of an understanding that it was tolerant and followed human rights protocols. Manolo, a political cartoonist who faced persecution because of his critique of the Partido Acción Nacional party, explained that he had based his decision to travel from Mexico City to Canada on "common knowledge." That knowledge included information that he had heard in the news and from people around him that depicted Canada as a safe and welcoming place: "I didn't need a visa, it's in the same continent, it's a country that speaks of human rights, supports other countries, protects other countries, well, that's what we had heard [laughs]. That's what I thought [laughs]. Those were the rumours." Manolo's laughter during the interview pointed to his critical view of Canada after having lived in the country for several years, particularly his experience of the refugee determination system.

Teresa had heard similar rumours and made her decision to migrate by comparing Canadian and US policies vis-à-vis LGBTQ rights and racism:

> I always imagined it [Canada] as a safe and *lejano* [faraway] country. Far away from all the problems that I was going through in Mexico and [a place] that was accepting of the homosexual community . . . The US definitely never was an option. It is a place that is also more open in terms of homosexuality. But at the same time, it is an extremely violent country. It is also extremely racist.

Teresa used a double meaning for the term *lejano*, referring to Canada as spatially far away as well as qualitatively different from the United States and Mexico. Before her departure, she thought that Canada could counteract the other two countries' negative qualities, considering the interlocking modes of oppression that she experienced: racism, homophobia, and lack of access to security. However, returning to Manolo's comments, Teresa had also based her decision on the rumours that she had heard about the country, which did not include information about immigration status or the lived reality of racialized queer residents in Toronto. Thus, Teresa exhibited what Puar (2007) has termed "homonationalism": the mobilization of exceptionality given queer rights in a country (in this case Canada) that occludes continued homophobia and its relationship to race and imperialism.

Crossing the Border

Pre-Migration Screening/Pre-Departure Illegalization

At the airport, before they depart for their destinations, migrants experience illegalization. As organizations that use technologies to determine legitimate travellers, airlines are part of an immigration management assemblage. For example, airline officials are responsible for conducting baggage and document checks and making sure that passengers will be allowed to enter a country. There is an economic rationale for airlines to accept this offloading of responsibility: they have to return those denied entry to the places from which they departed, often at their expense. As Lahav (2000, 222) argues, this nexus between travel and immigration enforcement is not new:

> Since the adoption of guidelines established by the 1944 Convention on International Civil Aviation (ICAO), transport companies have increasingly been forced to assume the role of international immigration officers imposed on them by states. The standards of the convention established the airline's responsibility to ensure that passengers have the necessary travel documents. Apart from ICAO guidelines, many countries have introduced laws that increase the responsibilities of carriers and levy fines against them for noncompliance.

The move to offload immigration enforcement to entities such as airlines leads to at least two results. First, immigration control becomes an income-generating/cost-reduction process. Second, immigration surveillance grows through a project to transnationalize and externalize border controls. Nation-states form partnerships that are then applied to the business of air travel. Thus, migration management is not only about an individual nation-state's work at the border but also part of a transnationalized nationalism to protect an imagined global community of nations (Arat-Koc 2010).

The Border Encounter

The interaction between would-be entrants and immigration officers has been discussed as a "border encounter" (Dzenovska 2014; Villegas 2015b). Despite the transnationalization of immigration enforcement, this encounter demonstrates the continued role of sovereignty – a country's control over what happens within its territory. Sovereignty takes work, often enacted or performed by border officials (Friedman 2010). But how does this sovereignty occur on the ground? Often border guards follow protocols about who can enter or not enter depending on a person's migration history, luggage, and intent. However, this work also involves discretion, sensing who might become a "public charge" or "risk" (Friedman 2010; Pratt and Thompson 2008). Potential entrants also participate in the performance of sovereignty to negotiate their ability to enter a country. They utilize strategies to produce coherent and acceptable travel narratives, including the production of paperealities (White 2014). However, this evidence is not always enough, and potential entrants have to be resourceful in how they navigate conversations with border officials.

In Canada, the actual process involves a number of steps. The first is "Primary Inspection," during which "you may be asked a series of questions to determine your Immigration status, the nature of any goods you are bringing with you, your duty-free allowance and personal exemption entitlements" (Canada Border Services Agency 2013). This step funnels those identified as "low risk" into Canada. Those who require more interrogation undergo an "Immigration Secondary Examination" (Citizenship and Immigration Canada 2013, 23). During secondary examination, officials can ask potential entrants to elaborate their answers during primary inspection as well as to provide material evidence, including showing their money, opening their luggage, demonstrating their ability to return to gainful employment in their country of origin, and placating any health or criminal inadmissibility concerns (Citizenship and Immigration Canada 2013, 31–32). Although sovereignty is paramount, officers also contend with the high volume of people whom they see every day, the need to maintain a certain number of tourist entries, and perhaps an exploitable, deportable workforce.

Juan Nadie, whose pseudonym means John Doe, travelled from Queretaro to Canada to reunite with his father, living in Toronto. He planned to find secure work, having had a series of precarious work experiences in his hometown. He explained the spatial organization of the immigration sorting process:

> [The immigration officer] asked me some questions, and I answered everything, and they sent me to someone else who said "okay" and put a stamp on my paper and told me "go through there" through a hallway. Then in that hallway another agent told me "let me see your paper," and I showed it to him, and he told me "go there." And other people showed him their papers, and he told them "go the other way." He like directed them, right? They sent me to a big room with a lot of tables where there was another person, another agent.

Juan Nadie described being shuffled around a carefully orchestrated assembly line, where, at each point, he was evaluated, his papers were stamped, read, and/or sealed, and he was sent to one of several available options. For those without migration experience, this maze can be daunting and confusing.This is not an accident. The objective is for potential entrants to reveal their intentions by being fully transparent (Hall 2015) and for officers to use that information to make a decision about entry.

Evaluating Arrivals: Sex and Morality

One example of the daunting sorting process involved Rebeca, who along with her children sought to reunite with Eduardo in Toronto in the late 2000s. Upon her arrival, officials asked her a series of questions, then told her to wait before secondary examination. This waiting is "dead time" (Dow 2007): that is, moments of waiting experienced during immigration detention that I extend to refer to the moments of waiting by migrants during a border encounter, including before primary inspection, between primary and secondary examinations, waiting for an interpreter, and waiting for a decision. Dead time is an affective process in which fear and anxiety circulate among potential entrants, and distrust can circulate among border officials who feel a need to enforce sovereignty and protect the nation (Pratt and Thompson 2008).

Rebeca recounted her experience during secondary examination:

> They didn't open my luggage, but they asked me if I had a letter from my kids' schools giving them permission to travel. They found out how much money I had. Questions: what I did for a living, what I did, what I had. Obviously, I said everything right. Whatever they asked me, there were a lot of questions. I felt like, it feels like one is a criminal when you are there.

Although Rebeca sought to stay and work in Canada, she had constructed a "papereality" using a letter from her children's school and a letter of invitation from Eduardo's employer acting as a "family friend" (White 2014). Having a letter of invitation is a common way to facilitate entry given that the host takes responsibility for the tourist, particularly in terms of accommodation (Vancouver Sun 2014). However, Rebeca described the border inspection as a process akin to confession (Salter 2007), whereby she felt guilty despite having documents to "prove" that she was travelling temporarily.

The interrogation took a turn because of the letter of invitation. Immigration officials interpreted the letter as a sign that Rebeca was having an affair with the man who had invited her. They asked, "Where did I meet him? Why did he know me if he was married? Why was I coming to visit him?" In her view, the interview's moral tone exceeded immigration officers' duties regarding immigration management. Even if Rebeca were having an affair, that did not demonstrate a threat to national security or an immigration offence. As Salter (2007, 58) explains, "the border represents an important site of examination for criminal, sexual, class or labor-related deviance." The encounter demonstrates a tension in which officials' affective response to protecting the nation's morality could be resolved if Rebeca confessed, which she did not do because doing so would have meant putting her border crossing as well as her husband's continued stay in jeopardy.

Corroborating Stories

Like Rebeca, other participants had experiences at the border that involved officers who wanted to corroborate their stories. For instance, Berenice and her partner travelled together, yet they underwent the immigration interrogation separately because of a lack of understanding of border-crossing protocols:

> It was more difficult for me than for my . . . partner . . . We didn't know that we could go together to speak to an official. So we each went to a different one, . . . and the one I had acted very special [finicky].
>
> He sa[id], "What do you do in Mexico?"
>
> I said, "I'm a lawyer."
>
> "How can you prove it?"
>
> I said, "Well, here it is," and I gave him my card . . .
>
> "Mmmm, sit down" . . .
>
> Ah! They went and compared information because [they asked] "Who are you with?"
>
> I said "With her" [her partner], and the [official] went to the other [official who had spoken with her partner] to see if we had said the truth. Then they made me show them how much money I had. To take it out and all the credit cards I had.

The rationale for this mode of interrogation was to verify that Berenice and her partner articulated the same version of their reason for travelling to Canada and provided similar types of evidence: money to spend in the country as well as a job and possessions in Mexico.

Maria Pérez, who travelled to Canada with her then boyfriend to find decent work and pay off a debt, told me about a different experience of corroboration. After living in Canada for some time, she broke up with her boyfriend and co-traveller, and he returned to Mexico. He later tried to re-enter Canada:

> My boyfriend was returned twice. Ex-boyfriend. He left, we, he was here a year. He left and then came back. He tried to come to Canada again,

> and it was during the time when they were imposing the visas. So they treated him very, very bad. And, when he tried to return, they went through all his things, his computer, everything. They found cards from places here where he might have had contact, business cards of restaurants and other acquaintances. And they told him that he didn't come to visit, that they knew he came to work. They detained him like twelve hours in a room, they sent him to the, that centre, the detention centre. And he said they had him handcuffed practically the whole time. And they returned him the next day.

Maria Pérez's description demonstrates the interpretation of evidence during the border encounter. Successful evidence is not only about the facts but also about their perceived "quality," as Sara Ahmed (2016) reminds us:

> Evidence is often understood as something that relates to objects (to have evidence is to have evidence *of* something) but also to subjects (someone *has* evidence of something). Evidence can also be a trace of where someone or something has been [or will go]. However even a trace can be disputed, even crumbs can be debated: how did they get there? Who left them there? Even: are they crumbs? Evidence has to be spoken of: the crumbs do not speak for themselves.

The crumbs were contacts that Maria Pérez's ex-boyfriend had in Canada, which, for the border official, were "proof" of his intention to work in Canada without legal entitlement despite the possibility of alternative explanations. They were coupled with the fact that they were held by a Mexican man. Because of this evidence, he was returned to Mexico, also prompting the archiving of the refusal of entry into Canadian immigration databases, a process that influences subsequent entries.

Interpretation and Rude Intermediaries

One of the barriers that participants faced during the border encounter involved language. Several participants already knew English, identifying a class privilege. Those who did not either pretended that they understood English or asked for an interpreter. Maria Nueva, who travelled with her boyfriend to Canada "to see the world" and "get rich," had language difficulties during her border encounter:

> MN: [They spoke] in English. So I think that's what they asked and what we answered [laughs] because we really didn't know much English. My then boyfriend knew more English, so he answered a bit more than I did, also because the way they asked questions intimidated me a lot, the way they asked [questions], how they cornered you with questions:
>
> "How much money do you have?"
>
> "Well, we have, I don't know, a thousand dollars"
>
> So, she asked, "You know, you know that you can't work or study, right?"
>
> And my boyfriend would say, "Yes, yes, yes."
>
> "No, no, no, I'm telling you that you can't work or study. Are you going to work or study?"
>
> And my boyfriend would say, "Yes, yes" [laughs].
>
> So, she said, "I don't think you're understanding. I'm telling you, you can't work or study."
>
> And he repeated that, yes, he was going to work [laughs] and study. But it was really obvious that he wasn't understanding the question.
>
> P: And did they provide an interpreter?
>
> MN: No, . . . they didn't even offer us one. Or maybe they offered it, and we didn't realize. The point is that I think she got tired [laughs] and said, "Fine, go through, go through." So we did.

Maria Nueva's story illustrates the reality that immigration officials do not turn everyone who seems to be inadmissible away given the benefit that tourists provide to the economy. It also demonstrates the lack of clear protocols for when an interpreter is required during an immigration interview. This discretionary power might be explained by the limited time that officers have with entrants and the number of entrants whom officers see each day – leading them to make decisions based on "gut" feelings (Eggebø 2013).

Some participants did get access to interpreters. For instance, Sergio was happy to have a Mexican interpreter during his questioning. However, when he interacted with her, his perception changed. He recalled that she acted rudely, even yelling at him and questioning the validity of his answers. As an Indigenous *campesino,* Sergio was not a stereotypical cosmopolitan traveller, leading the immigration officer and interpreter to question his intention to stay and work in the country. During this encounter, he told the interpreter, "Look, *paisanita* [literally, little/dear fellow countrywoman], you're Mexican, you should help me, not speak to me in that way."

Aquetzalli, who emigrated to Canada given her inability to find a job and her desire to help her family financially, also experienced a rude interpreter: "She was Hispanic. Rude. Arrogant . . . Like 'I'm only going to translate for you. For whatever she [the border official] asks you, you answer, and I tell her. But that's it.' She didn't say, 'Don't be nervous or anything.'" Aquetzalli expected someone to provide encouragement during a difficult time and was resentful of the interpreter's behaviour. Similarly, Güero referred to his interpreter as a despot: "She reminded me of public servants in Mexico. They do the same thing every day. So there's nothing, they disengage from being human. They do things grudgingly and are there only to do their time." Güero's impression mirrored Libertad's perception of Canadian refugee determination officials.

Border Encounter Negotiations, Strategies, and Resourcefulness

As the above examples illustrate, border encounters are organized events orchestrated by officials' evaluations and discretion. Cisneros (2012, 134) notes that bordering policy produces "the immigrant body as fearful and threatening and it makes illegality a performative affect emanating from the bodies of suspected immigrants." Despite this dehumanizing process, participants anticipated some illegalizing questions and procedures by gathering documents, saving money, and understanding the requirements to secure entry. Money is key because having too little or too much can be used as evidence that a person might overstay. Potential entrants also strategized what to do or say during immigration interviews, knowing that, if they fully "confessed" their intention to stay and work in Canada, they would be turned away.

One characteristic that benefited some participants was their perceived social class. Arne Saknussemm, a journalist and musician in Mexico, explained that his entry into Canada was very easy, which, coupled with his refugee claim experience, influenced his general perception of the country. Libertad also had an easy time despite not knowing English fluently:

> The interview with immigration officials that finalizes the process of arriving in Canada . . . was in English. It was very brief, the immigration official didn't seem to care too much about me, I think it has to do with the pre-judgment they do [before the flight leaves] . . . And of course I arrived with journalist identification, so they didn't ask me a lot of questions . . . I didn't look like a *mojada* [wetback] . . . I didn't look like an undocumented migrant.

Not looking like a "wetback" can involve class-based stereotypes of *campesinxs,* day labourers, and unskilled workers, as well as racialized stereotypes of Mexicanness. Libertad thought that she did not fit the "wetback" stereotype despite being a brown-skinned mestiza, demonstrating how her class privilege trumped other stereotypes.

However, not everyone had such an easy time. Liz, who received information from the Mexican Ministry of Foreign Affairs about her rights as a traveller, used that information to negotiate an encounter with a rude officer. During the primary inspection, she listed some museums that she planned to visit as a strategy to demonstrate that she was a legitimate tourist. At the secondary examination, Liz corroborated where she worked by providing a business card and company website (despite no longer working there). The officer then asked her how much money she had brought with her:

> L: I said, "Cash, I have $800."
> She says, "Can you show it to me?" . . .
> [Liz says to herself] "This is crossing the line." That's when I began to get irritated . . . When she asked me to show the money, it seemed to be in bad taste, that they demand it. I had it. It was simply the way she spoke to me that I didn't like, because I had read about all my rights, you know? I had studied it. I know what they could do and what they couldn't do.
>
> P: Had you read whether you had to show them your money?

> L: No, only if they arrested me. If they handcuffed me. Or if there was something more intimidating where they had to say, "You have to show us everything," you understand? But not during the interview.
>
> So I said, "No." I said, "Do I have to do it?"
>
> She said, "Yes, don't you speak English?"
>
> I said, "No."

At that time, Liz refused to continue to speak English and asked for an interpreter. The officer became exasperated since no interpreter was available. Liz then said,

> "Look, I don't have to *aguantarte* [put up with you]." I told her, "I don't have to *aguantarte*, I come to your country. That's it. And you are rude." I told her [in English], "You are very rude." I turned around and said [in English], "I don't care, send me to Mexico." I was very angry . . . Well, I think the woman saw my attitude and got tired of asking to see my money, so she stamped my passport.

Liz's self-presentation as a tourist who planned to spend her money in Canada, and her externalization of how indignant she was, comprise an example of resourcefulness and agency. Although her behaviour might have meant refused entry into Canada, the opposite occurred. However, the strategy is contingent on the officer, airport, and socio-political situation.

For those who did not have perceived class privilege, one strategy was to have a clear itinerary, including hotel reservations and places to visit. For instance, Maria Pérez reflected on her and her then boyfriend's border encounter:

> We were lucky. Because during that time the Mexican wave was starting, and we came on Mexicana [Airlines]. So obviously we were practically all Mexican . . . You see how they ask you to wait, right? You wait to talk to, how do you say, the immigration official. And we saw how they were asking them questions . . . [We didn't hear] what they asked them . . . But [given] how long they took to decide, . . . we got the idea that it wasn't so easy. In that regard, what my friend told us was useful: "You say that

> you are going to visit. Bring your itinerary of the places you plan to visit and make a reservation." I had made a reservation online and paid for it and everything.

Maria Pérez used the language of a Mexican "wave" to discuss the increasing number of Mexicans who travelled to Canada in the mid- to late 2000s, what Santa Ana (2002) has referred to as a "dangerous waters" metaphor. This was a prominent discourse in the late 2000s and influenced immigration officials' decisions. However, the "dead time" (Dow 2007) that Maria Pérez experienced was beneficial because she learned about the interrogation process.

Following a recommendation from a friend, Juan Nadie chose to land in Montreal and "finish" his trip in Toronto so that officials would not link him to family members living in the latter city:

> The plan was to come as a tourist, right? Even if my real plan was to stay, but to pretend to be a tourist, so I planned it . . . I bought a tour. Like a tour you buy, and they take you to different places. I went to Montreal, . . . then Ottawa and Quebec, . . . and at the end Toronto . . . I knew that immigration agents did ask you if you had a one-way ticket [and] it looked suspicious, that you would stay or something. So I decided to save more money and buy the return ticket . . . So when I arrived, they asked me "Where are you going?" But in reality I didn't have to, I did answer them, but in reality I showed them a paper that had the itinerary of everything I was going to do, you know? And I came with a group of people, two buses, like forty people per bus, and we all came for the same thing.
>
> Well, I didn't, but the others did.
>
> . . . When I got off the plane, three, they looked like police officers, I imagine, they stared at me, and I held my passport in my hand and the itinerary, . . . but they didn't say anything. So I kept going, and I thought that "Was it right?" . . . So then you go down an escalator, and you go to like two desks, and there were some guys who were on the same plane being interviewed at the desk next to me.

Although everyone looked like they were on vacation, Juan Nadie knew that his "vacation" was a performance. His itinerary, a "papereality" (White

2014), made him confident since he could just show the paper instead of having to explain himself. However, it meant the added cost of a return ticket. And his effort did not satisfy immigration officials, who also learn about and from the strategies that migrants use: "They needed to see what I brought. And I said, 'Okay.' And during that check, they took out everything I had in my backpack. Absolutely everything. And during that process, they kept asking me what I did in Mexico and millions of questions." Returning to Ahmed's (2016) discussion of the limits of evidence, certain people need more than documents and explanations to "prove" themselves. Juan Nadie, as a Mexican national, who also had a distinctive look affiliated with a specific music subculture, perceived that "illegality" "emanated from his body" (Cisneros 2012).

Güero shared an anecdote demonstrating that border performances are strategies used by a number of potential migrants. When he travelled to Canada, he wore his Sunday best, seeking to convince border officials of his "genuineness":

> When I arrived, there were two filters . . . When you arrive, everyone was nervous, the plane was full of Mexicans, and all, well, it's a migration process among Mexicans, right? Like *coyotes* [smugglers/migration facilitators], at some point I imagine they train you to cross: how you should dress, who knows? Here too. Everyone on the plane, we were all Mexicans, . . . we all came well dressed, some wearing ties. We looked like tourists . . . We all spoke about coming on vacation for two weeks. Even to each other, we didn't say that we came to *chambear* [work]. We all had, like someone had already told us, "You say you are coming on vacation, bring little clothing, come with a small backpack so they don't see you came to work. Come well dressed, with your most expensive and prettiest things you have, so they see you have money." And that's how everyone looked. It was funny because, after this happened, I think maybe a year later, I happened to see a man with whom I had spoken, wearing a tie and everything, on the plane. I happened to see him on the street, all dirty. Dirty from working. That's the thing.

Güero's anecdote demonstrates the alienation produced through some migration channels whereby potential migrants are wary of sharing too much information with co-nationals or other individuals lest that information reach immigration officials. With emerging technologies and the push to have travellers provide phone and social media account passwords, the surveillant assemblage can be used to illegalize them further (Haggerty and Ericson 2000).

***

Transit is a textured and layered process that involves making plans, drawing on networks, and sometimes engaging in quick departures. The process of being in transit, including border encounters, demonstrates the assemblage of bordering and illegalization. At ports of entry, officials organize and archive information about potential entrants and use it to make entry decisions. They do so by using technologies, including databases and biometrics. Airlines are pulled into this border work, demonstrating a transnational, pre-migration process of illegalization. Once migrants arrive for immigration inspection, another type of evaluation occurs, one that funnels believable entrants into the country and interrogates others more stringently. Affect, or a social way of feeling, permeates these border encounters. Specifically, fear, distrust, and disbelief circulate through interrogations, experiences of "dead" or "suspended" time, and the presentation of evidence (Dow 2007; Griffiths 2014). Actors involved in this process include potential entrants, immigration officials, other travellers, and interpreters. Potential entrants engage in strategies to counteract their potential illegalization by carefully crafting itineraries, packing only the necessities, and having appropriate documentation, in short "paperealities" (White 2014).

If successful, potential migrants gain entry into the country. However, the border work does not end there. Transit experiences affect how migrants experience their lives in their new context. In Chapter 3, I elaborate on this by examining what happens when state officials enforce additional borders that discursively identify migrants as illegal and work to prevent or re-assemble existing migration routes.

3

Assembling Discursive and Affective Productions of "Illegality" through Visa Restrictions

On July 14, 2009, the Canadian government announced that it would require Mexican and Czech nationals to have an entry visa to visit Canada (Citizenship and Immigration Canada 2009b). Prior to the announcement, travellers from those countries only needed a valid passport. Officials explained the requirement as a public policy response to an increasing number of refugee applications from both countries (Citizenship and Immigration Canada 2009b). In fact, the government had identified significant numbers of Mexican and Roma Czech refugee claimants as "bogus" for years leading up to the announcement (Galloway 2007; Keung 2007; Teves 2008), preparing travellers for the eventual visa imposition.

I began my interviews with participants soon after the announcement. Many participants, and the larger Mexican population in Toronto, expressed surprise and anger given the purported close ties between the two countries. After all, they shared extensive trade and migrant labour agreements (the North American Free Trade Agreement and a bilateral Seasonal Agricultural Worker Program, respectively). Libertad, who travelled to Canada to flee persecution because of her journalism and labour organizing, described her initial response:

> It was a shock for me because I know that Mexico and Canada are strong business partners. They need each other, but I think Canada really needs Mexican labour. Its temporary workers come from there [Mexico]. And I think it was more, . . . it was [immigration] officials who said it was to stop the wave of Mexican applicants. Therefore, my first reaction was to be angry. I was indignant.

Libertad understood the visa as a migration management strategy, controlling who could travel to Canada and under which conditions. Given this context, in this chapter I examine the 2009 visa requirement as a bordering tool to enforce and maintain the illegalization of Mexicans. I pay particular attention to media, politicians', migrants', and business representatives' understandings and reactions (the ways of knowing and feeling) to the visa. I conceptualize the visa not as a one-time event but as a *process* that began with news coverage of so-called bogus refugees and extended Mexican migrant illegalization even after its revocation in 2016. I begin by discussing the deployment of the bogus refugee as an affective and discursive category of exclusion. I then outline the work that went into constructing Mexicans as bogus refugees, how that work influenced the visa policy, and reactions from different stakeholders.

"Bogus" Refugees

Central to the identification of Mexican migrants/refugee claimants as bogus are affective proclamations about their threat to what Anderson (2013) has termed the "community of value": that is, "good citizens" who uphold the nation's purported values. Such responses are part of the "ordinary work of reproducing the nation" (Ahmed 2004a, 121–22). In this process, the "bogus" refugee becomes a "figure of hate" (Ahmed 2004a) compared with a "legitimate" refugee, framed as abject and pitied. These representations are not only invested in specific bodies but also circulate, interpellate, and essentialize refugee claimants as deserving or undeserving, with the former predominating. This process is also territorially organized. The circulation by politicians and citizens of words such as *overwhelmed* and *swamped* to describe the effects on nation-states from refugee claimants produces the perception of invasion (see Ahmed 2004a, 122).

The categorization of refugee claimants as legitimate or illegitimate also depends on racial logics. Inda (2006, 18) discusses the racialized responsibilization of undocumented migrants in the United States:

> The way to understand ... [racial technologies of exclusion] is to think about them in relation to the responsibilization of the subject ... Post-social regimes of rule ... produced a division between active citizens and anti-prudential, unethical subjects ... [The latter are those] who are

> judged incapable of managing their own risks . . . And this is very much a racialized division: the subjects most often deemed irresponsible . . . are those whose phenomenal/cultural characteristics serve to distinguish them from the dominant "white" population.

Constructing migrants/refugee claimants as irresponsible allows for the legitimization of their social exclusion (by rejecting their refugee claims and issuing removal orders).

The main drivers of the racialized responsibilization directed at Mexican im/migrants in Canada in the late 2000s were the media and politicians. For example, US television and film promote specific tropes about Mexicans and Latinxs. Pendleton Jiménez (2005, 97) states that "Hollywood stereotypes of Latina/os have important repercussions for Canadian audiences." The racial curriculum embedded in media representations, particularly the link between Mexicanness, illegalization, and criminalization, can influence perceptions of migrant deservingness to secure immigration status.

News media are another important avenue for the circulation of discourses regarding migrants (Chavez 2001; Li 2001; Mahtani 2008; Mountz 2004; Santa Ana 2002). The media not only report information but also are active in constructing what is newsworthy, sometimes in conversation with state representatives. Therefore, the media can serve to funnel state discourse as well as affect it. Mountz (2004, 328) argues that in Canada the media have "become the primary method of image-building into which the federal government pours significant resources." Similarly, Mahtani (2008, 232) notes that "what Canadians read and hear about immigrants largely influences their perspective on immigration in this country. In other words, news help[s] people learn about the world around them."

Affective Crises

To have the Canadian public buy in to the visa policy, the government participated in the construction of an affective crisis, mainly via the media, regarding Mexican refugee claimants and their purported threat to Canadians. Media coverage of immigration issues in Canada, unlike in the United States, is not a continuous phenomenon. In fact, Goldring et al. (2009) and Hier and Greenberg (2002) refer to the coverage of immigration events in Canada as "crises" that emerge periodically in the national/regional consciousness. When these crises emerge, however, they influence audiences to think about migration in particular ways.

Vukov (2003, 339) uses the language of "affective epidemics" to conceptualize these moments, noting that they occur

> when specific resonances become particularly acute, attaining a heightened level or pitch and triggering an accelerated circulation among peoples, as occurs when media spectacles around insecurity irrupt. Indeed, media culture is a key site for the proliferation of affective epidemics because of the ways in which mass media constitute such a backdrop to daily life and because of the intensified circulation of affect that they facilitate.

Through such a "narrative of uncertainty and crisis," the figure of the refugee or asylum seeker can become the target of a diverse set of discourses and fears about immigrants, the economy, race, gender, and sexuality (Ahmed 2004a, 122).

These crises demonstrate that policy shifts involve continued work and that their goals are not always coherent. De Genova (2002, 425) explains this:

> The intricate history of law-making is distinguished above all by the constitutive restlessness and relative incoherence of various strategies, tactics, and compromises that nation-states implement at particular historical moments, precisely to mediate the contradictions immanent in social crises and political struggles . . . By emphasizing this "tactical" character of the law, it is imperative to recall that tactics that aim to make a disciplined and manageable object of any given social group are conjunctural and can never be assured of the certainty of their realization.

De Genova's focus on a "tactical character" implies that, though a specific policy or policy outcome does not need to be in the minds of policy makers, their actions gesture in particular political directions. This was the case in the mid- to late 2000s in relation to Mexican refugees, when we can track instances branding Mexicans as bogus before the visa was implemented.

This pre-visa affective crisis, which played out in the media, linked ideas about illegitimate and irresponsible modes of immigration to racial and national markers. News stories focused on the growing numbers of Mexican refugee claimants in Canada. One strand of such stories referred to Mexicans arriving from the United States. For example, a 2007 *Globe and Mail* article described the arrival of a number of Mexican and Haitian nationals who had been living undocumented in the United States to Windsor, Ontario, to apply for asylum (Waldie, Freeman, and Perkins 2007). In an article by the *Naples News,* a Florida newspaper, the event was described as a scheme by US immigration consultants to "cheat" the Canadian refugee determination system (Delcorto 2007). Alba (2010) also described a 2005 process whereby "enterprising Canadian immigration lawyers saw an opportunity when border enforcement became a hot political topic in the United States. They began advertising legal migration to Canada, both in Mexico and Arizona." Although articles blamed immigration consultants on both sides of the border, they also placed responsibility on migrants, depicting their arrival as an invasion, with references to "flocks" and "tides" (Delcorto 2007). Layering immigration and economic concerns, Canadians expressed fears that such migration patterns would become common, imposing a burden on border cities' economies (Delcorto 2007).

Another strand involved a "tactical" response to a presumed problem. In 2007, an article in the *Globe and Mail* entitled "Flood of Mexicans Delays Other Refuge-Seekers" reported that Mexican refugee cases were being heard faster than other claims because Mexico was considered a safe place by Canadian immigration officials (Galloway 2007). This led to news stories of Mexican cases becoming a "top priority" for the refugee board, not because of claimants' needs for protection in a timely manner, but to resolve them quickly (Keung 2007; Teves 2008). One story in the *Toronto Star* reported that, instead of taking twelve to eighteen months, hearings occurred within six months (Keung 2007). The article did not cite a formal policy on Mexican refugee claimants, though several news reports noted the occurrence (Segura Loarte 2007). I also heard the same rumours through interactions with community workers and participants. For instance, when I interviewed Leonel in 2009, he stated, "I remember hearing at that time that Mexicans did not receive refugee status. Mexicans didn't get it. Mexicans were rejected."

In the spring of 2009, months before the visa requirement was implemented, a freedom of information request to the Immigration and Refugee Board (IRB) in Toronto asked for the number of Mexican refugee cases placed under a fast-track trajectory. The response stipulated that Mexico was not a fast-track country and that for the central region (Toronto, Niagara Falls) from 2007 to July 2009

> the average time for a Mexican claim, from referral to disposition, under the regular hearing process . . . [was] 368 days from time of referral to date decisions mailed . . . The average processing time of 368 days is based on cases finalized with a positive or negative decision. It does not include cases withdrawn, abandoned, or transferred out to another region. There are a total of 719 cases that fall under these categories. The average time from date of referral to date of decision in these cases is 197 days. (Immigration and Refugee Board of Canada 2009)

Although the IRB reported no fast-tracking of Mexican cases, news reports and rumours of the story influenced audiences, given that they highlighted the rising number of claims by Mexican migrants and informed the public about the steps that the government might have taken to restrict their success. In fact, rumours of a potential visa implementation appeared in the media as early as 2007 since visas were a common government strategy applied to countries with high rates of refugee claims (Segura Loarte 2007).

"Experts" in the immigration industry also informed public opinion. One story published in the *Toronto Star* included an interview with a social/settlement worker about the increase in Mexican refugee applications. Such experts appear to speak with authority about immigration issues even if they are not government representatives, and they can do so from a "human rights" perspective. When asked about the increase in Mexican refugee applications, the worker stated that "my concern is we're going to be swarmed by Mexicans" (Keung 2007). Because of his position, the newspaper's audience was likely to take the social/settlement worker's concerns seriously, leading to concerns about Mexicans overcrowding the "system" and the national space. Therefore, his words, when coupled with remarks made by other actors, helped to set the tone for how to imagine Mexican refugee claimants: that is, as a burden on the system. In addition, the image of a "swarm" draws on the considerable number of metaphors used to refer to migrants and migration as dangerous, including images of floods, waves, tides, infection, and animalization (Chavez 2001; Mountz 2004; Santa Ana 2002; Vaughan-Williams 2015). The comment dehumanized Mexican migrants and contributed to the racialized project to depict Mexican claimants as irresponsible and a threat to Canadians and the Canadian nation-state.

Media "crises" and their inevitable use of metaphors intensified early in 2009 when Minister of Immigration Jason Kenney began a public relations campaign against refugee claimants from low-acceptance countries and specifically targeted Mexico. Articles in the *National Post* and *Toronto Sun* in February and March 2009, respectively, cited Kenney, who stated that the claims were "systemic abuse" (Edwards 2009) and argued that they were "clogging up" the system (Thompson 2009). Kenney also referred to Mexican claimants entering through "the back door," inciting news audiences to feel outrage and producing a nationalist affect against those threatening the refugee system (CBC News 2009b). Kenney repeated the theme in a *National Post* article in April 2009: "It's just not fair. It's not right for people to jump on a plane, come here, and make a refugee application, even if they don't meet the definition of a refugee" (quoted in Fekete 2009). These stories reinforced the identification of Mexican refugee claimants with "cheating" the system and acting irresponsibly.

Such events demonstrate the shift from understanding Mexican refugee claims as an isolated phenomenon to their construction as a general "problem." That work culminated not in an analysis of the reasons that Mexican migrants were seeking protection at an increased rate but in the implementation of a visa to dissuade new applications and process existing ones faster.

Implementing the Entry Visa

The lack of a visa requirement for Mexicans before 2009 can be understood as a way for Canada to promote a borderless North America that extended to Mexico. As such, during negotiations for NAFTA in the early 1990s, the Canadian government explicitly stated its intention not to require an entry visa for Mexicans (Portal for North America 2009).

Not needing a visa allowed Mexican nationals who might not have otherwise been able to visit Canada if they could afford the trip. In addition, Mexican airlines increased direct flights to Canadian destinations. Because the United States requires Mexicans to have a visa to enter the country, a number of Mexican migrants elected to fly non-stop to Canada, despite the higher cost (CBC News 2009b; Fekete 2009). Airlines providing direct flights began branching out to less traditional destinations such as Calgary and Edmonton in 2008 (CBC News 2009b).

However, a commitment to "open borders" can shift over time. The issue for Canada was how to close or externalize its borders without alienating a close partner. Inaction meant increased visibility that Mexican citizens were coming to Canada to seek protection, which highlighted Mexico as undemocratic and created more work for the Immigration and Refugee Board. Therefore, on July 14, 2009, the Canadian government announced that it would institute a visa requirement on Mexican nationals visiting the country (Citizenship and Immigration Canada 2009b). The press release announcing the requirement illustrates the enactment and externalization of borders, requiring visa applicants to apply from Mexico and prove that "they [would] not overstay their approved time in Canada" (Citizenship and Immigration Canada 2009b). This meant not only having enough money and ties to return to Mexico but also not "looking" like a potential refugee applicant or undocumented migrant.

Although the objective of the press release was to announce the visa requirement, it also discussed the high numbers of Mexican refugee applicants, linking the two:

> Refugee claims from Mexico have almost tripled since 2005, making it the number one source country for claims. In 2008, more than 9,400 claims filed in Canada came from Mexican nationals, representing 25 per cent of all claims received. Of the Mexican claims reviewed and finalized in 2008 by the Immigration and Refugee Board, an independent administrative tribunal, only 11 per cent were accepted. (Citizenship and Immigration Canada 2009b, para 2)

Figures 3.1 and 3.2 outline the growth of Mexican refugee claims and their associated acceptance rates. By making the high number of refugee

FIGURE 3.1
Refugee claims received in Canada: Mexico versus all other countries, 1999–2008

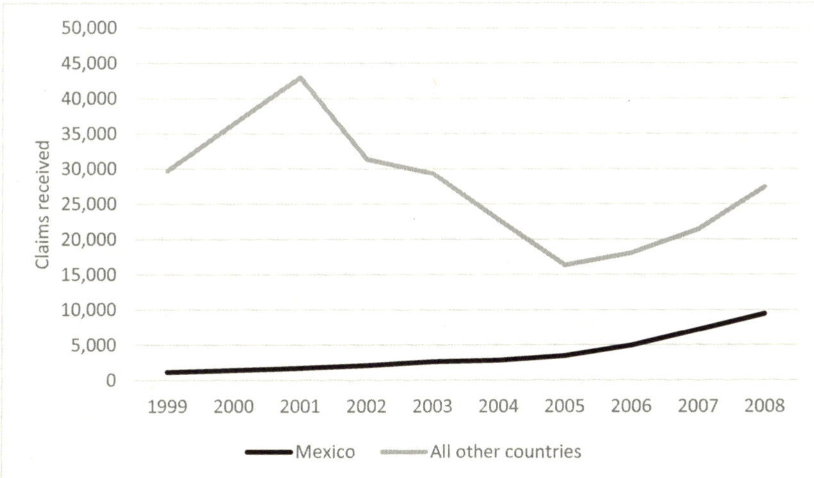

Source: Citizenship and Immigration Canada 2009a.

FIGURE 3.2
Acceptance rates of refugee claims, Mexico versus other countries, 2005–08

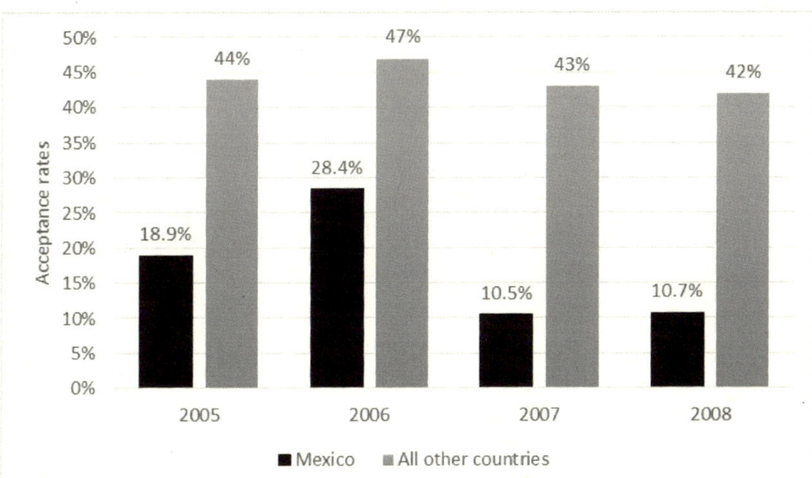

Sources: Citizenship and Immigration Canada 2009a; Schwartz 2015.

TABLE 3.1
Removals 2005–09

Removal year	Mexican citizens	Overall removals	Percentage
2005	1,490	11,291	13.25
2006	1,901	12,672	15
2007	2,963	12,509	23.7
2008	3,821	12,853	29.7
2009	4,708	14,865	31.7

Source: Canada Border Services Agency 2017.

applications the rationale for the visa requirement, the press release alluded to disciplining all Mexican travellers for the lack of responsibility of (some) refugee claimants.

The press release also continued the work of illegalizing Mexicans by citing Minister Kenney, who argued that applications for protection made by Mexican nationals affected Canada's "ability to help people fleeing *real* persecution" (Citizenship and Immigration Canada 2009b; emphasis added). By discussing "real" persecution, Kenney alluded to its opposite, false persecution. In doing so, he identified Mexican claims as false and therefore Mexicans as falsifiers. Although the evidence provided was the 11 percent acceptance rate, the press release did not explain the reasons for denied claims. In other words, it took for granted the impartiality of those who hear and decide refugee cases.

Another way to visualize the experience of Mexicans in Canada during that time is through removal statistics. Table 3.1 outlines the increase in removals in the years leading up to the requirement. These statistics branded refugee claimants as "fraudulent" (both morally and economically), informing audiences and contributing to the affective crisis. A poll conducted just days after the visa implementation found that 69 percent of Canadians agreed with the move, including 39 percent who strongly agreed (Fong 2009).

The result of the visa was an extension or externalization of the physical border to Mexico. Specifically, this border externalization allowed visa officers in Mexico to identify Mexicans with the potential to become illegal in Canada and provided them with the discretion to deny applications based on that assumption. Therefore, the process institutionalized class stereotyping into consular policy, leading applicants to experience illegalization before migration, thus demonstrating a transnational aspect to migrant illegalization.

At the same time, the Canadian government continued its bilateral temporary labour agreement with Mexico through the Seasonal Agricultural Worker Program, in place since 1974 (Basok 2003). In that sense, the message could be interpreted as Mexican migration is welcome in Canada if it is temporary, managed, and productive for the nation. Thus, the visa shifted the emphasis from one type of precarious status to another.

Transnational Responses

Canada's visa implementation was not without controversy. After the announcement, the Mexican consulate issued a press release stating that it would cooperate with the Canadian government and blaming fraudulent immigration consultants who duped well-intentioned migrants into cheating the system:

> Mexican authorities have detected that refugee claims lacking legitimate bases arise largely in response to the unrestricted operation of intermediary groups and organizations. These organizations have encouraged this practice among Mexicans acting in good faith, charging fees for advisory, logistical and training services to then present fraudulent cases. (Consulate General of Mexico in Toronto 2009)

Words such as *detect* and *legitimate* are reminiscent of Minister Kenney's comments and the Citizenship and Immigration Canada (CIC) press release explaining the visa requirement. They present a logically and legally sound tone. However, in contrast to the Canadian government response, the Mexican consulate seemed to place the blame on unknown consultants instead of refugee claimants.

However, Leonel reacted to the Mexican consulate response, arguing that it was not only shocking but also offensive:

> And now, with the visa implementation, I think that the Mexican government reacted in such a mediocre way . . . It almost criminalized Mexican migrants by saying that it was the Canadian government that

> creates the conditions for Mexicans to apply for refugee status. Put a better way, [the consulate seemed to say to the Canadian government] "You were stupid enough to let the [Mexican refugee claimants in]. Mexicans abused [the system], but you were asking for it."

Leonel referred to the "logic" used in the consulate's press release. Following that logic, the consultants who encouraged fraudulent claims were acting "illegally." Although the investment to deflect the blame, and make Mexican applicants look like they were innocently "acting in good faith," can be seen as a move to ameliorate the situation, it also mobilized strategies of illegalization. In fact, by agreeing that almost 90 percent of claims were fraudulent, the consulate aligned itself with the Canadian government. The move deflected the blame from refugee claimants and only implicated the Canadian government indirectly by blaming it for not regulating immigration consultants. It also maintained the mirage that Mexico was safe.

Although the consulate's response was one of cooperation and damage control, Mexican officials in Mexico proposed imposing similar measures for Canadians. This put Mexico between the proverbial rock and hard place. Mexican politicians' desire to counteract the measure was limited since Mexico's economy is dependent, in part, on tourism. Imposing a visa requirement would have reduced the entry of Canadian tourists. As a result, Mexico's recourse was to apply a visa on Canadian diplomats, a largely symbolic move (Mayeda 2009).

Finally, US officials in Mexico also reacted to the requirement. In a document released by WikiLeaks, an official working at the American Embassy in Mexico referred to the requirement as the "July Surprise," meaning the month that the Canadian government announced the requirement (Press 2011). The leaked document stated that the United States "has long been aware that numerous Mexican nationals have benefitted from Canada's lack of tourist visa requirements to cross into and assume residence in the U.S. illegally" and that the requirement "could improve Canadian-U.S. border security" (Press 2011). The response is another example of the transnationalization of "homeland security" and migration management practices (Arat-Koc 2010).

Effects on Canadian Businesses/Provincial Governments

Along with Mexican officials, some politicians and stakeholders in the business sector voiced their concerns about the effects that the visa decision would have on the agricultural and tourism sectors, particularly since the global recession was still in full force. One report explained the economic loss:

> For years, the absence of such requirements has served as a comparative advantage for Canada's tourism industry. In recent years, the number of visitors from Mexico has surpassed those from Japan and Germany and made Mexicans the third greatest source of Toronto tourism. Approximately 266,000 Mexicans visited Canada last year . . . and brought with them an estimated annual revenue of $256 million for Canada's tourism sector. (Portal for North America 2009)

Because of the fears of revenue loss, officials from the federal New Democratic Party (NDP) and the Alberta premier asked the government to reconsider its decision or at least to delay it until the end of the summer (CBC News 2009a), the latter also fearing a lack of Mexican workers in Alberta (Henton 2009). The fear mobilized by these actors demonstrates an economic nationalist affect. Stakeholders were afraid that the already fragile economy would suffer from a loss of tourism and farmworker labour. Therefore, in an interesting turn of events, migrants previously constructed as irresponsible become responsible consumers and producers – but only if they stayed temporarily.

Six months after the requirement was implemented, an opinion piece in the *Globe and Mail* entitled "While Mexicans Fume, Canada's Reputation and Revenues Take a Hit" conducted a cost-benefit analysis of the visa requirement, continuing the debate about the cost to Canadian enterprises (Simpson 2010). The piece estimated a loss of over $300 million, considering the loss of tourism revenue and the cost of processing visas in Mexico. The article also estimated the money saved on refugee applications at $38.5 million, leading to a net loss. Not surprisingly, the article calculated the loss in relation to Canada and the Canadian economy, again mobilizing a nationalist affect that ignored the effects of the visa on Mexican migrants.

Disrupted Flows: Locking Migrants into Place

The media coverage leading to the visa requirement depicted refugee claimants from Mexico as illegal not because of their lack of permission to be in Canada (refugee claimants have permission to stay in the country until their cases are finalized) but because they were assumed to be "cheating the system." However, since it is difficult to identify refugee claimants without asking for specific forms of identification, the visa affected other Mexican precarious status migrants, including all of the participants whom I interviewed.

For some, the effect was a result of their inability to continue circular migrations between Mexico and Canada. Lencho and Emiliana Zapata visited Canada for short periods (to work and visit friends and family members) more than once, a practice that the visa ended. Lencho arrived in Canada just months before the requirement. This was also a time when the H1N1 "epidemic" was in full force. He recounted his arrival in Canada as an enforced border performance in which he was paraded through the airport wearing a surgical mask, making bystanders afraid of him. When the visa was announced, he decided to stay in Canada given his family's declining business in Mexico and the limited possibility of his being able to return to Canada in the future.

Similarly, Emiliana Zapata described how circular migration had benefited her and her family in the past: "You come [to Canada] and do things, and you can go back [to Mexico], right? When something happens, you can say, 'I'm going.' Or you can say, 'There's a problem there [in Mexico], I'm sending . . . some money.' Or I can come back [to Canada] and work hard again, and I can help in that way." However, with the advent of the visa, Emiliana Zapata also chose to "overstay" in Canada since she did not foresee the Canadian government granting her entry in the future. The decision to overstay resulted in participants feeling and literally becoming "locked" into place in Canada, augmenting their experiences of illegalization and demonstrating how precarious status migrants become "spatially bounded" despite their transnational experiences (Espiritu 2003, 2). Their length of illegalization and temporariness became indefinite (only amendable through deportation or adjustment of status), making their precarity also indefinite in terms of access to decent work and social goods.

Another effect was increased visibility. That visibility manifested itself not only in relation to immigration officials but also in relation to anyone who heard about the requirement. Teresa, who emigrated to Canada to avoid being implicated in narcotrafficking in Mexico, discussed this shift. According to her, the visa

> was also a way . . . to see how they keep trying to control the migration of Mexicans and to find out the routes under which that migration takes place. I immediately thought that none of my relatives would be able to visit, even if they meet all the requirements [for a visa] . . . because what the visa does is to more completely and comprehensively document the migration of people. This makes it easier to link who is here and where. And this puts us [precarious status migrants] at a greater risk.

Teresa identified several ways in which the requirement illegalized migrants. First, it involved racialization through a sequential process: it conflated Mexicans, regardless of their actual status, with refugee claimants and then identified them as suspect, drawing on discourses of bogus refugees. This process occurred in both the Latinx community and the mainstream media. Therefore, though the bogus refugee construct can be mobilized for different racialized and/or migrant communities, the visa resulted in Mexican nationality being read as code for claiming refugee status and therefore being an irresponsible subject. A consequence for Mexican precarious status migrants was that it opened the door to "uncomfortable questions" about their immigration status (Bernhard et al. 2007), leading some to isolate themselves from their communities.

Second, Teresa identified the increased recording of information about migrants as an effect of the visa, a process that can be attributed to a surveillant assemblage of migrant illegalization (Villegas 2015a). She predicted that, if any of her relatives travelled to Canada, the Canada Border Services Agency (CBSA) could track her through them. For those migrants who were actively sought by the state through deportation warrants, this was concerning. Teresa had applied for immigration status and been denied, leading to a deportation order. The potential that family members visiting Canada could lead to her identification made her feel nervous and hypervisible.

Moments of Negotiation

Media coverage of the visa requirement rarely included the voices of Mexican migrants, particularly those with precarious status. This was especially the case for "mainstream media." "Ethnic media" did provide some coverage. For instance, in the summer of 2009, I was invited to an action organized by a newly created (and short-lived) group called Mexicanos Unidos en Acción (Mexicans United in Action), in response to the visa policy. The action, held at Toronto City Hall, was covered by *El Correo Canadiense,* a Spanish-language newspaper published in the city:

> Mexicans United in Action was immediately organized to resist the onslaught against Mexicans and added itself to the group of refugees, people without immigration status, temporary workers, permanent residents, and anyone who wanted to raise their voice against the decision . . . To begin, on July 25, the group organized a symbolic protest in front of Toronto City Hall. Although the next steps for resistance are not clear . . . they will try to "influence the makers of immigration policy."
>
> According to Mexicans United in Action, "the Canadian Minister of Immigration and Multiculturalism, Jason Kenney, . . . announced this arbitrary and illegal action of closing the borders to those who need asylum and protection."
>
> According to this group, Kenney has been attacking the Mexican community since he was named [minister]. (Vasquez 2009)

Although the action did not attract a large number of protesters, for those present and those who read its coverage in the news, it was not merely "symbolic." It countered the hypervisibilization of Mexicans, not through invisibilization but through an alternative portrayal, shifting the discourse away from Mexican illegalization and toward an analysis of the legality of the actions of the minister of immigration. This reversal questioned his power in redrawing policies unilaterally. It also demonstrated that membership within a national community and the demand for inclusion does not necessarily require citizenship status (Coll 2010).

Most of the participants whom I interviewed did not participate in such actions given their visibility. Protests can always attract police interaction and intervention. For example, during the action, the police asked organizers to leave because they did not have a permit for the demonstration. Therefore, we can link participants' decisions not to participate in such actions to Teresa's comments about the visa being both a tool to close borders and a surveillance mechanism to track deportable Mexican migrants. For those participants, the action also generated a feeling of solidarity. Despite their lack of public participation, during interviews they voiced a range of feelings related to the visa. Mexicano en Acción called the decision makers "wretched." Berenice identified feeling fear because she saw the visa as "part of the measures taken to stop immigration," adding and perhaps foreshadowing that "this is going to get worse."

Continued Work and Reassemblage

The implementation of borders and their accompanying divisions among "citizens," "guests," and "aliens" necessitate constant maintenance. Although the visa requirement led to fear for Mexicans and the enhancement of racist surveillance of them, it would be incorrect to identify it as the origin or end of racialized illegalization of Mexicans in Canada. As I described above, the work of racializing and visibilizing Mexicans began years before. In fact, participants identified hearing stories about Mexicans not being able to enter Canada before implementation of the visa. Leonel reflected on this process:

> Now it's going to be even worse, [but] I feel that the entry [in]to Canada was hardened . . . There were visas in place [already]. Supposedly, Mexicans had the right to be here. But . . . I knew there were many, many who were deported at the airport. And others weren't allowed to leave Mexico: that is, they didn't let them board the plane in Mexico.

Leonel described the visa as a hardening of the Canada-Mexico "border" but warned against the assumption that it had been open before. In fact, he argued that the visa had been in place in an implicit way before 2009, allowing immigration officials to reject and return potential entrants.

Although the visa was an extension of an existing "border," one thing that it changed was control over where the determination of travel eligibility took place, granting power to visa officers in Mexico to select those who could demonstrate their willingness to return to the country. Given the fees, bureaucratic scheduling, and the fact that initially applicants could apply for a visa only in Mexico City, the number of Mexican travellers to Canada decreased post-2009.

The visa therefore led to a decrease in refugee claims. In May 2010, an article in the *Globe and Mail* reported that the number of refugee claims by Mexicans had decreased by 80 percent from the year before (Jimenez 2010). This was indeed the case, as CIC figures in Figure 3.3 illustrate. The total number of Mexican removals and its proportion of overall removals also decreased after 2009. The Conservative federal government saw the decrease as a victory, particularly because, as the application rate decreased, the acceptance rate began to increase (up to 28 percent in 2014) (Keung 2015).

Given this "success," Canadian officials did not heed continued calls by Mexican officials to rescind the visa (Blanchfield 2013; El Universal 2017). The former maintained that the high number of refugee applications, high rate of "immigration violations," possibility of fraudulent documents

FIGURE 3.3
Refugee applications by and removals of Mexican nationals 1999–2017

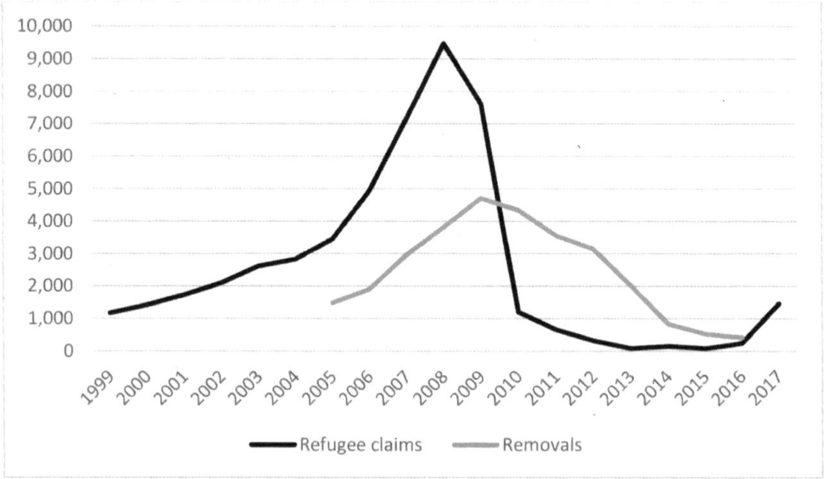

Sources: Citizenship and Immigration Canada 2009a, 2014, 2015; Canada Border Services Agency 2017; Rehaag 2017, 2018.

available in Mexico, and possibility of organized crime travelling north to Canada were continued threats (Bell 2013; Government of Canada 2009, 2016; McGregor 2016b). The response continued to impose an inherent criminality on Mexicans.

The government also reinforced the bordering process through other policy options. One example was the designation of certain countries as safe for the purpose of refugee determination through the 2012 Protecting Canada's Immigration System Act. The act outlined different application procedures depending on whether someone came from a "safe" or an "unsafe" country. According to the CIC, safe-designated countries were those "that do not normally produce refugees, that have a robust human rights record and offer strong state protection. States with strong democratic, judicial and accountability systems are likely to provide the necessary protection to their citizens" (Citizenship and Immigration Canada 2013). The safe country designation was reminiscent of the rumours of fast-tracking Mexican applications in the mid-2000s (Keung 2007). It also granted the minister of immigration discretion to identify and place countries on the list. Mexico made the list on February 14, 2013. This policy response put an end to the piecemeal response to high levels of refugee applicants. For example, after visas were imposed on Mexican and Czech nationals in 2009, the Canadian government warned Hungarian nationals that it might impose a visa for them as well after refugee applications from Hungary increased (Scoffield 2010). Changing the refugee determination system also allowed an integrated approach to decreasing application rates, thereby ensuring a decrease in positive outcomes.

Lifting the Visa

In the summer of 2016, after a change in the federal leadership the previous year, Liberal Prime Minister Justin Trudeau announced that he would revoke the Mexican visa requirement in December of that year. The decision was motivated by a projected growth in the Canadian tourism industry and an agreement with the Mexican government to remove a ban on some Canadian beef products in place since 2003 (Government of Canada 2017a; Mas 2016; McGregor 2016a). In preparation for the change, the government noted that it had evaluated potential consequences, particularly after the US election and rumours of increased claims from undocumented migrants looking for protection (Harris 2016a). For instance, the government sought assurances from Mexican President Enrique Peña Nieto that he would issue a warning about following Canadian laws (Fife and McCarthy 2016). Officials also met with the immigration department's area director for Latin America, Olivier Jacques, who, according to a news report, "acknowledged that more Mexicans could arrive from the U.S., and others directly from Mexico, due to changes. Jacques said various criteria are reviewed to assess a country's 'readiness' for a visa lift. In Mexico's case, those risks were measured against Canada's 'unique relationship' with the country, including geographic proximity and the close trade relationship within NAFTA" (Harris 2016b).

Those opposed to lifting the visa argued that the Trudeau government had not thought through potential consequences (Harris 2016a; Malcolm 2016). For instance, a Conservative Party member stated, "You don't impose a visa on a nation that's close to us in terms of trade unless there's a serious, discernible problem. And there was" (Harris 2016a). One op-ed piece commented on a perceived lapse in the procedures of implementation: "Typically, Canadian rules only allow the government to lift a visa requirement for countries that make up less than 2% of the total refugee claims" (Malcolm 2016).

Opponents also mobilized affective responses, with news stories describing fears of a "surge" and "potential flood" of Mexican refugee claimants re-emerging in media outlets as well as from Conservative politicians, immigration officials, and lawyers (CBC News 2017; Harris 2016a, 2017). Some estimated an average of 1,000 claims per month (Malcolm 2016). "Dangerous water" metaphors (Santa Ana 2002) again worked to promote moral panic about Mexicans in Canada, particularly after the US election. Critics also feared "that asylum seekers in other Latin American countries, wishing to gain entry to Canada, could take advantage of Mexico's weak passport system without having to undergo Canada's rigorous visa screening" (Fife and McCarthy 2016). Alternatively, the fear was that organized crime would find a pathway through Canada with revocation of the visa (CTV News 2018; Government of Canada 2016; Immigration, Refugees and Citizenship Canada 2018; McGregor 2016b).

The Mexican community in Canada also aided the re-emergence of this moral panic. For example, on December 1, 2016, an online Mexican outlet, *W Radio,* posted a news story by a Mexican journalist living in Canada. The story was titled "Elimination de visa canadiense para mexicanos incrementará la residencia ilegal" (Eliminating the Canadian Visa for Mexicans Will Increase Illegal Residence) (Basulto 2016). It portrayed Mexicans as "scheming" to get into Canada to live without documents. It also cited "expert" Mexicans with secure status, despite a lack of background in immigration policy or scholarship, who admonished their co-nationals for asking Toronto residents about the best way to arrive and stay in Canada through Facebook groups (Paloma Villegas 2016). An opinion piece by a Mexican writer living in Canada continued this narrative:

> It's true that Mexico has dangerous places, but people are still free to move from one city to another in search of safety. There are still many places where a decent, hard-working person can start over. Thus, for most it's not imperative to flee the country . . . Canadian taxpayers foot the bill to help refugees. I couldn't be happier or more proud of this. Unfortunately, Mexicans have cried wolf too many times in Canada . . . It horrifies me when I see pages on Facebook where Mexicans living in Canada advise their fellow countrymen to come ". . . illegally, whatever, who cares?" and say, "Everyone has a right to search for a better life." And they attack those who, like me, protest and say, "Don't do that; come legally." . . . I categorically disagree with the idea of entitlement. You don't have a right to invent a story in order to be accepted into Canada. No one does. (Batiz 2017)

The idea that safe places (what are called internal flight alternatives for those seeking protection) are readily available in Mexico can be disputed. Although Mexican insecuritization should not be equated with the war in Syria in the 2010s, Batiz's description was not accurate. During our interview in 2009, Mexicano en Acción refuted this criminalization:

> I obviously don't see that Mexicans came and abused [the system], for example asking for protection, for example those people who did not meet all . . . the requirements for whatever reason decide[d] to leave the country, . . . decided to leave Mexico. For me, that's valid because it might

> not be a direct persecution, but it is a persecution that is global, you see, or that goes beyond us [as individuals].

Mexicano en Acción disrupted the binary construction between refugees and "economic migrants," pointing to the fact that persecution and insecuritization operate in complicated and interlocking ways. Mexicans face growing economic and general insecuritization while facing limited emigration options given the hardening of the US-Mexico border. In fact, a news report stated that one reason immigration officials were against the lifting of the visa was that "Mexico's low standard of living, *poor human-rights record* and high crime rates will drive Mexicans to seek refuge in Canada" (Fife and McCarthy 2016; emphasis added). Instead of recognizing this, Batiz's op-ed criminalized potential im/migrants and refugee claimants, using words such as *decent* and *hard-working* to allude to fraudulent claimants who "cry wolf too many times" and feel "entitled." These accounts also constructed Mexicans with stable legal status in Canada as a deserving moral compass to discipline their co-nationals.

Responding to critiques, the government pledged to monitor regularly Mexican flows and to respond accordingly. A spokesperson for Minister of Immigration Ahmed Hussen stated that "we continually and carefully monitor migration trends to ensure the integrity of Canada's immigration system" (quoted in CBC News 2017). Leading up to the lifting of the visa, previous minister of immigration John McCallum said that he would reimpose the visa if a certain number was reached (rumoured to be 3,500 per year though never verified) (Harris 2016a). McCallum explained that "Canada retains its sovereignty on this issue. There comes a point where it would become unsustainable, but we are hoping that point will not arrive" (quoted in Harris 2016b). In another example, a Vancouver lawyer critiqued the strategy, referring to it as a "'close the barn door after the horse has bolted' policy" (quoted in Harris 2016a), also promoting the animalization of migrant flows (Vaughan-Williams 2015).

And, though touted as opening the border, the removal of the Mexican visa was anything but that. Travellers still had to apply for an electronic travel authorization, which evaluates their admissibility before their departure and can be described as a visa by another name. They also had to undergo border inspections and interrogations. All of this led to a disconnect between projections and reality. More Mexicans did travel to Canada, but they did not apply for protection in similar numbers as in the late 2000s. On January 10, 2017, the CBC reported that "at least 70 Mexicans claimed refugee status in Canada the first month after the federal government lifted a visa requirement . . . The one-month figure brings the total number of Mexican refugee claims for 2016 to 248, compared to 111 in 2015, according to figures provided by the Canada Border Services Agency" (Harris 2017). In the first few months of 2017, figures continued to rise, with 71 claims in January, 85 in February, and 110 in March (Levitz 2017). However, these figures were well below the estimated thousands per month.

Another point of discussion regarding the revocation was the cost as estimated by a 2016 government regulatory cost analysis (Government of Canada 2016; Harris 2017). Over ten years, the analysis calculated that a total of $433.5 million would be spent, with $262 million in net cost and $171.6 million in new revenue (Government of Canada 2016; Harris 2017). Costs taken into account included "receiving and processing asylum claims," "front-end security screening," "processing of claims at ports of entry," "investigations, hearings, detentions, litigation and removals of failed asylum claimants," and "issuing operational bulletins and implementing systems changes" (Harris 2016c). Revenue would come from opening Mexico's markets to Canadian beef (Harris 2016a) and a growth in tourism and air travel (Harris 2016c). However, the revenue estimate did not consider the benefit from an increased exploitable workforce of Mexicans who might travel to Canada but be wary of applying for refugee status.

In the period after revocation of the visa requirement, events related to the United States presidential election in 2016 affected the perception of Mexican migrants in Canada. The first event involved US-Canada relations vis-à-vis trade, including tariffs and NAFTA renegotiations. Government officials were concerned about "a significant risk that the United States would see Canada as a weak security partner, leading the Americans to thicken the border with Canada, imposing more regulations and inspection that could slow down the cross-border trade" (McGregor 2016b). An example emerged in 2018 with what were described as "tariff wars" initiated by the United States and imposed globally, including Canada and Mexico.

The second event involved the cancelling of limited protections for specific precarious status groups in the United States – those with Temporary Protected Status (TPS) and Deferred Action for Childhood Arrivals (DACA) – which influenced US-Canada migration. Prime Minister Trudeau had campaigned under a banner of "refugees welcome" in 2015. Although celebrated internationally, the degree to which this agenda was open and welcoming is debatable. However, by 2017, when the cancelling of TPS and DACA occurred, the immigration agenda shifted away from a mirage of "welcoming" given a rise in migrant arrivals from the southern border seeking protection in Canada (Forrest 2017; Scotti 2017; Selley 2017). In the summer of 2017, the Ad Hoc Intergovernmental Task Force on Irregular Migration was created to respond to this perceived "problem" (Goverment of Canada 2017). Interestingly, as the name of the task force suggests, at this time the Canadian government began to use the language of "irregular" migration instead of refugee claimants or undocumented/non-status migrants. Suggested responses included amending the Safe Third Country Agreement (STCA) between the United States and Canada, an agreement that prevents the making of a refugee claim in one country if a person has already landed in the other country. Because the STCA applied only to official border crossings, irregular arrivals were able to make claims once inside the country, prompting Canada to ask the United States to agree to apply the policy to the entire land border (Paperny 2018).

In relation to Mexicans, the government approved increased funding to police potential irregular arrivals and refugee claimants (Government of Canada 2017a). However, by October 2017, only thirteen Mexican irregular arrivals were identified (Scotti 2017). Another strategy was to send a member of Parliament of Argentinian descent to Los Angeles to detract potential Latinx migrants from attempting to travel to Canada and applying for protection (Forrest 2017).

***

In the 2000s and 2010s, the convergence of discursive, affective, and transnational strategies illegalized Mexican migrants and refugee claimants in Canada as irresponsible subjects and therefore illegal in the eyes of the nation. The representation continued in the 2010s, extending to associate

Mexicans with drug trafficking. This framing of Mexicans was imposed by specific actors – government officials, business representatives, and im/migrants – and organizations – mainstream and alternative media outlets, Citizenship and Immigration Canada (now Immigration, Refugees and Citizenship Canada), the Canada Border Services Agency, and the Mexican consulate – and obscured alternative representations.

On the side of the Canadian government, the visa requirement and later its revocation involved a number of "tactical" strategies (De Genova 2002) and discursive/affective circulations. The strategies involved the workings of flexible borders: preventing the entry of some Mexicans while keeping the doors open for temporary and controlled migrations (in the form of classed tourism or temporary exploitable labour). These borders externalized traveller scrutiny to Mexico, reformatting the process into the electronic travel authorization when the visa was revoked. After the American election in 2016 and associated immigration policy changes, new borders were erected in Canada to control or prohibit the entry of migrants who sought protection from its neighbour to the south. However, the Canadian government also re-evaluated its relationship with Mexico vis-à-vis diplomacy and trade given growing hostility from the United States, a process that began before the visa requirement revocation (Gutiérrez-Haces 2015) and continued after the 2016 US presidential election. Finally, though less visible because of the modes of exclusion mobilized alongside the visa requirement, Mexican precarious status migrants also intervened in the situation and strategized ways to negotiate their depiction as irresponsible subjects. In the next section, I discuss the production of the Mexican failed or bogus refugee claimant and the strategies that participants used to negotiate their illegalization and pursue secure legal status.

PART II

Immigration Status Trajectories

Esta mañana llego la migra
A mi trabajo Uniforme gris
documentos Con fotografía en
mano. Me preguntaron Si con-
ocía a la persona del Apartamen-
to 608 No recuerdo el nombre.
"¿OK ve usted ese edificio? ¿Color
café? Pues ahí no es, vaya mas
adelante Y de vuelta a la dere-
cha, al East" Pensaría usted . . .
"Hasta encontrar la primera autopista
Y diríjase hacia el sur Hasta llegar
a la primera intersección . . ."
"Estacione su auto en cualquier
lugar Y camine, olvide Y consí-
gase un trabajo de verdad Sinies-
tro y repugnante personaje."
Pero, le sonreí, mientras Mirándole
a los ojos Le respondí que no . . .
No conocía a quien buscaba. En
ingles, claro.

This morning the "migra" showed
up at my workplace. Grey uni-
forms, documents, a photograph
in hand. They asked me if I knew
the person from apartment 608, I
don't recall his name.
"OK, do you see this building?
The brown one? That's not it, go
further Then turn right, toward
the East" I thought . . .
"Until you reach the first highway
and then head south until you
hit the first intersection . . ."
"Park your car anywhere and walk,
forget. Get yourself a real job
Evil and repugnant individual."

That's what I wanted to say but in-
stead I just smiled while, staring
into his eyes, I said no – I didn't
know who he was looking for –
In English, of course.

– "Mi mundo visto desde el ground floor" (My World Seen from the Ground Floor) (Maya 2012, 66), translated by Jeannine Pitas

Maya's (2012, 66) poem describes the circulation of hate or disgust for immigration authorities who police precarious status migrants and are often pivotal in their removal from Canada. Immigration authorities are part of a surveillant assemblage of illegalization that includes IRB members, lawyers, settlement workers, and the police (Paloma Villegas 2015a). This type of surveillance is particularly pertinent when examining immigration status trajectories, which, unlike immigration trajectories, do not necessarily involve the crossing of international borders. They do involve crossing the boundaries or "gradations" of citizenship status or "legal status transitions" (Goldring, Berinstein, and Bernhard 2009; Goldring and Landolt 2013).

Immigration status trajectories affect migrants' lives and their conceptions of themselves. For instance, I interviewed Manolo, who had applied for refugee protection but had been refused, days after his scheduled removal date. During the interview, he defined illegality and how it related to his life: "Illegality is when you do something that goes against the norms and the principles dictated by the law. That's the definition. Why am I illegal? Because I have been ordered to return to my country, which I will not do. Therefore, since I no longer have any legal status in this country, I lose protection and end up as illegal." Manolo could pinpoint the exact date that he became illegal, demonstrating the productive power of migrant illegalization. Legal documents, such as the deportation order, create categories of identification. By indicating that he was illegal, Manolo accepted that the deportation order produced his illegality. However, his illegalization began before this time.

In the chapters in this section, I outline the interlocking of immigration policy and practice that produces limited opportunities for precarious status migrants to achieve secure immigration status. As discussed in Part I, immigration policy has not followed a unified or coherent approach to surveilling and policing non-citizens. Instead, it operates through a "tactical character" that involves "intricate and calculated interventions" (De Genova 2002, 424). In Chapter 4, I outline participants' experiences while navigating the refugee determination system and illustrate the legal status transitions that precarious status migrants can experience, for instance from tourist to refugee claimant to refused refugee claimant

(Goldring and Landolt 2013). This process is time sensitive and onerous. It takes work to meet strict deadlines, particularly given language barriers and irresponsible legal representatives. The dead or sticky time (Dow 2007; Griffiths 2014) experienced by those who apply for refugee protection also contributes to an affective process that circulates fear and anxiety among claimants, particularly given media representations of refugee claimants as bogus. This dead or sticky time, however, also "buys" applicants time to strategize and look for alternatives. Finally, I discuss the reorganization of immigration and refugee policy in the early 2010s and its effects on future Mexican claimants, a process that paved the way for revocation of the visa requirement in 2016.

In Chapter 5, I focus on other avenues that migrants use to apply for secure status. Given the borders created through changes to the refugee determination system and the effects of the visa policy and its revocation, I argue that humanitarian and compassionate application and spousal sponsorship became more prevalent strategies to achieve secure status. I draw on the concept of yearning (Burman 2010). Participants, yearning for secure status and a more equitable existence, evaluated the different options available to them and chose the "best" option in terms of affordability and the chance of approval. However, as in the refugee determination system, legal representatives, immigration officials, and third parties such as employers and sponsoring spouses affected participants' outcomes. Given these difficulties, participants sometimes applied to more than one option, extending their deportability and precarity over time. This process again points to the ways that migrant illegalization becomes multiplied through "gradations of status" as well as legal status transitions (Goldring, Berinstein, and Bernhard 2009; Goldring and Landolt 2013).

Returning to Maya's (2012) poem, participants' experiences of applying for secure status have an (unintended) consequence. Their application information becomes stored in databases that can be pulled up at any time, particularly if an application is refused and a removal order is issued. This illustrates the work of illegalization and deportability through technologies of identification and surveillance inside the borders of a nation-state. These "surveillant assemblages" of migrant illegalization (Haggerty and Ericson

2000; Villegas 2015a) include archives of photographs, applications, and other documents that, as Maya (2012) describes, encourage community members such as the poem's protagonist to participate in identifying illegalized individuals for immigration officials. Therefore, though immigration applications are an important strategy to achieve secure status, they can also be the avenue through which to heighten precarious status migrants' deportability.

4

Navigating a Shifting and Exclusionary Refugee Determination System

I met Berenice in her home one afternoon. She welcomed me and opened up about her migration and status trajectories, triggered by the violence that she suffered in Mexico and Canada. During the interview, she also reflected on the development of her political consciousness. Like other participants, Berenice was critical of the immigration system and its exclusionary measures. As a queer racialized woman, she used the lens of intersectionality to think through this experience:

> Becoming illegal in another country when you have your own country, why do you do it? To live a better life? When I arrived in Canada, I still used the same term, right? . . . To refer to someone who did not have papers: "I think so and so is illegal because he doesn't want to work with a social [insurance number]," right? Like that . . . So, for instance, I called anyone illegal who did not have refugee status or anything. Someone who was not here with permission, right? So I, yes I, speculated a lot in that sense, and everyone around me speculated that way . . . When I begin to participate more in the migrant community, at a political level, . . . we begin to talk about these issues, we begin to . . . understand colonization, how it happened, how borders were created, how divisions among countries were created, and their policies – imperialism, all those things, globalization, neoliberalism . . . And you begin to realize that borders were created by countries for economic purposes. When I learn about [the organization] No One Is Illegal, I realize that in reality no one is illegal, right? And a phrase that I love, when we chant at marches, is

> "We didn't cross the borders, the borders crossed us." And I said, "Wow, that's true." So I stopped saying illegal, it's offensive, it's, when you say, "That person is illegal," you become part of the system and say, "You, you are not, you don't deserve anything, you don't have rights, you are nothing, because you don't have a paper, the paper that this racist government demands."

Berenice explained how understandings of illegality, a process of knowledge production, can shift through encounters with new ideas and individuals. She discussed how association with criminality – that is, illegalization – justifies punitive detention and deportation policies to "protect" the nation-state and its citizens and withholds agency from migrants.

The identification of Mexican refugee claimants as bogus provided a rationale for the implementation of the 2009 visa requirement. But how did Mexican migrants experience the refugee determination system at this time? When I interviewed Mexicano en Acción, who applied for protection because of his sexual orientation and persecution in Aguascalientes, he discussed how he thought mainstream audiences saw refugee claimants: "They see us refugees like the mainstream media depicts us. You see? That we're abusing [the system] ... I say, you know these people have another way of thinking, and maybe don't understand, they don't grasp power dynamics one bit and the lack of balance in the world, you see, but, well, it's on them."

Given this framing, in this chapter I examine the Canadian refugee determination system as an assembled process that involves immigration policies, institutional practices, and discursive understandings of refugee claimants and the countries/contexts from which they are seeking protection. The process is organized temporally and transnationally. Temporally, it demonstrates instances of frenzied, ruptured, dead, and sticky times (Dow 2007; Griffiths 2014) as well as what I refer to as the strategic buying of time. Sometimes wait times are long, as if they are suspended or dead, though the process is moving forward (sticky time). In other instances, times are frenzied, such as when applicants have to submit applications and additional evidence. Ruptures occur through negative (or positive) decisions, forcing migrants to strategize new options.

The Canadian refugee determination system has also become re*assembled* given policy directives, such as the 2009 visa requirement, as well as more comprehensive policy changes in the Canadian immigration system in the 2010s. For Mexicans and other claimants identified as coming from safe countries, the result has been a hardening of access to secure immigration status and an increase in deportability. This process produces a "permanent temporariness" (Bailey et al. 2002). However, as I illustrate, migrants are not frozen in place during this time of limbo; they negotiate and strategize for secure status.

The Refugee Determination System and Its Reassemblage

The Immigration and Refugee Board has overseen refugee determination since 1989 and is "currently the largest administrative tribunal in Canada" (Soennecken 2013, 293). The IRB defines protected persons as those "whose removal to their home country would subject them personally to a danger of torture, a risk to their life, or risk of cruel and unusual treatment or punishment" (IRB Communications Directorate 2006). More specifically, the Refugee Protection Division of the IRB decides inland claims, made at the Canadian border or once claimants are inside Canadian territory. The process has specific criteria. To be determined as at risk, the violence needs to occur in the country from which the person is seeking protection, it must be personal and not general, it cannot come from having committed a crime (e.g., murder), and it cannot be as a result of "the country's inability to provide adequate health or medical care" (IRB Communications Directorate 2006).

Before 2012, when the participants whom I interviewed made their refugee claims, refugee claimants initiated the process by speaking with an immigration officer, who determined whether a claim could move forward. The applicant underwent a security check to determine admissibility and whether she or he was a "flight risk." Applicants allowed to move forward filled out a Personal Information Form (PIF) outlining their cases within twenty-eight days of applying for protection (Citizenship and Immigration Canada 2016a).

In 2012, Protecting Canada's Immigration System Act changed this process. Instead of a PIF, claimants now had to fill out a Basis of Claim (BOC) form within fifteen days of asking for protection (Citizenship and Immigration Canada 2016a). The government also implemented a two-stream system based on a person's country of origin: one for those coming from countries deemed safe (designated countries of origin or DCOs, a list that includes Mexico), and one for countries not deemed safe (Citizenship and Immigration Canada 2013). The process for claimants coming from DCOs made it increasingly more difficult to compile "evidence" and submit documents on time, producing "frenzied time" for claimants (Griffiths 2014). It also stereotyped applicants as potentially fraudulent. The Canadian government ended the DCO system in 2019 (Immigration and Refugee Board of Canada 2019).

Discursive Framing of Refugees

Immigration policy is often legitimized through the language of national security. Building upon my discussion of the bogus refugee, the framing of refugee claimants as potential threats to the nation is part of that process. For instance, the 2002 Immigration Reform and Protection Act (IRPA), the policy organizing federal immigration practice, describes a "dual mandate" – "closing the back door to criminals and others who would abuse Canada's openness and generosity while opening the front door to genuine refugees and to the immigrants the country needs" (Citizenship and Immigration Canada 2002, as cited in Ibrahim 2005). The front door–back door metaphor is a common trope that reinforces discourses of legitimate versus illegitimate migration. Legitimate entry is depicted as occurring through the front door. The government criminalizes entry through what it calls the back door despite stringent border/immigration controls that narrow who is determined a skilled migrant or can apply and receive protection in Canada. This framing also ignores the explosion of temporary foreign worker recruitment in a variety of occupations (all easily deportable) and the narrowing of access to sponsor migrants to Canada.

Pratt and Valverde (2002, 146) discuss this process by comparing refugee claimant representations to those of "welfare cheats":

> Refugee claimants . . . are rarely able to claim the deserving victim spot regardless of the conditions from which they are fleeing. Instead, they are presented as opportunistic rational-choice decision makers who have "freely chosen" . . . to come to Canada. By virtue of this allegedly free choice they become "rational" calculators and hence potential

system abusers, who need to be deterred through clearly laid out disincentives.

Depictions of welfare cheats and bogus refugee claimants, and their representation as rational actors, allow for the latter's positioning as threats to the economic and moral viability of the Canadian nation-state through the language of "queue jumpers, uninvited guests, threats to public security, and drains on public resources" (Huot et al. 2016, 131). This framing makes it very difficult to see that claimants are subjected to persecution and violence. It also often aligns itself with the perception that the refugee determination system is too welcoming and open to fraud and unable to distinguish between what are constructed as honest and dishonest refugee claimants. Finally, refugee claimants are often depicted as being unproductive given their reliance on social services and their difficulty finding work. These practices disrupt the idea of the Canadian refugee determination system as welcoming and open that has predominated domestically and internationally in the past few decades.

Entitlements Associated with a Refugee Claim: Practice versus Reality

Manolo, a cartoonist from Mexico City, described refugee determination in the following way: "It's like a funnel. They receive you with the cone this big. With their arms wide open, well somewhat open, somewhat open." Manolo's description of the system as wide and open is important for two reasons. First, the entitlements associated with making a claim in Canada are substantial, even if they have been regularly eroded. Second, Manolo also mentioned that the funnel is not as wide as one would imagine, foreshadowing the narrowing that can happen as time passes, albeit slowly (Griffiths 2014), and applicants develop a greater understanding of the system.

Participants who met specific criteria had access to health coverage through the Interim Federal Health Benefits Plan (IFH), legal aid, social assistance, and a work permit. These entitlements had a positive effect. For instance, Arne Saknussemm described arriving in Canada after experiencing political persecution: "I was overwhelmed by . . . the reception we had. To find that there was an infrastructure to receive people in need as was my case." These feelings extended to the IRB, which he also evaluated as fair, an experience that was potentially mediated by his class status. As a professional musician and journalist, he recounted not having difficulties entering Canada and asking for protection.

Arne Saknussemm also accessed adult education. He attended ESL classes to better his English skills and subsequently received a scholarship to attend a local college and become an immigration consultant. However, his experience was unique. Access to postsecondary schooling for precarious status migrants is often difficult because of immigration status restrictions, the evaluation of credentials from migrants' countries of origin, and the cost (Villegas 2019a). In terms of cost, those accepted are often asked to pay international fees that they are unable to cover given limited access to decent work. Other participants were unable to access additional forms of schooling, and some, including Berenice and Libertad, did not even take ESL courses.

Furthermore, because refugee claimants might have left their places of residence quickly, they might not be able to afford to live in a new country and pay for the services necessary to make a claim. This makes the social assistance provided even more welcome. Like Arne Saknussemm, Manolo was not aware of the possibility of asking for protection before his arrival in Canada. Although critical of the refugee determination system, he found the support system that accompanied it a good surprise:

> When you leave [the immigration office] with your immigration [information] packet, they tell you you have rights, that you need to contact your lawyer, that the state can pay for that. They tell you they can pay and find [these services] for you, that you can find translators in certain places, they give you a list . . . I can't complain. I'm still alive. The system does push you aside to a life of illegality . . . However, to some extent, they know that right now there is some money that the government puts aside to help people who don't have economic possibilities.

The availability of social assistance signals that the Canadian government makes provisions for the fact that people lead lives *during* their refugee claims. However, if something happens during their stay in Canada, such as experiencing abuse or violence, those experiences are not counted in the refugee claim process. This means that, despite the entitlements available, the refugee determination system is not always welcoming, particularly given the discursive framing of refugees and the specific outcomes of participants' claims. In fact, for most participants, the refugee determination system was a violent process that produced instances of stress and temporal limbo.

Specifically, participants articulated several barriers that illustrate the difference between the projected view of the refugee determination system as open and welcoming and lived reality. First, services (e.g., legal aid, social assistance, employment eligibility, health care) are temporally limited. They are contingent on the refugee claim remaining open or a positive decision.

Second, the government can amend or cut services at any point, particularly given discourses of austerity. For instance, in 2012 the government cut IFH services through which refugee claimants receive health care (Canadian Healthcare Association 2012). During this period, some refugee claimants who came from designated countries of origin were only eligible for emergency services or application-related exams. Those services were not fully reimplemented until 2016. Similarly, in recent years, cuts and proposed cuts to legal aid services in Ontario also affected refugee claimants' ability to access affordable legal services (Keung 2013b, 2016a).

Third, entitlement does not always lead to access, as Manolo discussed in relation to transportation and time: "The transportation is not cheap, and you don't know the city, so in order to make it to appointments, and if you don't get there because it's late, and you should have submitted it yesterday, . . . it's a bit difficult. It's not that easy." Given this, claimants have to learn quickly to navigate the geographic space of the city, its transportation services, and their schedules to make use of entitlements, another example of "frenzied time" (Griffiths 2014).

Fourth, the provision of entitlements is a mode of social control. Accessing services is a way for people to build networks, some of which are officially recorded and which immigration authorities can exploit when executing an immigration warrant through a surveillant assemblage of illegalization (Villegas 2015a). The provision of entitlements is also a biopolitical process to control populations in the name of public health and security. For instance, the government froze Johann's application for a work permit until Johann received treatment for tuberculosis, given the public health risk. Finally, refugee applicants who receive social assistance soon become privy to what many people with full immigration status also realize, that the money designated per person on social assistance is not enough to live in Canada (Colour of Poverty Campaign 2007).

Institutional Actors and Legal Representatives

Judges/Members

Institutional actors, including IRB members, immigration officials, and legal representatives, also play a role in creating an un/welcoming environment. IRB members are judge-like figures who decide refugee cases. In the name of efficiency, the 2002 IRPA limited the number of IRB members adjudicating a case to one (prior to the IRPA, two-member panels heard and decided cases) (Soennecken 2013). Therefore, the outcome is dependent on the decision making of *one* individual.

Another factor that makes IRB members controversial is that they are appointed by the ruling political party, through the "Governor in Council, based on the recommendation of the Minister of Citizenship and Immigration Canada" (Colaiacovo 2013, 124). Colaiacovo (2013, 214) found that members "were administered written tests, screened and interviewed by IRB officials, external experts and panels 'representative of Canadians,' before being recommended by the Minister for appointment." However, critics argue that the member selection process affects IRB members' neutrality (Showler 2009). In 2009, the union representing IRB staff criticized what it called a "giant sinkhole" sucking efficiency and credibility from the board, referring to the practices used for appointing members:

> The IRB has been raked over the coals by two impartial government auditing agencies for its failure to maintain transparency and merit in its appointment practices. Previously criticized by the Office of the Auditor General (OAG), a recent audit by the non-partisan Public Service Commission (PSC) revealed that barely one in three appointments met merit and guiding values requirements.
>
> "The PSC found an outrageously high use of governor-in-council appointments in a clear effort to circumvent merit-based hiring practices," Meunier-McKay [the national president of the Canada

> Employment and Immigration Union] said. "This not only raises questions of competence and political patronage, it serves to demoralize the great majority of IRB staff who have proved their suitability for their positions through a rigorous, merit-based staffing process." (Canada Newswire 2009)

The failure to meet requirements through the appointment process affects refugee claim outcomes. IRB member decisions, not always impartial, are one example (Rousseau et al. 2002). Rehaag (2008, 2014) has demonstrated that IRB decision making is inconsistent at best, with some members approving 80 percent of their cases, whereas others approve none. Such disparities affect how claimants navigate the system, whittling down their chances for protection to luck. Similarly, Colaiacovo (2013, 144) examined IRB member decision making and found that it was influenced by social location, which can include political leanings: "Board members are not approaching cases tabula rasa but rather their decisions are influenced by their educational and professional backgrounds."

These processes support Razack's (1998, 88) argument that "the refugee hearing is a profoundly racialized event." In relation to Mexican claimants, Showler (2009, 16) examined members' ability to make decisions without government interference: "With a few exceptions, the principle of independence has generally been respected by the Canadian government and IRB management who also has a duty to ensure consistency in its decision-making process. However, the government's recent public declarations about the invalidity of Czech and Mexican refugee claims may be an exception to that principle." Showler's reference to the public comments made about Mexican and Czech (Roma) claimants supports Razack's argument and how racialized framings of bogus refugees were mobilized by the government and potentially internalized by IRB members.

Given this process, participants shared negative impressions about immigration officials whom they encountered through the refugee determination process. For instance, Manolo told me, "They talk to you in a rude manner. At the airport, they don't baby you and say, 'Come here little one.'" Other participants, including Libertad, described having to negotiate and endure interactions with rude or disrespectful immigration officials:

> It would seem as if we are begging, it's my personal interpretation, but I remember those times often during my immigration process. They see a lot of cases daily that they must sometimes be tired, and some even in a bad mood because of it, as if it were something they do for free and by force. As if it were a crime, no, not a crime, a punishment they are paying for. Because their attitude is hostile. I have had the opportunity to accompany other people during their immigration process, and the treatment [by immigration officials] is sometimes inappropriate. Not to say rude and hostile.

Not expecting to be treated with contempt by someone paid to do a service, Libertad compared the work that immigration officials do with penitence. Manolo referred to this treatment from members, immigration officers, and other actors as a way to demonstrate how the system "te va orillando" (it begins to push you to the margins). Their responses mirror Güero's depiction of Canadian border officials as similar to the dehumanizing work of Mexican bureaucrats. Such references demonstrate a transnational process of exclusion of marginalized communities that encounter states and their institutions.

Lawyers, Consultants, and Other Representatives

Participants also experienced barriers finding adequate legal representation. Some had difficulties sifting through the large amount of information that immigration authorities gave to them when they applied for protection, including the fact that they had the right to legal aid. Others were unsure where to find a lawyer whom they could trust. Libertad thought that this uncertainty affected how representatives treated her:

> I didn't know that I could receive free counsel . . . So I didn't find, look for, help. I didn't have a lawyer, I didn't know I had the right to apply for legal aid, they must have told me, but I forgot, or I didn't retain it. I went with people who had never studied to be interpreters and who charged $100 to interpret each document page and people who wanted to do my

> PIF [personal information form] and people who wanted to take me to their lawyers.

Libertad arrived in Canada with post-traumatic stress disorder after undergoing a number of near-miss encounters with her persecutors and an internal relocation to Acapulco. During our interview, she stated, "I think I was going through one of the most difficult moments of my life because I wasn't able to understand even why I was going through that." Given her mental health situation, she found it difficult to retain information about her application, opening up the possibility for unscrupulous persons to take advantage of her.

Similarly, Mexicano en Acción had a difficult time finding a lawyer, in his case because he wanted someone to whom he could relate:

> I almost, almost opened the yellow pages and chose the first immigration lawyer . . . She was someone whom I don't think had much knowledge, we were both Hispanic, and so she filed my refugee application . . . I think my [PIF] was one page long . . . My friend asked me, "Hey, why did you choose that person? I know a lawyer, and he's gay and good, and he has experience." . . . Well, when I [went] to this lawyer and showed him a copy of my PIF, he almost threw it in my face [laughs] . . . We later found out she wasn't even a lawyer . . . She wanted to charge me . . . $4,000, and she guaranteed me permanent residence.

Mexicano en Acción's experience demonstrates the workings of internal borders and parallels my discussion of participants' difficulties in finding health care, in terms of both lack of information and high cost. Believing that it was the going rate, Mexicano en Acción planned to pay the unscrupulous legal representative's fee by working under the table. Fortuitously, the IRB tribunal allowed his new lawyer to amend the application and include additional materials in his file. And his new lawyer was paid through legal aid.

Legal representatives who try to take such an advantage comprised a running thread for refugee claimant participants. And it extended beyond the filing of documents and charging of fees. Manolo also chose a lawyer who spoke his language, thinking that doing so would facilitate his claim.

However, reflecting on his hearing, he began to wonder whether a lack of effort by his representative had to do with ulterior motives:

> You have a Latino lawyer because you look for someone similar to you, right? Someone who knows your language . . . And if you tell them I don't have money, they take legal aid, . . . and they tell you, "Don't worry, everything is fine." And when they get there [to the hearing], they don't speak. They don't say anything. They don't work for you. Why? Because if you lose, you can appeal, and its more money for them. If you lose the appeal, . . . it's more money.

Refugee claimants have access to several appeal and risk assessment processes before they are removed from Canada. Each involves filling out an application and potentially having legal representation present. Although it is difficult to prove whether legal representatives purposefully fail clients, in a capitalist marketplace it makes business sense to extend a case for increased profit.

When Armando arrived in Montreal, he found work with a family who acted as migration facilitators, bringing Mexicans to Canada, finding them work cleaning office spaces and other businesses, and convincing them to apply for refugee status: "That was their business . . . They would bring them, get them to ask for refugee status, and then pay them cash, but they paid them six to seven dollars [per hour] . . . They would tell them, 'You should ask for refugee status.' The government is going to give you money, and what you get from work is for you." The migration facilitators convinced Armando to apply for protection despite not fully understanding what applying entailed. Although he did not think that his lawyer behaved in an improper manner, he thought that the lawyer gave him false hopes: "My lawyer was always very positive. He was always positive, . . . so I got my hopes up. It was a difficult time because my lawyer was 80 percent sure." When his case was denied, Armando's lawyer blamed the denial on the IRB member's anti-Mexican bias. However, during the mid- to late 2000s, it was clear to the legal community that Mexican cases were being heard faster and denied in large numbers, yet the lawyer still took the case and promised a positive outcome. This was the reason that several participants chose not to apply for refugee protection.

Negative Decisions: Internal Flight Alternatives, State Protection, and Member Discretion

Participants' case decisions reflected Mexicans' low acceptance rates. In fact, nine of ten participants who applied for protection received a negative decision (the only positive decision was Arne Saknussemm). Two common and interrelated responses that the IRB utilizes to explain negative decisions are access to an internal flight alternative (IFA) and state protection. These two responses demonstrate the transnational dimensions of refugee determination: members, consultants, and applicants utilize information from/about claimants' countries of origin, including reports and other evidence, and popular discourses and stereotypes, to make their decisions.

An internal flight alternative refers to an area in a country where a person can go into hiding and live safely. A case on the Federal Court of Canada website explains the legal perspective on an IFA:

> The concept of an IFA is "inherent" in the definition of a Convention refugee ... By definition a Convention refugee must be a refugee from a country, not from some subdivision or region of a country, [and] a claimant cannot be a Convention refugee if there is an IFA. It follows that the determination of whether or not there is an IFA is integral to the determination of whether or not a claimant is a Convention refugee. (*Gallo Farias v. Canada (Citizenship and Immigration)* 2008)

Fleeing from a whole country does not mean that claimants have to flee state persecution; Canada recognizes non-state perpetrators of violence as also producing refugees. What it does imply, however, is that, regardless of the perpetrator, an applicant must exhaust *all* internal flight alternatives. In other words, applicants are responsible for proving that no IFA exists where they can relocate and remake their lives safely. This can be difficult since a number of IFAs are available in theory for people who face persecution, including densely populated urban areas or areas unconnected to a person's persecutor(s). For instance, participants mentioned that members often told Mexican applicants that Mexico City was a good IFA given the metropolitan area's population of over 20 million.

Berenice, who applied for protection from her partner's brother, a transnational migration merchant (Kyle 2000), as well as her employer at a government agency, was one of those applicants. During the hearing, the IRB member presiding over her case hinted that his ruling would recommend Mexico City as an IFA:

> I think he already had the answer [ruling]. He gave me that impression by the questions he asked. For instance, he would say, "How far is your city from Mexico City?"
>
> And I [said], "Four hours."
>
> "Do you have family in Mexico City? Would it be difficult for you to live in Mexico City?"
>
> And I said, "Well, the headquarters of the office for which I worked is in Mexico City. The office, its headquarters, [is] in Mexico City. I can't be in Mexico City."

Although Berenice thought that she thoroughly explained why Mexico City or other sites were not appropriate IFAs, she did not think that the member considered her arguments. Because Berenice worked for a government agency that granted loans to working-class Mexicans, her former boss had access to government records that could track her presence if she used identification or accessed a bank. In addition, even if her boss did not have access to such records, he could purchase them in the underground market (Gonzalez 2010). Despite this information, when the decision arrived, it cited Mexico City as an IFA.

Mexicano en Acción had a similar experience. He described a difference in the IRB member's behaviour during the hearing and in his subsequent explanation for rejecting the case: "The guy was very sympathetic during the hearing, very nice and everything . . . He surprised me by saying 'No.' His reasons were that I had lived in Aguascalientes, and I could have gone to live in Mexico City, you know, because the Zona Rosa [pink zone] is there, because human rights are respected and valued in Mexico."

The Zona Rosa in Mexico City is "a middle- to high-class neighbourhood. For many years, it has been a gay gathering centre with many gay bars, clubs, discotheques and shopping centres" (Infante, Sosa-Rubi, and Cuadra 2009, 131). The IRB member's response demonstrates a limited knowledge of the social and political contexts in Mexico vis-à-vis queer rights. By proposing the Zona Rosa as an IFA, he implied that Mexicano en Acción had access to a small neighbourhood in which he could be openly gay. The decision is reminiscent of the "discretion argument," whereby refugee adjudicators explain their decisions to deny claims by arguing that claimants need only be "discreet" (i.e., "pass" as straight) to navigate homophobic conditions in their country of origin (Kendall 2003; Lewis 2013). For the member, it was perfectly acceptable for Mexicano en Acción to perform heteronormativity outside the Zona Rosa and visit that neighbourhood only when he "needed to be gay," a notion of identity that assumes sexual orientation is performed in specifically stereotypical ways. Kendall (2003, 740), citing Casswell (1996), deems it a double standard since, "in Canada, the state of the law is such that 'a lesbian or gay man is certainly not expected to hide their sexual orientation in order to be safe somewhere in their country.'" Finally, as a middle-class neighbourhood, Zona Rosa is not accessible to many working-class Mexicans.

The decision also ignored systemic barriers faced by queer Mexicans. Although discrimination based on sexual orientation is illegal in Mexico, policies do not erase homophobic practices and violence or ensure state protection. Queer Mexicans highly distrust the police given their lack of action during homophobic violence by citizens or the fact that police are often the perpetrators (Ortiz-Hernández and Granados-Cosme 2006; Rotman and Marshall 2016).

In addition to IFAs, a criterion that IRB members use is whether a person has exhausted appeals to state protection in the country where the persecution occurred. The IRB evaluates protection in relation to relative safety in a country and accessible police services. Therefore, a country has to be infamous for not protecting its citizens and residents, or an applicant has to prove that he or she exhausted appeals to state protection and still underwent persecution. The following excerpt outlines the process:

> In *Kadenko v. Canada (Solicitor General)* (1996), 206 N.R. 272 (F.C.A.), the Federal Court of Appeal held ... that in order to rebut the presumption of state protection, refugee claimants must make "reasonable efforts" at seeking out state protection, and that the burden on the claimant increases where the state in question is democratic. (*Gallo Farias v. Canada (Citizenship and Immigration)* 2008)

Claimants must prove not only that they went to the police but also that the police refused to protect them. In addition, IRB members measure an applicant's credibility in relation to the evidence provided and their perception of a country's "democratic" performance. Canada's classification of Mexico, its trading partner, as safe demonstrates the transnational production of a specific notion of Mexico: safe for Mexicans. This was particularly the case given the warnings issued to Canadian citizens travelling to Mexico, particularly because of violence stemming from organized crime since the mid-2000s (Rotman and Marshall 2016).

Manolo, Arne Saknussemm, and Johann were unable to seek or receive police protection given that the police or unmarked attackers who had ties to the police, they believed, were involved in the violence perpetrated against them. Alternatively, Berenice had proof of visiting the police for protection after her partner's brother attacked her. She also went to the police after several instances of abuse and sexual harassment by her boss. Her experience demonstrates what Rotman and Marshall (2016, 2) highlight as a specific group who face limits to protection, queer Mexicans:

> In June 2015, a few days before Mexico City hosted a massive Pride parade, unknown armed assailants savagely beat and shot in the head a transgender woman in Chihuahua. The victim's body was wrapped in a Mexican flag – apparently a protest against the Supreme Court's June ruling allowing gay marriage. According to the UN Special Rapporteur on extrajudicial, summary or arbitrary executions, between 2005 and 2013 in Mexico, 555 homicides targeting individuals because of their sexual orientation or gender identity were reported. The actual number is likely greater, as many crimes of violence in Mexico go unreported due to a lack of confidence in the justice system.

This form of extreme violence was a daily reality for queer participants while they lived in Mexico, including Berenice, Mexicano en Acción, and Teresa. This meant that, even if claimants such as Berenice sought state protection and provided evidence of its limitations, IRB members had clear ideas about Mexico's safety. For example, the member presiding over Libertad's case cited Mexico's commitment to democracy and the government's predisposition to better Mexico in his decision: "Even if there are problems with corruption, ... Mexico is considered [democratic]." For Libertad, the comment did not come as a shock. She recounted cases in which the response was more blatantly biased: "I have heard some people say that during their hearing the judge [IRB member] ask[ed] them 'Which Mexico are you talking about? I just came back from Cancún, and it was beautiful.'"

Right to an Appeal?

The refugee determination process does not end with a negative decision. Claimants with a negative decision have several legal options to prevent their removal and/or ask that their case be reviewed. One example is the Refugee Appeals Division (RAD). Although the RAD was promised in the 2002 IRPA, it was not implemented until December 2012 through the Balanced Refugee Reform Act (Immigration and Refugee Board of Canada 2016). The RAD gives a refugee claimant the ability to have someone other than the original IRB member evaluate their case. This is particularly important because only one person makes the initial decision. Although the appeals process is also conducted by political appointees (Citizenship and Immigration Canada 2011b), it nonetheless signifies an opening up of avenues to secure status. However, the RAD implementation raised concerns similar to those directed at the refugee determination process. A report by CBC News found that "the average rate of positive decisions by adjudicators now at the appeal division is significantly lower than that of all members of the Refugee Protection Division" (Elliott 2014).

Because participants applied for refugee protection before 2012, they did not benefit from the RAD. The most common option for them was Judicial Review, which occurred through a two-stage process. The first is called "leave" and entails a person proving "that an error was made in the decision, or the decision was not fair or reasonable" (Citizenship and Immigration Canada 2009d). The criteria used to move a case into the leave stage are narrow. Judges review not the case evidence itself but technicalities and how IRB members conduct themselves. More specifically, to provide leave and have the case reassessed, there has to be an explicit mistake (Becklumb 2008). That process is limited since "the FCC

[Federal Court of Canada] typically defers to the IRB, with official court records showing that only 10 to 15 percent of cases are granted leave" (Gould, Sheppard, and Wheeldon 2010, 459). If successful, the second part is a more detailed "application for Judicial Review," which includes a hearing. The outcome is either agreement with the original decision or reassessment of the claim at the IRB. No participants were granted a reassessment.

Like IRB members, Federal Court judges are politically appointed. In 2011, the *Ottawa Citizen* studied 480 immigration and refugee-related Federal Court decisions and found that "Federal Court of Canada judges appointed by Conservatives are significantly less likely to overturn decisions by government officers and tribunals to deny refugee claims or deport non-citizens than are judges appointed by past Liberal administrations" (Butler 2011). The newspaper's findings point to a narrowing of legal access to secure status not only in relation to individual cases but also in relation to the refugee determination system.

The process also involved a quick turnaround or "frenzied time" (Griffiths 2014) because of the short time period between when a claim is denied and when the Judicial Review application needs to be submitted, fifteen days, as Mexicano en Acción explained:

> You only have fifteen days to submit the application, and then you have thirty days to submit new evidence or the reason why you are submitting the application. And I remember that my lawyer told me, "You know, there's very little chance, but I suggest you do it, to win some time, and perhaps you might get a positive result." But, no, the Federal Court did not find any errors with this guy [the IRB member who handed down the negative decision].

Another factor that a Federal Court judge might consider when deciding a case is new evidence (judges do not reconsider submitted evidence). Although Mexicano en Acción knew that the success rate was low, he saw Judicial Review as a literal way to buy time to plan his next step (the application has a fee). This was because, while the case undergoes review, the removal process is paused, allowing applicants with negative decisions time to look for other avenues to defer deportation.

Like other hearings, Judicial Reviews are also subjective. When Manolo received a negative decision from the IRB, he noticed an important error:

> When my case was presented, . . . in the response they made huge mistakes . . . The response I got for my case was that I was not eligible [for refugee status] and that I could return to Colombia, my country of origin [laughs]. I'm Mexican. That means that the IRB only copied the letter that they sent someone, they copied and pasted, right? They copied [the text] and put it in my letter. They didn't even take the time to read what they were sending me. That is a huge mistake because it means that they are not giving people the time they supposedly give you.

Although the typo on the letter explaining the negative decision was considerable, the appeal judge did not grant a reassessment: "I appealed, and they said that error was only a typo." Manolo called attention to another important point: for the IRB, refugee claimants become file numbers with mapped-out endings, copied and pasted from previous responses. In that moment, the claimant exists only insofar as the file and case exist and becomes devoid of other characteristics, in sum dehumanized. In the name of streamlining or efficiency, claimants and their cases become something to overcome to move on to the next case (Soennecken 2013).

Pre-Removal Risk Assessment

After claimants have exhausted all avenues to remain in Canada, the last option to protect them from the potential danger of returning to persecution is the Pre-Removal Risk Assessment (PRRA). The PRRA consists of an application process to determine the risk that a person will experience if removed from Canada. The Citizenship and Immigration Canada (2010) website outlines the process: "An officer will review your application, as well as documents and other evidence you provide in support of it. If you previously made a refugee claim, the officer will limit their consideration to new evidence, or that which you were not able to present at your refugee hearing. You may be asked to attend an interview." Before 2012, refused refugee claimants received a PRRA application when CBSA considered them "removal ready." Removal ready meant that a person had a valid passport or travel document, or that CBSA believed the person could obtain one reasonably quickly, meaning that the removal order could be enforced swiftly (Community Legal Education Ontario 2008). Once that occurred, a person had fifteen days to apply for the PRRA, again demonstrating how "frenzied time" can affect outcomes (Griffiths 2014). Immigration officials paused a removal until the PRRA decision.

The PRRA does work similar to the refugee application without the need to promise more secure forms of status. It allows applicants to prolong their stay in Canada, like the Judicial Review process, thus allowing them more leeway to plan their departure or make other plans. However, the success rate of staying a removal with a positive PRRA decision is low. For instance, between 2002 and 2014, the PRRA approval rate did not go over 3.3 percent (Citizenship and Immigration Canada 2009c; Immigration, Refugees and Citizenship Canada 2016). Several reasons exist for this low rate. First, like the Judicial Review, an applicant can only submit new evidence to support the PRRA. Second, the PRRA is not an independent review, and immigration officials who might be predisposed to reject applications perform evaluations. Third, like other applications, the PRRA is time sensitive, making it difficult to compile new evidence. Fourth, though a removal is stayed for fifteen days, applying for a PRRA is contingent on receiving the documents within the allotted time. If applicants have moved, then they might miss that opportunity.

In addition to general issues regarding the low acceptance rate, Libertad identified something that affected her application. After receiving the documents in the mail, she went to the immigration office. There the immigration official tried to convince her to sign her right to the PRRA away and accept a voluntary removal:

> I didn't know what the PRRA was, I said. They are asking me to go to put me on a plane. Well, I went. I've always tried to have a good disposition and follow the rules. So they say to me, "Because your application to Federal Court was rejected, and your refugee application was negative, we are going to give you the option of doing a PRRA. But if you don't want to do it, you can sign here" [laughs]. They pressured me, saying, "Very few people [win the PRRA], it's tiring, very few people, it's not worth it, you don't get help, you don't get legal aid, nothing." Like saying,

> "It's your right, and we are telling you about it because it's your right," but trying to talk me out of it. Like saying, "We'll give you the answer tomorrow or the day after. Better to make things easier. Sign here that you don't want to apply for the PRRA, and we'll take care of everything." . . . As if they are so generous . . . So I said, "No, I'm going to do the PRRA. There are a lot of reasons why I need to show that my country is not the place where I should be."

During our initial interview in 2009, Libertad thought that she needed to exhibit a *disposición de cumplir,* a willingness to follow the rules, to obtain a more stable status. However, as time passed, hope also began to diminish, a process directly related to how she was treated by immigration officials, who are meant in theory to be impartial and objective. After the PRRA, eventually denied, Libertad's notion of following the rules changed slightly, for Libertad realized that the system was not there to help her but to eliminate her presence from Canada.

The immigration official's attempt to dissuade Libertad from applying to the PRRA demonstrates a push to increase deportation efficiency, something desirable in bureaucracies. Not having to process extra documents decreases immigration agents' workload (Soennecken 2013). Efficiency through deportation is also a facet of nation building: filtering "undesirables" out of the territory. Finally, the attempt to dissuade migrants from applying tests whether they are truly afraid to go back. In her interaction with the immigration official, Libertad countered that test by stating that there were many reasons why she thought Mexico was unsafe. Therefore, though the law has built-in controls to make sure that people do not fall through the cracks and are deported to dangerous places (in this case the PRRA), immigration officers can make people more easily deportable by trying to convince them to voluntarily depart. Canada ran an Assisted Voluntary Return and Reintegration (AVRR) program from 2012 to 2015 (Aberman 2018).

Armando described a similar encounter with an immigration official:

> [The immigration official said,] "Look, it's over, you applied for this, and that, and your time is up." So he told me "In about a month," he says, "you're

> going to get a departure date, so you have to come and prepare your departure, your return to Mexico." He told me in about a month. He told me, "So any change you have in your cell phone, address, please notify us." And … before I left, he told me "If you decide to stay," he says, "remember that sooner or later you're going to end up here. Sooner or later everyone who [over] stays returns here." He says, "So think long and hard. Do things right."

The encounter points to a surveillant assemblage of illegalization whereby immigration policing institutions demand that any change in personal information be reported and input into the system to guarantee that a person will submit to removal. Furthermore, like Libertad, Armando was threatened that, if he stayed, the surveillance web would eventually catch up to him, also signalling the fact that he would have to bear (aguantar) deportability on a day-to-day basis after the removal date passed.

Such moments of rejection can also lead to negotiations and attempts to change the system. For Mexicano en Acción, the denial of his refugee claim, his Judicial Review, and the arrival of the PRRA incited him to action. He began a public campaign that he elected to call "Let Him Stay" during our interview to protect his confidentiality. He recounted how he came to the decision:

> I said, "If they have been fighting me to stay here, I'm also going to fight them. And I hope it costs them to make me leave." … At that time, I was already part of [a migrant rights organization], and so … I met a member through another group, and I told him and another guy, "Listen, they're going to deport me." … Obviously I didn't work on this campaign alone, obviously I can't ever take full credit, it wouldn't have been possible without so many people that helped me, that supported me … The campaign had two objectives. Yes, obviously to allow Mexicano en Acción to stay in Canada and obtain status, but also to raise more consciousness and education about the situation in which we live, right? To confront, as LGBT refugees, as Latino refugees, Hispanic refugees, you understand? Not only as one thing but everything, … like the intersection of everything.

Mexicano en Acción explained his decision to visibilize his impending deportation through the clause "I hope it costs them to remove me." One can interpret the reference to cost in two ways. The first meaning involves financial cost. As I discussed above in relation to the representation of welfare cheats and bogus refugees, costs to the nation usually involve a negative moral evaluation. However, Mexicano en Acción's comments turn that perception on its head. We can compare the cost to the Canadian nation to the cost accrued by refugee claimants in terms of money, effort, time, and emotion. In that way, his comments involved public defiance and an alternative interpretation of the cost-benefit analyses imposed on refugee claimants.

The second meaning involves effort. Mexicano en Acción's campaign utilized the internet and media appearances, appealing to the public and politicians to allow Mexicano en Acción to stay in Canada. However, he was aware that his was not an isolated situation. Therefore, the campaign highlighted his efforts as part of a web of activities to combat the illegalization and deportation of *all* migrants. The lens through which he examined his experience is also important. He was interested in making visible the experiences of differently situated migrants, pointing out that queer and racialized migrants undergo forms of oppression that interlock with immigration status. Thus, we can see that, though limited, the funnelling of refugee claimants toward deportability also includes moments of negotiation. The campaign influenced audiences to think about immigration and migrants' status differently, reassembling normative discourses and inserting less visible explanations for why migration and status trajectories occur the way that they do.

Reassembling Refugee Determination

The 2012 Protecting Canada's Immigration System Act led to the creation of two streams of applicants: those from designated countries of origin (DCO) and those from non-DCO. The change is another example of law-making as a "tactical character" or contingent process that involves "intricate and calculated interventions" (De Genova 2002, 424). This process of knowledge production is an element of the migration assemblage produced in relation to Mexican migrants in Canada. It interlocks with visa policy and practice and internal bordering practices.

The DCO policy produced several effects, mainly targeting DCO claimants, including a fast-tracking of applications and limits to the appeals process. For instance, regarding the Refugee Appeals Division established in 2012,

> until July 2015, refugee claimants from DCO countries were barred from access to appeal a negative refugee determination . . . It was also possible to deport failed DCO claimants from Canada immediately after a negative decision on their refugee claim; they did not have a right to an automatic suspension of deportation when they pursued review of a negative decision at the Federal Court. (Rotman and Marshall 2016, 28)

The government implemented the RAD ban, arguing that DCO claimants were bogus and therefore should not be granted additional entitlements. However, the Federal Court, in *Y.Z. v. Canada,* found that not allowing DCO claimants access to the RAD constituted a violation of the Canadian Charter of Rights and Freedoms (*Y.Z. v. Canada [Citizenship and Immigration]* 2015). Specifically, the policy discriminated against claimants based on their nationality (Canadian Council for Refugees 2015).

A second outcome was the limiting of a PRRA application for all refugee claimants. In fact, non-DCO claimants were barred for twelve months after a negative decision, whereas DCO claimants were barred for thirty-six months (Rotman and Marshall 2016). Citizenship and Immigration Canada (2012c) explains the changes as a way to "streamline the asylum system, eliminate duplication and enable faster removal of failed refugee claimants." This reorganization of policy and practice demonstrated a rise in deportability in general as well as the way that it was applied in the refugee determination system. Refugee claimants faced deportability sooner in the process and had fewer avenues to "buy" time to look for alternatives.

The DCO policy was terminated in May 2019. The government explained its decision in the following way: "The DCO policy did not fulfil its objective of discouraging misuse of the asylum system and of processing refugee claims from these countries faster. Additionally, several Federal Court decisions struck down certain provisions of the DCO policy, ruling that they did not comply with the Canadian Charter of Rights and

Freedoms" (Immigration and Refugee Board of Canada 2019). The decision came after repeated calls from migrants, lawyers, and other stakeholders claiming that the system was discriminatory. However, the explanation provided continued the practice of criminalizing claimants for what it called "misuse." Thus, the government decided to end the policy not because it was discriminatory but because of a calculated decision about the efficiency of this specific bordering practice.

***

The refugee determination process in Canada is onerous and illegalizes precarious status migrants who do not fit norms for successful applicants. This process is organized through specific ways of knowing: refugee policy and discourse about which claimants are "legitimate" or not depending on their geographic location and how that location is understood as "safe" or "unsafe," the basis of their claim, and their social locations (race, gender, sexual orientation, etc.). Claimants receive instructions from legal representatives, non-governmental organizations, and the Immigration and Refugee Board and its representatives, and they have to make quick decisions about submitting appropriate applications and documents. IRB members and judges actively engage in restricting access to secure status, as evident from inconsistent decision making and discretionary power. Mexican claimants are often directed to internal flight alternatives, particularly in Mexico City, and told that state protection exists in their country. During this process, applicants' personal information is stockpiled in databases and saved in case it might prove to be useful during removal proceedings.

For participants, the process initially seemed to be fair and welcoming. However, this idea began to erode for those who encountered rude immigration officials and IRB members as well as after experiencing moments of sticky, frenzied, and ruptured time because of negative decisions (Griffiths 2014). Given ruptures, migrants strategically engage in the buying of time, by appealing applications or making new applications, to defer removal orders. These processes are emotionally draining, producing instances of insecurity, fear, and distrust. Finally, another temporal rupture occurred through the reorganization (reassemblage) of refugee policy and practice post-2012. Changes limited the amount of time that claimants had protection from deportation and sped up "frenzied" time through fast-tracked applications, making it more difficult for claimants to collect evidence to make their cases. The result, as I discuss in the next chapter, was a shifting of strategies, whereby Mexicans opted to apply for refugee protection less and less and acted on, or planned, other avenues for obtaining secure status.

5

Yearning for Secure Status

When I interviewed Leonel, whose refugee claim was refused in the late 2000s, he described living without status and his desire for stability:

> Perhaps many of us are looking for a little bit more rights because perhaps, by trying to find a way to fix your papers, you are trying to stop it a bit, right? The things you have to *aguantar* (bear) day to day, right? Who doesn't want to improve? The difficulty is doing it when you don't have status ... They could say, "You're living what you deserve." Perhaps, [but] many of us are finding a way, another way.

This affective process, a *hope, desire,* or *yearning* for a dignified existence, and the strategies that migrants use to approximate it through obtaining secure immigration status, motivate this chapter. Given the narrowing of access to the refugee determination system for Mexican migrants with precarious status because of the 2009 visa requirement and subsequent changes to refugee determination, this yearning for status led to a shifting of strategies, whereby participants focused on humanitarian and compassionate applications, marriage sponsorship, and study and work permits. These strategies operated alongside existing ways of knowing: immigration law, discourses about deservingness, "good citizenship," and "fraudulent marriage" sponsorship. Participants' relationships with these ways of knowing were sometimes contradictory: challenging bogus refugee discourses while sometimes upholding ideas about fraudulent marriages. In doing so, they navigated a system in which lawyers, immigration officials, spouses, and employers sometimes opened up access to secure status and at other times produced and upheld internal borders. Regulatory bodies, such as those for immigration consultants and government institutions, also participated in this border work. For instance, government institutions continued to store precarious status migrant information, looping it back onto ways of knowing and augmenting migrant deportability. Anticipating barriers, participants presented themselves through curated "paperealities" (White 2014): archives of documents or photographs and experiences to have the best chance at obtaining secure immigration status.

Theorizing Yearning

Yearning is a point of departure to explore how ways of feeling circulate among and through precarious status migrants. Burman (2010, 10) argues that, whereas nostalgia refers to an intense longing for something, and an orientation toward the past, yearning "opens up visions of a more equitable future." She goes on to state that "yearning is manifest when people express critical desires for justice and change, and try to make the conditions of their involvement in a globalized socioeconomic setting more equitable. This might happen through organized opposition and/or political mobilization, individual practices of transmigration, or creative work articulating a vision of diasporic subjecthood" (8). Burman frames yearning as a process that makes room for the strategies in which a number of migrants engage as they navigate their way in a new context and through their legal status transitions.

Power is an important aspect of yearning since "yearnings are shaped by a culture of migration" (Ibarra 2003, 266). Pessar and Mahler (2003) propose that initiative and resourcefulness are important aspects of this process. Linking agency to yearning, they note that "much of what people actually do transnationally is foregrounded by imaging, planning, and strategizing; these must be valued and factored into people's agency" (447). As in Burman (2010), this focus points to a desire to create social change even if that change is not always achieved.

Yearnings often involve disillusionment (Ibarra 2003, 266). In his "Undocumented Alphabet," Ledesma (2017, 97) discusses this:

> "Y" is for the word "Yearning," that intense longing that all undocumented immigrants feel for a more just world where their suffering and hard

> work might be rewarded. It is a desperate hope that if you work hard enough you can actually change your life. But, this yearning is fickle, often dissipating into the nihilistic realization that no matter how much you may want it or how much you may work for it, that divine justice you are hoping for is just an illusion.

Ledesma points to the fragile link among yearning, imagining, and belonging, a process that involves the circulation of emotions across and through spaces and bodies. This process also involves aguantar or bearing abuse from partners, employers, and the immigration system, as well as from the circulation of hate, fear, and national love mobilized against migrants. For participants, the yearning for status did not always materialize in *arreglar papeles* (literally, to fix one's papers or become documented). However, even if they did not achieve secure status through one application, some participants continued to work for and hope for better outcomes.

Application for Permanent Residence through Humanitarian and Compassionate Grounds

The application for permanent residence through humanitarian and compassionate (H&C) grounds is one option for migrants living in Canada to obtain secure status. Determination of eligibility under an H&C application is different from that of the refugee application. It evaluates an applicant's risk if deported as well as their level of establishment in Canada: "Persons who apply for H&C in Canada may have spent an extended time in Canada and may claim to be well established. There is no hard and fast rule relating to the period of time in Canada but it is expected that a significant degree of establishment takes several years to achieve" (Immigration, Refugees and Citizenship Canada 2017). Factors considered in evaluating establishment include length of time in Canada, why a person remained in Canada without secure status, which often involves measuring the risk involved in returning to the home country, and what applicants have done that contributes to Canadian society: stable work, taxes paid, use of welfare services (or lack thereof), language skills, efforts to improve education and skills, assets (bank accounts, etc.), community involvement, volunteer work, contacts in Canada who write reference letters (including family members, employers, co-workers, and community members), and finally the best interest of any child involved (Buahene 2004). Claimants must show evidence of these actions: receipts, accounts, letters of support. These archives do at least two types of work. First, they temporalize applicants' presence (Coutin 2000), literally outlining how long applicants have been in the country and when they did what. The problem arises when applicants have gaps in time that they cannot explain: lack of receipts, work under the table, insecure housing, et cetera (Mattingly 1997). Second, they provide immigration authorities with information to update their databases and extend surveillant assemblages of migrant illegalization (Villegas 2015a).

The reassemblage of policy and practice through the passing of the Balanced Refugee Reform Act (BRRA) in 2010 changed H&C determination such that "H&C decision makers may not consider the risks that are assessed within the refugee protection process, i.e. risk of persecution based on grounds set out in the Refugee Convention or risk of torture, to life or of cruel and unusual treatment or punishment, but must continue to consider elements related to the hardships that affect the foreign national" (Citizenship and Immigration Canada 2011a). This change sought to differentiate the H&C from a refugee claim and to focus the evaluation on establishment. However, officers still have to evaluate whether applicants will experience "'unusual and undeserved or disproportionate hardship' if their applications were refused" (Meurrens 2016). Similarly, a 2015 Supreme Court decision in *Kanthasamy v. Canada* stated that immigration officers should evaluate cases "holistically" and "weigh *all* the relevant facts before them, and not just evaluate them against overly rigid and strict criteria" (Meurrens 2016). The BRRA also narrowed access to H&C applications for refugee claimants with negative decisions, who cannot apply until twelve months have elapsed (Citizenship and Immigration Canada 2012b). This means that refused refugee claimants have to endure living underground and avoid deportation before having access to the application.

Other barriers exist with the application. First, unlike the refugee application and the subsequent right to judicial review and Pre-Removal Risk Assessment (PRRA), an H&C application does not protect one from deportation. Police or immigration agents can profile, stop, and deport applicants. Second, applicants pay a fee of $550 for adults and $150 for minors, making it financially prohibitive for many potential applicants, particularly those with large families. Third, applicants must pay for their legal representation. Given the fees for such representation, immigration consultants might convince clients to submit applications without providing them with sufficient information or presenting false hopes. In the past decade, a number of changes have been made to regulate the immigration consulting profession (Friesen and Clark 2010; Keung 2010). However, "ghost consultants," unregulated representatives who do not register with the government and Immigration Consultants of Canada Regulatory Council (ICCRC) but represent clients, continue to operate (Quan 2016). Even if a consultant belongs to the ICCRC, it is not illegal for someone to convince a client to apply, even if the chance of acceptance is low. Fourth, approval rates vary across time, making it difficult to plan for the best time to apply.

Yearning for Status/Claiming Deservingness

Despite such barriers, several participants submitted an H&C application or planned to do so. For instance, by the time Mexicano en Acción received his PRRA documents after his unsuccessful refugee claim based on persecution because of his sexual orientation, he had already applied for permanent residence under an H&C application. He described what he told the immigration official during his PRRA meeting:

> "I'm trying to better my English, I'm trying to integrate into the community. I'm doing practically everything you are asking me to do," right? Practically, for the H&C. "Not to be on welfare, to be working, to be studying English, to volunteer." ... So they told me, ... "Okay, we're going to wait for the H&C [outcome], and we're going to see which decision has more weight, and we'll continue to evaluate you."

Because of this, Mexicano en Acción never received a removal order. In addition, the PRRA meeting was a catalyst for the public "Let Him Stay" campaign that he organized alongside migrant justice organizations and allied supporters. The campaign had two objectives:

> [first] ... to have Mexicano en Acción stay in Canada and receive status but [second] ... to create more consciousness about what we experience,

> right? What we face as refugees, as LGBT refugees, as Latin American refugees, . . . the intersection of all of that. And [to fight against] what you already are aware of, [comments such as] "Refugees only come to steal our jobs and live off welfare." No, we contribute, we work, we volunteer, we do a bit of everything, so that was also something we were working for.

Through his political mobilization, Mexicano en Acción presented a yearning for an equitable future. However, in doing so, he framed his right to receive secure status through the language of deservingness – "we contribute, we work, we volunteer, we do a bit of everything." Such a narrative has limits given that it excludes migrants who are not seen as contributing or are unable to work. Despite aligning himself with this contribution-as-deservingness discourse, Mexicano en Acción also demonstrated an understanding of the relational nature of his immigration status and queer and Latinx identities. Thus, his words were also a yearning for recognition of all aspects of his existence, something that immigration systems often ignore.

His application was approved, and Mexicano en Acción received permanent residence in 2010. The campaign allowed him to navigate the system and produce beneficial results without sacrificing his commitment to systemic change. However, his case is not the norm. Visibility often increases deportability.

In contrast, Leonel received a removal order upon the rejection of his refugee claim and subsequent appeals. He had already experienced the pain of deportation when his sister, who had invited him to Canada in the early 2000s, was deported in the mid-2000s along with her husband and children. Because of his own removal order, Leonel opted to go into hiding at the same time that he submitted his H&C application, demonstrating a downward legal status transition (Goldring and Landolt 2013). His H&C application demonstrated a yearning to regain some of the entitlements that he lost when his refugee claim was refused as well as new ones, including the right to stay in Canada. The application was also a way to disrupt understandings of deserving status. His comment at the beginning of this chapter – "they could say, 'You're living what you deserve.' Perhaps, [but] many of us are finding a way, another way" – illustrates this. It counters the idea that some migrants are undeserving of status because of the legal system or because of an inability to fit into the "good" immigrant frame that Mexicano en Acción projected above. The reference to "they" includes not only the immigration system and the nation's "community of value" (Anderson 2013) but also Leonel's co-nationals with secure status, who, Leonel thought, policed him and other precarious status migrants as a way for them to show good citizenship and belonging.

When I first interviewed him in 2009, the removal order was still in effect, and Leonel had been waiting for an H&C decision for several years, extending his illegalization and precarity and demonstrating how the sticky time of immigration applications affected his yearning (Griffiths 2014). In the meantime, Leonel sent updates to support his application on two occasions. The practice of submitting updated information, he believed, was a way to keep track of his whereabouts in order to deport him eventually (Villegas 2015a). For instance, one year he submitted a tax form that contained his employer's address. Subsequently, Canada Border Services Agency (CBSA) officials appeared at his job site as well as his sister's home, showing that applicants cannot demonstrate their ability to become established if those actions increase their deportability. Several years later the application was refused, stating that the evidence used to determine establishment – letters of support from employers, community members, family members, and acquaintances – was not sufficient. Although Leonel had the choice to appeal, given his lack of success in appealing his refugee decision and the cost associated with the process (including the lawyer's fees), he opted not to do so and continued to live in a state of precarity and deportability.

The Best Interests of Children?

Libertad also made an H&C application after her refugee claim was refused. When I interviewed her the first time in 2010, her removal date was imminent. In fact, our interview took place a few days before she was set to leave. She was packing up her place without having decided whether to stay in Canada or to allow the Canadian government to deport her to Mexico, all while her young child napped in the adjacent room. Her yearning for status was also a yearning to make her child's life more comfortable, understanding that in mixed status families those with status often experience barriers similar to those of their precarious status family members (Enriquez 2015).

I interviewed Libertad again in 2015. During that time, she had remained in Canada, eluding immigration authorities as well as her child's father, who had been abusive during and after her pregnancy. Libertad filed criminal charges; however, given her increased deportability following her removal order, she was forced to withdraw them, thinking that if she appeared in criminal court she could be apprehended by immigration authorities. Her child's father had threatened to call them on several occasions.

Libertad's H&C application, like that of Leonel, was refused, despite the argument that her child, now elementary school age, would be affected by the deportation. Citizenship and Immigration Canada (2016b) explains the criteria that it uses to account for the best interests of children:

> The codification of the principle of "best interests of a child" into the legislation does not mean that the interests of the child outweigh all other factors in a case. While factors affecting children should be given substantial weight, the best interest of a child is only one of many important factors that the decision maker needs to consider when making an H&C decision that directly affects a child.

Similarly, Meloni et al. (2014, 5) discuss *Baker v. Canada*, a case that has influenced legal interpretation regarding the best interest of the child in removal proceedings:

> An undocumented Jamaican woman . . . was ordered to be deported with her four Canadian children in 1992. Ms Baker applied for an exemption on the basis of compassionate and humanitarian considerations, arguing that she was the sole caregiver for two of her Canadian-born children and that her two other children depended on her for emotional support. Her application was refused. Subsequently, Ms Baker applied to the Supreme Court for a review of the case, with the objective of determining whether federal immigration authorities must treat the best interest of the Canadian child as a primary consideration in assessing an applicant under the Immigration Act. The Supreme Court agreed that the Federal Court's decision was unreasonable and that, although the best interest

> was not of primary consideration, immigration authorities should "give substantial weight, and be alert, alive and sensitive to the rights of children, to their best interests, and to the hardship that may be caused to them by a negative decision." . . . [This] follow[ed] an approach that respects humanitarian and compassionate values.

Although *Baker* had a positive resolution, it did not definitively outline that best-interest-of-the-child considerations would mean a stay in deportation or the granting of permanent residence, only that the case would receive substantial reconsideration. Therefore, in the eyes of the law, the negative decision in Libertad's H&C application did not contravene precedent.

Another example came from Eduardo and Rebeca. In the early 2010s, Eduardo was fixing his bicycle outside his house when he was racially profiled by a police officer. The officer was looking for a neighbour and, upon hearing the accent of Eduardo, who spoke English fluently, asked him about his immigration status. Eduardo showed the officer a valid Canadian driver's licence, but it did not satisfy the officer, who then called immigration authorities. Eduardo was detained, prompting him and Rebeca to apply for refugee status as a strategy to buy time. They also submitted an H&C application before their refugee claim was resolved (as I discussed above, this is no longer an option). Their refugee claim and H&C decisions came around the same time, and both were negative. Having three young children, one Canadian born, did not affect the outcome, forcing them to decide whether to stay in Canada under a removal order or to return to Mexico. In 2012, they opted for the latter, returning to the economic precarity and insecuritization from which they had fled years before and which had only become worse in the interim.

Although advocating for the best interests of children is an important strategy to secure immigration status, it also has some limitations. The argument depends on discourses of deservingness, which construct children as worthy because of their age. This means that older children might not receive the same considerations. Racialized and immigrant children are also aged differently (Orellana and Johnson 2012). The construction of deservingness vis-à-vis childhood often uses the logic of "don't blame children for the sins of their parents," which criminalizes the yearning and strategies in which migrant parents engage to remain in Canada.

Plans to Apply and Reasons for Hesitating

Other participants planned to submit H&C applications, though they had not yet initiated the process. When I interviewed Aquetzalli in 2015, she had lived in Canada for almost a decade without status. She described an affective attachment, or yearning, to stay in Canada. Her yearning was related to the security that she felt in the country, her networks, as well as the cultural work in which she was engaged, which she thought counteracted some of the negative effects of her precarious status and working conditions.

During the interview, Aquetzalli described an incident that made her yearning more precarious. A few months earlier, she had become acquainted with a woman whom she initially considered a friend and who participated in the same cultural/artistic activity. One day Aquetzalli jokingly criticized the woman, who then accused her of being a bully and told her that she was going to call immigration authorities (she knew about Aquetzalli's status). Although aware that this could happen anytime, when retelling the incident, Aquetzalli reflected on her deportability:

> Having to see myself involved in this, particularly in a cultural space [laughs], that's the last place you would think it would happen. And to see how that person abused her power. I don't even think she has papers, well, no, but because she's a[n international] student one could say she's a bit more protected, right? And, if not, the fact that someone sees you as vulnerable and says I will go after her, well, it's sad, no? It's ugly for people to abuse their power . . . I don't wish it on anyone, because you think about it: what if they deport me? And I've grown to love it here. So it was a big shock. I was afraid when I went [to the cultural space]. I didn't want to go [there] anymore . . . Without papers, I'm left defenceless. That is, I am an open target for anyone. Yes, that situation made me think about, well, I want to have status, obviously, like anyone. I want to have my papers and try harder. But at the end of the day, it hasn't been because of a lack of effort, right? It's been a lack of opportunities or money or – it's not that I don't want to.

After the loss of a loved one back home, and the inability to travel to the funeral and be with her family, Aquetzalli decided to take a chance and apply for permanent residence under the H&C. She hoped that her cultural work, which had garnered media coverage and public recognition, would be enough for her to receive secure status. However, her application was delayed because of financial difficulties and the prospect of applying for status through marriage sponsorship.

Juan Nadie also discussed his yearning for secure status. He had lived in Canada for seven years when I interviewed him in 2014. He told me that

> some time ago I went to see a lawyer, and she told me to apply for a, what's it called? For humanitarian reasons. The lawyer told me that I had strong possibilities of obtaining it that way. Because they look at the time you've been here. I think that, well, I have been here seven years. And they look for people who have been here for five years or something like that. Who have more than five years. And she gave me other criteria, like paying your taxes, doing community service, all of that, making donations to institutions, and what else? Speaking the language. Having had studied something. Things like that. Various points that are key for them to look and say, "Oh, yes, he's a good citizen, I'm going to give him papers." Uh huh. So that would be . . . one of the options. That or getting married, but I think that's a bit more difficult.

Juan Nadie understood that the H&C application evaluated whether a person was a good deserving citizen. After the interview, we discussed potential volunteering opportunities for him to engage in to strengthen his application, but he was unable to participate in any of them given his long working hours in the construction industry. Presenting oneself as a good citizen takes time and money. To have time to study, one must have a flexible schedule. Thus, like Leonel, Juan Nadie had a difficult time demonstrating his "good" citizenship because of the nature of his work.

Sponsorship: "Real Marriages," "Marriages of Convenience," and the Work of Applying

Another option to remain in Canada is a sponsorship application. Although Canadian permanent residents and citizens can sponsor children, parents, or grandparents, no participant had such relatives with legal status in

Canada, making marriage the most viable option. The sponsorship application can be time consuming given that, in addition to filling out immigration documents, applicants have to compile "evidence" of the legitimacy of the marriage, what White (2014) calls an "archive of intimacy" to produce a "papereality" – a version of the relationship narrated on paper. This archive, through which affect circulates as a manifestation of love (or distrust among officials evaluating it), includes letters, emails, and other exchanges between spouses; letters of support from friends and family members; and photos, videos, and any other materials that might be relevant (White 2014). The rationale for producing this archive is to prove that sponsor and sponsored are not committing fraud.

According to Citizenship and Immigration Canada (2012a), "marriage fraud" can take two forms:

> A couple pretends to be in a genuine relationship, so that the sponsored spouse can come to or stay in Canada. In some cases, the sponsor may be given a financial or other kind of benefit in exchange for the sponsorship; or [o]ne of the partners enters the relationship in good faith, while the other is using the relationship only to gain permanent status in Canada. This victimizes the sponsor.

In fact, in 2011, Citizenship and Immigration Canada launched an anti–marriage fraud campaign to counteract what it saw as a growing issue, using the language of "marriages of convenience" (Gaucher 2014) as opposed to "real marriages." The social debate that ensued is an important way to frame some participants' reflections on their sponsorship applications or their reasons for choosing to apply or not apply via this route. Participants were influenced by understandings of marriage, love, and marriages of convenience as either a strategy or a criminal act.

Marriages of convenience are often depicted as antithetical to real marriages even though the former are difficult to prove (Gaucher 2014). Real marriage often relies on specific understandings of the reasons for entering into a marriage contract, namely love. It also involves a reinforcing of heteronormativity even when same-sex sponsorship is legally allowed (Luibhéid 2008). Although participants understood that there was a business "out there" whereby one could find a sponsor, pay that person a certain amount of money, and enter into a marriage contract for the purpose of receiving status (they related figures ranging from $5,000 to $20,000), many were wary of the possibility of abuse.

In October 2012, amendments to the Immigration and Refugee Protection Act imposed a policy that awarded sponsored spouses conditional permanent residence for two years before they received full permanent resident rights. This conditionality meant that sponsored spouses had to cohabitate "in a legitimate relationship with their sponsor" or risk losing their permanent residence status (Citizenship and Immigration Canada 2012a). The probationary period made it difficult to leave a marriage in cases of abuse. It also reinforced understandings of marriage that centre on cohabitating, ignoring the many other families and marriages divided by Canada's immigration policies. The conditional requirement was revoked in April 2017 (Keung 2016b). The decision continued to employ illegalizing language, stating that, though "non-genuine relationships" existed, "most spousal sponsorship applications are made in good faith" (Government of Canada 2017b). A second rationale was a "commitment to family reunification and supports gender equality and combating gender violence. As a result of the requirement for the sponsored spouse or partner to live with their sponsor, an imbalance between the sponsor and the sponsored spouse or partner could have been created, potentially making the sponsored spouse or partner more vulnerable" (Government of Canada 2017b).

Sponsorship as a Strategy/Yearning for Status

A sponsorship process does not protect migrants from illegalization and precarity. Not only are they deportable if their applications are denied, but also they now have to depend on a third party, their spouse or common law partner, to obtain status (Goldring, Berinstein, and Bernhard 2009). They also have to contend with discursive forms of illegalization that depict them as potentially participating in fraudulent marriages. Johann submitted his sponsorship application when his refugee claim was refused. Although he was in a happy relationship with his partner, he could not help but think about this fact:

> It's not living, having to wait [for the process to be finalized]. As you know, I'm going to submit my sponsorship application. I hadn't done it

> before because in human relationships there is the possibility that people create, perhaps not my partner or her family, because they know me, they've known me for two years and a bit, but society in general can . . . always say, "He surely only got together with this woman to get his papers." . . . So I said, no, I'm going to wait out my own process [refugee claim]. If they say no, then my partner can voluntarily tell me, "I don't want you to go." So that she doesn't feel used like many people can be used. Because it happens both ways. Couples who just pretend or those that only say, "She's my girlfriend, I get my papers, and then I can treat her badly," or those who are sponsoring someone can also be abusive. If they fight, they can say, "I'm going to withdraw the sponsorship." And you live in a fucking uncertainty where you say, "Shit, when is this going to end?"

The temporal limbo in which Johann found himself as he waited to receive secure status was prolonged because he started a new application (the H&C) when his refugee claim was refused. In fact, by 2016, he had still not received permanent residence, which he thought was a punitive response from immigration authorities who prolonged the sticky time of precarious status indefinitely (Griffiths 2014). As a result, Johann articulated a yearning for stability and reprieve from the restrictions that migrants experience during the sponsorship process. Being in limbo marks individuals not only in terms of the ever-present threat of deportability but also because it restricts a person's ability to go to school, work in her or his profession, and participate in other activities.

Johann also related feeling that he needed to go through all the steps of the refugee determination system despite having a partner who was a Canadian citizen. Two reasons influenced his choice. The first reason was that he wanted the historical record to show that his case and the persecution that he experienced really had occurred. This was a yearning for justice. The second reason related to his partner. Johann did not want her to think that he was using her. As I discussed above, the notion of using someone to receive immigration status is prevalent in immigration discourse mobilized by the state (Citizenship and Immigration Canada 2008). However, his comments illustrate how, though critical of other means through which the immigration system illegalized him, in this instance

Johann aligned himself with official discourse against marriage fraud, accepting not only that it existed but also that it was reproachable.

Berenice did not experience this moral valuation. After her refugee claim was refused, she and her partner broke up, meaning that Berenice went through the appeal process alone:

> I lost my [refugee] appeal. [Some friends] told me, "Well, we love you, we don't want you to go . . . What if we offer you a sponsorship?" They were two Canadians. One girl was born here, white, and the other was nationalized. Naturalized, naturalized. So they tell me, they tell me that, and so I said, "Okay, I'll think about it." I never thought that they would be sending me the PRRA in a week and asking me to appear at the airport in fifteen days. I said, "Wow," I called my friends, and I told them, "You know what, let's do it."

Sponsorship was an appropriate strategy to avoid deportation for Berenice given that Canada recognizes same-sex unions. However, the process requires specific documentation on the relationship, an "archive of intimacy" (White 2014), and a certain degree of planning, particularly when the marriage is not "romantic." Berenice did not have much time to get married and file the application given the swift issuing of her PRRA date. When deciding which of her friends would sponsor her, they initially chose the naturalized Canadian, a Latina. The rationale was that they would have more things in common and could convince the government that the marriage was legitimate. However, at the last minute, Berenice's friends decided that the white woman would be a better choice since she had a higher-paying job and a family history in Canada.

During her sponsorship process, Berenice's spouse engaged in harassment and emotional violence:

> So she began to sexually harass me. Horrible. It was horrible . . . Because we had a close relationship since we were friends, we saw each other at parties and so on, right? She drank and then did it. So, every time she was drunk, she accosted me. So it was horrible because my friend [her partner] noticed it but didn't want to see it. So she invisibilized it, and in many instances I could swear that she blamed me, and then she acted

> badly toward me. On one occasion . . . we went to a women-only party, and we were at the bar, and she was really drunk. Then she grabbed me from behind . . . I didn't move. After all I experienced in Mexico, and all my life I have had problems with sexual harassment, what I do when someone tries to do something to me is that I become paralyzed . . . Then a friend came over and told her, "Leave her alone, don't touch her, leave her alone."

Berenice's experience of sexual harassment had several effects. The first effect was that it made Berenice question whether the sponsorship application was worth the violence that she experienced. This was especially traumatic because part of the reason that she applied for refugee status was the sexual harassment and violence that she had experienced in Mexico, demonstrating the transnational extension of insecuritization. However, knowing that a sponsorship application was her only option, she put up with the violence, another example of aguantar.

The second effect involved the uncertainty of the application and knowing that the sponsor could change her mind at any point, which she threatened to do after the party described above. The constant fear of deportability followed Berenice until her case was resolved. The fear had an additional effect: it led her to withdraw from the Latinx community in Toronto in order to avoid the abuse. Although her friends tempered the sexual harassment, going to parties and events meant the possibility of another incident, which would involve not only additional violence but also the threat of losing her application. Luckily, Berenice did not cohabitate with her spouse, and immigration officials never attempted to verify their relationship. Her application was approved, and she received permanent residence.

Lencho had a similar experience but with a very different outcome. He married a woman, recommended by family members, who was willing to sponsor him. The process of compiling "evidence" was lengthy, illustrating sticky time (Griffiths 2014). There were also issues given that the couple did not initially cohabitate and were not involved romantically, and Lencho thought that his sponsor engaged in manipulative practices, dictating where he should work and live. The result was that the sponsor reneged on her promise to sponsor him, leaving Lencho married but without an avenue for secure status.

Legal Representatives

The sponsorship application is another way to illustrate the effects that legal representatives have on immigration proceedings. For example, when Maria Pérez and her husband decided to apply, she felt inundated with the paperwork and criteria: "It was long and complicated because they have so many requirements. Well, it's not as easy as get married and then apply, right? . . . It took a long time, it took me a long time, because my husband doesn't really care. It took me a long time to start, to be proactive." She measured the sponsorship process temporally, also indicating her need to take the lead given what she thought was her husband's lack of interest. This process was made more difficult because of her initial legal representation:

> Unfortunately, I went to a lawyer who was not professional and told us that, after a year of having us go to meetings and everything, told us what the law and requirements were and the documents required of him. Because they always do an assessment of the sponsor . . . he has to be good, has to work, and all that. And one of the requirements was to not have a criminal record. And my lovely husband had one . . . So at the end she told us, "No, he doesn't qualify as a sponsor. You're going to have to do other things." She said, "If you are working at a restaurant, your boss can sponsor you." And we paid her every time we saw her . . . We lost a year because we didn't do anything, then the year she made us lose. And I was desperate because I wanted to do other things. I wanted to go to school in a formal way instead of taking a course here and a course there. So I found another lawyer, very good, a friend recommended her . . . She helped us, and everything was super quick, super professional. Not cheap, it was about $7,500.

The first legal representative misinformed Maria Pérez twice. First, the criminal record policy did not apply to her husband. Yet, because she was not an expert on immigration policy, Maria Pérez had no way of knowing that. Second, the advice that her boss could sponsor her could have led Maria Pérez down the wrong path given the difficulty in sponsoring workers who participate in "unskilled" jobs in the service economy. The erroneous advice also affected her timelines. This intersected with the fact that the year she submitted the application immigration workers went on strike, which added extra processing time. Furthermore, extended timelines can open the possibility for immigration policies to change and close off opportunities for secure status.

Reservations with Sponsorship

Like Johann, other participants were wary of applying for permanent residence through a sponsorship application, particularly if it was a business transaction like Lencho's failed one and not a romantic relationship. As discussed above, Juan Nadie related that, if he applied for permanent residence, it would be through an H&C application. His reasoning was that a spousal sponsorship would be more difficult. I asked him to explain this choice:

> Because, well, not that difficult, I don't know, well, to begin, I'm not interested in marrying, for love or something else. And second, well, it's difficult to decide to marry just like that. It would be really bad for me to marry someone like that only for . . . papers and then get divorced and live a lie during a certain amount of time. No, I wouldn't like it, to tell you the truth. There's the option of paying someone to reach an agreement. But I don't know anyone who can do that. I have friends who have, have offered me, a friend offered it. But the majority of the people I know always work with, don't even work, they're on welfare and things like that. It's difficult for both of us, right? Because they may be willing to do it, but they don't meet the requirements . . . They are not "good citizens." . . . But if someone whom I trusted would offer me, I think I would do it. For money, not for, not because I love them or they love me . . . Apparently marrying is quicker and a bit more secure, but you also need time.

Juan Nadie differentiated between a business transaction, in which both parties agree, and pretending to be in love with someone for the purpose of receiving legal status. He was wary of cheating anyone, yet as he spoke he became open to a business agreement in ways that he had not earlier in our conversation.

Other participants also had reservations related to their well-being and security: Maria Nueva was successfully sponsored by her husband after living without status for years. Despite having achieved a more secure status, she recognized what it might feel like when a sponsor takes advantage of the person sponsored or rescinds a sponsorship offer: "[They might say,] 'If you don't do what I say, I'm not going to sponsor you' or whatever. I think that that is super difficult as well [to deal with]. And it's very, very difficult to live with that fear, that paranoia, all the time." Her use of the term "paranoia" alludes to an irrational feeling. However, given Lencho's and Berenice's experiences, the possibility that a sponsor might rescind an offer or act in an abusive manner is real, as Liz articulated:

> I've tried in a million ways. I've visited a lawyer who charges a lot of money, almost 7,000 to 9,000 dollars to fix your papers. But according to her, I don't have another option but to get married . . . And I'm not going to get married. There are a lot of issues [associated with it], yes, there are a lot of issues . . . It scares me that they'll take advantage.

Taking advantage is facilitated by limited government protection and the ever-present circulation of discourses of fraud around marriage sponsorship. The fear can lead migrants to continue to endure what Griffiths (2014) refers to as "suspended time" – when a person is not moving, even slowly, toward a more secure status but stuck in limbo and deportability.

Armando, who initially lived in Montreal, then in eastern Ontario for some time before moving to Toronto, articulated the fear that can lead to inaction. He chose to move to Toronto after his refugee claim was denied, thinking that a deportation order would be easier to carry out in a small town versus a metropolitan area. Like Aquetzalli, he discussed the reasons for his yearning to stay in Canada:

> I've been here, and the truth is that I've liked it, and I'm staying. And I had to make this decision. That is, I made the decision to make plans . . . Plans to look for, get my papers, another way. I came to Toronto with that plan. I came to Toronto with the plan of getting married. Afterward, given the situation, I don't know. It didn't work out. It didn't happen because I felt there was a risk, and I became scared. I was scared, and in the end I didn't do anything. I said, "It's better to not do it." So that was it, and I'm still here.

Armando drew on the notion of risk, linking it to his deportability. He identified his apprehension about participating in a system that he had already experienced as violent, opting to continue his current version of precarity instead of risking making the wrong decision.

Other Difficulties

For some participants, finding a sponsor was not the problem; rather, it was acquiring documentation for their "archive of intimacy" (White 2014). Güero travelled to Canada to change the direction of his life, which he thought was going nowhere in Mexico City. In Canada, he entered into a relationship that eventually led to marriage and a sponsorship application:

> [The process] has been prolonged, or it has been at a standstill because of the fact that I have a son in Mexico. We're trying to include him in the application so that, when I receive my permanent residence, he does as well to make it easier for him to come visit me. But my relationship with his mother is not the best.

Often the literature on family reunification focuses on the difficulties imposed by the state, leading to transnational family arrangements (Abrego 2014). In Güero's case, a family member was responsible for the delay, prolonging his precarious status, his yearning to see his son more frequently, and the power to grant him the benefit of legal status in Canada.

Libertad, whose H&C application was denied even though her child was a Canadian citizen, planned to apply through a sponsorship, though she had not concretized that plan by the time of our second interview in 2015. One of her concerns, given that she had a negative refugee claim and an outstanding deportation order, had to do with identification. When her refugee claim was denied, her documents – including her passport – were not returned. It becomes difficult for precarious status migrants to apply for a new passport without a police report outlining that the passport was lost. Deportable migrants cannot obtain this report given the relationship between policing authorities and the CBSA in Toronto. This barrier made it difficult for Libertad to navigate the city and its institutions. One such institution was the City of Toronto and its application for a marriage licence, which requires two valid state-issued forms of identification. Libertad could only acquire a birth certificate. Although the Mexican consulate at one point had issued *matriculas consulares,* or consular identifications, popularized in the United States by their use in Mexican undocumented communities, Libertad noted that it had stopped issuing them years earlier.

Aquetzalli also explored the possibility of a sponsorship application, though she eventually decided on an H&C application. She was wary since the process had been difficult for her to navigate while, as she stated, "there are some people who arrive and a month later are already getting married or a year later." She explained that she found some "prospects" to marry, but they fell through for various reasons, such as the lack of ability to sponsor given income requirements or Aquetzalli's limited funds. As I mentioned above, a sponsorship agreement can involve a monetary exchange. For some, this can mean a certain amount of money up front and subsequent payments. In one of her "negotiations," the person expected more money up front than Aquetzalli had, making the arrangement prohibitive. Another concern is what happens if a person receives money up front and then rescinds the offer, as in the case of Lencho, whose wife reneged on the promise to sponsor him even though he had paid her a large sum. Given that this process is technically illegal, as well as the legal status of participants, they have little recourse if that happens.

Study Permits

Although an uncommon approach, one participant attempted to apply to remain in Canada, at least temporarily, as a student. Liz sought legal counsel and evaluated her options. Although she decided that she did not want to get married, in the past she had applied for a student visa. As she told me,

> I was accepted at the University of Toronto and George Brown [College], . . . but my student visa was not approved . . . During that time, I hired a lawyer that gave me bad advice . . . instead of telling me to go back to Mexico and to return or apply from there, something like that. I still had time and had status, but due to ignorance, I think, and trusting her, I applied from here, . . . and they said no. It was rejected, and around

> the same time I was left with nothing [no status]. My status ended right away. And it's been two years since then, two years without status.

Like other participants, Liz narrated how immigration representatives can unscrupulously make recommendations to their clients, to extract fees, that affect them negatively. In her case, had Liz applied for a study permit from abroad, she might have been able to enter Canada with a less precarious status, though given her economic situation the international student fees associated with that status might have been prohibitive, particularly given her economic situation in Mexico. In her comment, Liz identified a shift toward precarity: "I still had time and had status." However, given bad advice, she lost that status and prolonged her precarity.

Work Sponsorship

Other participants sought to stay in Canada because of their work experience, though this type of application is difficult when one participates in "unskilled" or unregulated employment. Zyanya worked in a warehouse in the late 2000s after she travelled to Canada to join her boyfriend. One day her employer recruited her to do some filing given a labour shortage. Because she did well, she was promoted to work in the office:

> Z: They gave me an office, right? So I was like, it was like, I felt different. I didn't feel like I was a robot but someone who contributed . . . I remember that during that time they said that there was a possibility [to sponsor me] but that we had to go to Mexico. I remember that I had been working there two and a half years. Yes, because I left in 2009. So I went to Mexico for just a weekend, to be able to have legal status [as a visitor] and do the paperwork with the company. But another company bought out that company, and they fired the woman who wanted to help us, and so they then fired everyone, and we were left without a job . . .
>
> P: So you didn't submit the paperwork?
>
> Z: We weren't able to do it.
>
> P: But the company was going to sponsor you?
>
> Z: The company would sponsor you. And they could; they met all the requirements.

Because Zyanya and her colleagues worked in "low-skilled" labour, it is unclear how the company planned to sponsor them, since work sponsorship emphasizes classed skills (schooling, training, and work experience) and the inability to find Canadians who can fill those jobs. It is possible that the company misled employees with false promises. However, it was never clear to Zyanya because she was fired, and the application was not filed.

Liz, who evaluated all her options and applied for a student visa, had also thought about work sponsorship, particularly because her work as a server had merged into the financial management of the restaurant, including preparing tax returns before her employer sent them to his accountant. As she told me, "because my [study permit] was denied, the owner of the place where I mentioned I'm managing this small restaurant also tried to sponsor me and get me my papers, to pay for everything. However, the lawyer said that they really didn't see the case in applying since they thought it would be rejected." Liz's experience demonstrates the deskilling that precarious status migrants experience because of their legal status. Liz was proud of her work experience in Mexico at an import-export company and how that experience was useful in her current employment. However, because of her status, she could not receive recognition in relation to that work and continued to be identified as a low-skilled worker. In fact, she experienced what Coutin (2003) has described as legal "nonexistence," a process whereby precarious status migrants are unable to document their presence and employment because of working under the table or using alternative names and documents. This becomes a problem when precarious status migrants want to use their labour and presence as rationales for receiving immigration status (Mattingly 1997).

***

In this chapter, I have discussed the different strategies that participants used to pursue secure immigration status given the closing of the refugee application for Mexican nationals in the early 2010s through the 2009 visa requirement and the 2013 identification of Mexico as a designated country of origin. Although not always successful, the strategizing demonstrates resourcefulness in the legal and temporal limbo of precarious status.

One way to view such strategies is through the lens of yearning: the hope to improve one's life that can also include a political commitment to equity. This forward-looking process is not straightforward, and participants often strategized and evaluated different types of applications, including sponsorship, H&C, and study and work permits, sometimes applying for more than one, demonstrating their transitioning across different legal statuses (Goldring and Landolt 2013). This process took work and involved engagement with specific institutions and organizations, including Citizenship and Immigration Canada, as well as specific actors, including legal representatives and sponsoring spouses. Such relationships were organized through power relations in which spouses and other sponsors had control over the outcome of an application, demonstrating the conditionality associated with immigration applications (Goldring and Landolt 2013). Furthermore, participants' deportability affected their decisions to make applications or persist in what Griffiths (2014) calls "suspended time." The implication is that, though options exist to apply for secure status, as in the refugee determination system, those options are restrictive, requiring archives of evidence and records of migrant information, which augment deportability. In the next section, I discuss the effects of internal borders given restrictions to secure legal status.

PART III

Internal and Interlocking Borders

Pintar la cocina de rosa mexicano La sala azul intenso, que nos de gusto llegar a casa Una recámara verde botella Y la nuestra, del color del barro.

Pintar una casa, tener un hogar Y soñar con otras cosas Con algún reencuentro Algún perdón Abrazos.

El Guernika, las máscaras Los cuadros, el gabán, los sombreros.

Tener trabajo, vacaciones Ir al dentista con regularidad Hacerse un chequeo medico.

Sentirnos seguros, Que no hubo redada. (En Canadá no existe la migra)

Caminar por las calles Preguntarle cualquier cosa a un Oficial de. policía, cualquier cosa . . . Por una calle o acusar que me pagaron Con un cheque sin fondos.

To paint the kitchen Mexican pink the living room bright blue, bringing joy to each homecoming the other bedroom bottle-green and ours, the color of earth.

To paint a house, to have a home and to dream of other things some joyous reunion some forgiveness an embrace.

The Guernica painting, masks, pictures, a jacket, hats.

To have work, vacations To see the dentist regularly Get your usual check-up.

To feel certain That there won't be a raid. (In Canada the "migra" doesn't exist)

To walk through the streets and ask a police officer anything, absolutely anything . . . or to go and tell them how you got paid with a bad check.

Quizás, todo se reduce a tener un hogar No quiero decir que la casa sea propia Solo querer el derecho de sentirme en casa.	Maybe it all comes down to having a home I won't say that I need to own it I just want a place to feel at home.
Soñar, con los momentos Que construyen esta vida Que ha de mantenernos en pie En todas partes.	To dream of the moments that build up our lives – these moments that make us stand firm always.

– "Pancho," by Jesús Maya (2013, 82), translated by Jeannine Pitas

Although borders exist at the edges of nation-states, they also extend to the everyday practices inside those territories. Maya's (2013) poem "Pancho" narrates the hopes and aspirations of living a dignified life: painting the house with lively colours, having meaningful objects, access to decent work, time off, health care, and security. Yet precarious status migrants face difficulties accessing such a life given internal borders, which emerge at the juncture of accessing social goods, decent work, security, and other interactions (Leerkes, Bachmeier, and Leach 2013; Mutsaers 2014; Francisco Villegas 2016). Maya illustrates this by debunking the myth that "la migra," immigration authorities, exist only in the United States.

Leerkes, Bachmeier, and Leach (2013, 912) define internal border controls as "all legally mandated practices that national, state, or local governments engage in or promote in their jurisdictions, but not at country borders, to exclude, either directly or through third parties, certain categories of noncitizens from the country's territory, or parts of that territory." In the chapters in this section, I discuss participants' experiences of such invasive and ever-present borders, which can become activated to interpellate precarious status migrants depending on their social and physical locations as well as their specific legal status. Thus, internal borders produce insecurity through an everydayness or *cotidianidad*.

Internal borders are assembled. They incorporate institutional representatives, employers, co-workers, acquaintances, policies, informal practices, popular understandings, and stereotypes about migrants. They also involve work and need constant reinforcement. The work is context specific and includes labour market segmentation, interlocking forms of discrimination, the ever-present reality of deportability, and the work of gatekeepers. Illustrating this assembled process, one report noted that the "undocumented population [in Canada] concerns the Canadian government, particularly with regard to the abuse of workers' rights, the interplay of undocumented migration, organized crime and fraud, as well as health and safety concerns" (MacLaren 2010, 3).

The extensive work performed by internal borders is often not executed by immigration officials and can include social service providers, school administrators, health-care providers, employers, social workers, and so on. These internal border control actors operate as gatekeepers, enforcing and/or negotiating borders for precarious status migrants. Welcoming policies such as those involved in the formation of sanctuary cities, and the specific work of intermediaries, can work to erode internal borders and illegalization somewhat.

In this section, I also discuss the circulation of affect and discourse. Institutional actors can mobilize hate or distrust and act as gatekeepers. Precarious status migrants can experience fear and anxiety in relation to deportability, which also produces risk as well as indignation (Reeves 2015, 123). Deportability is used to discipline or control individuals (Richard and Rudnyckyj 2009). For example, precarious status migrants might amend their actions to fit preconceived ideas of "passing" as citizens or looking like they "belong." They also mobilize the idea of *aguantarse*, bearing or tolerating abuse, when they come across internal borders. Teresa explained this process:

> First, I've thought about not exposing myself where they are looking for people. And second, yes, why not, to dress like people here. Even if that's not me. Yes, I can't be a blonde-haired person, I can't have blue eyes, I can't put on a *gringo* mask. But I won't stop being a Mexican, that is. You try to not speak Spanish in the streets because that is something that makes people turn their heads and quickly ask, "Are you Mexican?" And you say, "No, I'm Colombian." And then you realize that they can tell the difference [in your accent], and you say, "I don't think that worked" [laughs]. It does make you do that. It makes you want to hide, not only your language, but to cover up your physical characteristics. So you don't

> show that you are Mexican. Because whether you have status or not, you'll be questioned. You will be questioned.

Passing is limited given precarious status migrants' social locations, which, as Teresa mentioned, mean not being able to wear a "*gringo* mask." *Gringo* refers to white North Americans, mainly from the United States, though I have also heard the term used to refer to Canadians. Her words illustrate the limited strategies that precarious status migrants have to counteract the racial profiling that Leonel described and the emotional effects of that strategizing and failure. Finally, migrants also "dream of the moments that build our lives," to return to "Pancho" (Maya 2013), demonstrating a yearning for a more equitable future.

The Toronto context is important in understanding the internal bordering practices that participants experienced. Toronto is a large metropolitan and immigrant-receiving city. It has been at the forefront of immigration policing and immigrant justice in Canada. It is also located in the province of choice for most newcomers to Canada, Ontario. According to Human Resources and Social Development Canada (2006), about half of Latinx immigrants in Canada live in Ontario, with a large proportion in the Greater Toronto Area.

In Toronto, various institutions and actors, including the municipal government, schools, the police, health-care providers, and activist organizations, have a history of working with precarious status migrants to improve their situations, to various degrees of success (Berinstein et al. 2006; City of Toronto 2007; Mukherjee 2008; Sidhu 2008). In the 2000s, the City of Toronto passed a Don't Ask Don't Tell policy, whereby city representatives were instructed not to ask their clients about their immigration status (City of Toronto 2007). It became a sanctuary city in 2013 (Keung 2013a). However, several limitations exist related to eligibility criteria for social services and jurisdiction. For instance, having a specific status is often a requirement for receiving services (notably those programs under the jurisdiction of Immigration, Refugees and Citizenship Canada, a federal agency). Furthermore, even if institutional actors do not ask about a person's immigration status, other types of identification such as a driver's licence or health card are often required.

Similarly, in 2007, the Toronto District School Board unanimously passed the Students without Legal Immigration Status Policy (Toronto District School Board 2007). This policy clarified the types of migrant students who could enrol at schools without paying fees and the types of documents or information required given the board's interpretation of the Ontario Education Act (Sidhu 2008; Francisco Villegas 2013). Most precarious status students were eligible, with the exception of "visitors" or those with a student visa. For instance, Eduardo and Rebeca had to wait eight months until their tourist visa expired and a new school year began to enrol their children in school.

Toronto has also been the site of an active campaign to stop police officers from asking migrants about their immigration status as well as from disseminating that information to the Canada Border Services Agency, responsible for immigration enforcement (No One Is Illegal Toronto 2015). In 2008, the Toronto Police Services Board passed the Victims and Witnesses without Legal Status Policy (Mukherjee 2008). This policy stipulates that police officers should not ask victims and witnesses of a crime about their immigration status unless they have a bona fide reason to do so (Mukherjee 2008). However, the policy is largely ineffective because it continues to illegalize precarious status migrants regardless of whether or not they are victims or witnesses of a crime.

Discussing his deportability, Leonel related one example of interacting with police authorities in Toronto:

> I don't feel free to be in a park, for example. I also don't feel comfortable being in a street corner waiting for someone. I don't like to do those things . . . I don't like to, I . . . I feel that, well, it's happened to me. One time I was in a street corner, and the police came looking for someone. My friend was sitting next to me, and [the police officer] asked [my friend] about that person. And immediately [the police officer] began to ask him personal things. Why was he smiling, right? What was he doing here? Why was he here? Where was he working? Are you studying? My friend answered very politely. But I know that he asked him [those questions] because he looked Hispanic. The police officer was white. He would not have asked a Canadian, a white person, those questions.

Leonel described how internal borders permeate public spaces of rest such as parks and street corners. He also identified the interlocking of racialization with status that makes looking Latinx or Mexican an opening for interrogating someone about his or her presence and belonging. Internal borders thus affect the "life chances" of precarious status migrants, promoting their deportability and affecting their visibility (Leerkes, Bachmeier, and Leach 2013).

Responses to the barriers faced by precarious status migrants have emerged from grassroots organizations, including No One Is Illegal Toronto, the Don't Ask Don't Tell Coalition, and the Solidarity City Network. They have also come from educational advocacy groups, including the Education Rights Taskforce (Koehl 2007) and LAEN Latinx, Afro-Latin-America, Abya Yala Education Network, women's organizations (including the Rights of Non-Status Women's Network), and workplace rights organizations such as the Workers' Action Centre (2014).

In Chapter 6, I discuss participants' relationships with health-care access. I examine the role of information and networks in opening avenues to care. Participants who had limited access to information about affordable clinics often paid costs out of pocket or delayed care. Others accessed affordable services, but this often took some researching and building of trust with community clinics. However, despite having access, they often faced other types of barriers, including negative treatment from institutional workers.

In Chapter 7, I extend the discussion in the previous chapter and think through participants' experiences of precarious work and how their immigration status affected their positioning within the employment landscape. I outline a process whereby participants "learned" to find better jobs as they integrated into their new contexts and built networks. However, learning to navigate the employment landscape does not completely protect precarious status migrants from negative experiences: dirty, difficult, and dangerous jobs, wage theft, and being asked about status upon applying for work. Although participants understood their exploitation, they used the language of aguantarse, bearing and tolerating work conditions for fear of losing income and having to look for other work.

Finally, in Chapter 8, I examine another internal border, the one that prevents or excludes precarious status migrants from fully participating in creative projects. I bring together discussions of precarious work, status, and the particular experiences of the "artistic precariat" (Bain and McLean 2013). Participating in creative projects (paid and unpaid) brought meaning to participants' lives. This occurred not only because the participants were involved in things to which they felt connected, but also because the social interactions led to a deepening of their social networks and attenuated the effects of precarious working conditions. However, participants were also exposed to internal borders vis-à-vis their creative projects, sometimes also enforcing bordering practices themselves.

6

Access to Health Care and Temporal Negotiations of Internal Borders

I interviewed Emiliana Zapata in 2009. She came to my apartment and shared her experiences, while sipping tea, of coming to and living in Toronto. When I asked her about her health, she shared that she had started to develop chronic pain given the repetitive nature of her work, which at that time involved cleaning grocery stores. Given her interest in Indigenous languages and ways of being, Emiliana Zapata depended on her family's traditional cures when she was sick. However, she discussed the emotional and economic effects of getting sick while not having status:

> I'm alone here. I have to do everything by myself [rascarme con mis propias uñas or literally scratch herself with her own fingernails]. If I'm sick, there's no one like a brother or someone to make you atolito [a corn porridge] or at least some tea. No, so I have to get up, sick and cold, and wait to have the energy to make myself something and go back to bed, right? And to try to cure myself. And if I don't feel well, too bad, I have to go to work. Because not going to work a day or two as a result of being sick is the same as going to the doctor. It's a luxury, and you later say, "Shit!" One or two days do make a difference [in terms or earnings]. So you say no, unless it's that time I fell and I almost broke my arm [laughs], that time I did take the day off, but only one day, right? And one time when I had stomach pain, and I asked for a day, one day, off. Only one. I have never been off work more than two days.

Emiliana Zapata linked her health to social factors, including precarious work and limited money, themselves influenced by immigration, health care, and employment policy. She contrasted an affective process of having someone take care of her, for example through the provision of soothing food such as *atole*, to the isolation that she experienced when she felt sick in Canada.

Like Emiliana Zapata, participants often referred to accessing care through the concept of aguantarse: enduring, bearing, or putting up with something. They had to aguantar the pain involved in delaying care, which could be mitigated by receiving information about affordable care or through accessing secure immigration status. They also had to put up with the cost of receiving care and paying for medication. Aguantar therefore participates in the temporal and economic negotiations associated with receiving health care.

Given this context, access to health-care services for precarious status migrants in Toronto involves a process of finding information that is also assembled with eligibility requirements, cost, social interactions, and quality of treatment. According to Steele Gray et al. (2010b, 2), precarious status migrants in the city experience barriers to care because of fear, cost, knowledge/information gaps, language, culture, and discrimination, as well as "funding cuts to programs, [l]imitations and gaps in the current services available, [and] [s]tructural barriers." These multiple factors – service providers' ways of knowing vis-à-vis health-care provision; ideas and feelings about precarious status migrants' deservingness of care; barriers imposed by bureaucratic institutions, actors, and processing times; and access to money – produce and reinforce internal borders, making it difficult for some to access health care or producing a time gap for others to receive more accessible care. As opposed to the geographic edges of nation-states, internal borders extend into the everydayness of the lives of migrants once they are in a country and emerge through encounters with different actors, networks, and institutions.

Access to Care in Toronto

Hacker et al. (2015) identify three categories that influence access to and quality of care for precarious status migrants: the policy arena, the health-care system, and the individual level. This multiscalar approach lends itself to understanding access to health care in Toronto as an assembled process influenced by multiple and fluid elements.

In terms of the policy arena, access for precarious status migrants in Toronto varies depending on immigration status as well as other institutional and social barriers (Elgersma 2008; Larchanché 2012; Oxman-Martinez et al. 2005; Steele Gray et al. 2010b). Visitors, tourists, and those "out of status" or who have submitted an H&C application have little access to health-care services unless they pay out of pocket or can plug into certain (limited) networks that provide free care (Community Health Centres of Greater Toronto 2008; Elgersma 2008; Morris 2009; National Post 2007; Paloma Villegas 2013a). Refugee claimants have access to the Interim Federal Health Benefits Plan (IFHP) even if their claims are refused until the Canada Border Services Agency issues a removal order (Elgersma 2008). However, between 2012 and 2016, the federal government cut the IFHP for some refugee claimants (Canadian Council for Refugees 2013). Even if they are eligible for care, they are sometimes turned away because of lack of knowledge among gatekeepers or the fact that processing IFHP coverage is more onerous than provincial universal health care (Chase et al. 2017). Migrants' information is also recorded on every visit. Although privacy regulations prevent health-care providers from sharing information with immigration authorities, given that information is stored for several years before it is "disposed," it sits in a potential surveillant assemblage of illegalization (Villegas 2015a), waiting to be activated should regulations change.

Therefore, the health-care system imposes what Willen (2012, 807) has termed "multi-tiered . . . health care systems . . . that provide high quality care to citizens and authorized residents while shunting individuals with precarious status into patchy or unreliable networks of NGO- or charity-based care." An internal border emerges from the relationship between the health-care sector and the policy arena through bureaucratic operations, eligibility criteria, and other policies that restrict provision, as well as the specific practices of health-care providers. For instance, those who engage in service provision in the city note that limited funding sources, overwork, and overstretched networks affect their ability to provide comprehensive care to patients (Munro et al. 2013; Paloma Villegas 2013b). Some health-care workers act like "civilian soldiers" (Aberman 2018;

Orr 2004) or hold discriminatory assumptions about precarious status migrants, which can affect access to as well as quality of care (Ruiz-Casares et al. 2013; Rousseau et al. 2017; Steele Gray et al. 2010b).

Despite these barriers, the internal border is not straightforward. In Toronto, networks of health-care providers and institutions that seek to open up health care for uninsured patients exist, though often they face limited funding and eligibility restrictions (Community Health Centres of Greater Toronto 2008, 2011; Steele Gray et al. 2010c; Paloma Villegas 2013a). Health-care providers have come together under the banner of "OHIP for All" to expand eligibility requirements to the Ontario Health Insurance Plan (OHIP for All 2016). Community Health Centres receive pots of money that they can use to treat uninsured clients, including precarious status migrants (Atungo et al. 2010; Stanley 2014; Steele Gray et al. 2010a; Paloma Villegas 2013a). Finally, there are health clinics around Toronto that provide free or low-fee services for uninsured clients (Caulford and Vali 2006).

Individual participants in my research experienced a number of barriers in receiving care, which interlocked to produce material vulnerabilities. Lack of information about affordable health clinics structured participants' experiences. It often meant delaying treatment given the prohibitive costs (Stanley 2014). However, once participants overcame the barrier, information meant a pathway to health-care services. Yet some participants continued to face barriers in the health-care system, stemming from their treatment by health-care workers.

Lack of Information

Access to quality health-care options opens the path to well-being. Yet participants found that accessing information was not straightforward. Access to information is linked to institutional support, community engagement, and building social capital in a new context, as well as learning how to navigate precarious status. Reflecting this situation, the Toronto Board of Health (2013, 13) explains that "uninsured residents may not know how to access services that are available to them and staff are not consistently aware of the services that are available for this population." Other research suggests that newcomers, regardless of status, experience barriers to information when accessing social services (Toronto Public

Health and Access Alliance Multicultural Health and Community Services 2011).

Alternatively, Lai and Hynie (2010) find that community engagement is an important factor for immigrant well-being. Community engagement involves social and civic participation, which can be difficult for precarious status migrants given their need to work as much as possible to make ends meet as well as the difficulties that some experience with language acquisition, housing, and other processes of integration. Furthermore, most participants did not know many people when they arrived. Some, such as Maria Nueva and Eduardo, knew no one. It takes time to expand one's social circle, making it difficult to learn about what is available in the city. Finally, given deportability, some precarious status migrants might not be willing to share information about themselves or to ask about pertinent services for fear that they might be outed to immigration authorities.

Sergio, an Indigenous man with an expired tourist visa, had not visited a doctor during his stay in Canada. Although he had family members in Toronto, he did not know about affordable services. He explained his understanding of pathways to health care:

> There's a difference between getting sick and having an accident, right? Uh huh, so, for example, if my head hurts, I know something about medicine, pills, right? I go to the pharmacy and buy something that I know has cured me in Mexico . . . That's how I solve [the problem]. If I have a cough, . . . I buy some tea to drink, something that I can take. That helps. That's what I always do. Now an accident, that means having to go to the doctor, right? Or to a hospital . . . The problem is that it is going to be very expensive, that's what, that's all I know. But there are, there are doctors, or I mean the hospital. They can treat you, [but] since you don't have their cards, I don't know the type of things they ask for, but they do cost a lot, that's what people say.

Given a lack of information about emergency care and the availability of health-care clinics that might do more regular check-ups, Sergio had to assess his own health-care needs. He thought that he could visit a pharmacy and purchase over-the-counter medication to alleviate pain, a popular pathway given the lack of interaction with medical practitioners (Coffman,

Shobe, and O'Connell 2008). However, having an accident involved added planning (a temporal process) and action. Since Sergio was lucky not to have been in an accident, he did not have a full picture of what going to the hospital entailed, only that it would mean paying a lot of money. His limited access was compounded by the fact that he did not speak English, diminishing his ability to navigate the health-care system if he did need it in the future, though his relatives might have been able to help in that regard. He also assumed that he would need documentation, or one of "their cards," to be seen. Not having access to documents can elicit a feeling of being unable to access *any* public services. As a Toronto public health nurse working at a clinic for uninsured patients commented in an interview for the *National Post* (2007), "when you don't have a health card, you start to think you're not entitled to other things so when they get care, it's like it validates their existence." This feeling of being not entitled to care can lead precarious status migrants to endure (aguantar) being sick longer.

Scaling up, another reason for a lack of information is the (in)visibility of accessible clinics. Although information is readily available online, some participants did not know about them. This might be because of a mismatch between clinic and precarious status migrant networks. Or sometimes health-care workers want to avoid large-scale visibility in case their work in opening up access is attacked by policy makers, who can cut their funding (Paloma Villegas 2013a). Therefore, though increased visibility might be ideal to increase the number of people who know about services, it can have unintended effects that can lead to nationalist or anti-immigrant backlash or a depletion of resources.

Cost

For precarious status migrants without eligibility for public health insurance programs, the cost of health care is another important axis of exclusion and often interlocks with a lack of information. Several factors explain the prohibitive cost of care. First, paying for health care can mean not paying for other expenses such as housing, food, and sending remittances. Furthermore, precarious status migrants are often funnelled into precarious work if they do not have work eligibility (and, even if they do, they face deskilling or hiring discrimination) (Fudge 2012; Goldring and Landolt 2011; Teelucksingh and Galabuzi 2005). Second, the cost of health care is exclusionary because it involves the organization of fees for uninsured migrants in Ontario. Given a lack of regulation, out-of-pocket fees are significantly higher than standard fees for specific procedures or courses of treatment (Paloma Villegas 2013a; Wilson-Mitchell 2013). For instance, one hospital in Ontario in 2015 noted that an emergency room visit would cost $618 for uninsured residents of Canada (those who had been away from Canada and needed their health insurance reinstated) versus $927 for non-resident uninsured patients (Queensway Carleton Hospital 2015). And such fees are not standardized. As Wilson-Mitchell (2013, 38) argues, in relation to pregnant women, "physician and hospital fees are commonly unregulated for the uninsured; fees vary amongst hospitals, anesthesiologists, and obstetricians." Finally, cost overlaps with the lack of information discussed above, such that those whose networks are not developed often face paying out of pocket. Armando, who moved to Toronto from eastern Ontario after his refugee claim was refused, thought that his only option was to pay to receive services. He described the process of visiting a walk-in clinic: "I don't know. I have gone, for instance, to the [walk-in clinics] that have been recommended to me, right? Basically, they ask you [for] information. You simply go in, and if you have your things [documents] they see you; if you don't have them, they still see you. Pay and there's no problem."

Cost and lack of information intersected for Maria Nueva, who did not know about affordable services when she first arrived in Canada. I asked her if she had visited a doctor and paid for it out of pocket: "Yes, I don't remember why. But yes. My ear, my stomach . . . Yes, [I always paid]. No, I never found one [an affordable clinic for uninsured patients] . . . If I would have found out earlier, I would have saved a lot of money." Later Maria Nueva recounted paying $120 for x-rays of her hand because of pain caused while working at a factory.

Similarly, when I asked Leonel if he knew of clinics that treat uninsured patients, he told me,

> No. No. I think I've only been to a clinic that is free for women. But that's the only one. But for something that hurts me, if I have a cough or a cold or something like that, no. I always go to the walk-in clinic, and they always charge me . . . Imagine, a doctor's visit costs sixty dollars. And all

> the medicine is so expensive. There's medicine that I couldn't even dream to buy. It costs like $300, $350 for a treatment of [depression] . . . or more, it's so expensive. And it's covered by health insurance here. So of course it affects me. I only go to the doctor if I really need to . . . I try to take care of myself, take care at work.

As a refugee claimant, Leonel had health coverage that gave him access to depression medication, leading him to state that "it's *chido* [cool] to go . . . it's cool to go to the doctor each time you need it, right?" However, his claim was denied, and he received a removal order and lost his eligibility, depicting how transitions in legal status influence eligibility to receive social goods (Goldring and Landolt 2013) and produce ruptured time in relation to health and status (Griffiths 2014). Leonel then transitioned to paying for care out of pocket. In general, participants recounted that going to a walk-in clinic involved paying fifty to sixty dollars for the visit plus the cost of any exams and medications.

Liz, who worked in the restaurant industry and had been unable to find a pathway to apply for secure status, was also unaware of affordable clinics. When she felt ill, she asked her friends to take her to a hospital:

> L: One time my kidneys hurt really bad, and they, my friends, took me to the emergency room. And only to cross the door of the emergency room and receive treatment they were charging me $400. And I'm talking about four years ago.
>
> P: And when you got to the hospital, did they ask you for any type of information?
>
> L: Yes, they asked me for my social insurance number. That's why it was so expensive too. And they did help calm the pain and gave me antibiotics, which helped me wait [*aguantar*] to go to the walk-in clinic later . . . And I've been going to a walk-in clinic when I feel bad because I have no other social security option.

The cost of going to the emergency room is a lot higher than that of a walk-in clinic. Although legally hospitals have to provide emergency care, patients might have to provide money upfront. They then receive a large bill afterward, though some hospitals work out payment plans with patients

(Toronto Board of Health 2013). One exception is when patients are members of Community Health Centres or other clinics that have formalized agreements with hospitals. In that case, the former often pay for some or all of the cost (Steele Gray et al. 2010c).

Liz's account demonstrates a lack of knowledge of the type of information needed to procure health care. Hospital frontline workers automatically ask for health-care eligibility documents such as provincial health insurance cards (OHIP in Ontario). However, Liz mentioned a social insurance number, which relates to work eligibility. Her "error" makes sense given that she understood health as a part of the social security net provided to members of a society, a net to which she did not have access and would not know its intricacies. Given that her network did not extend to those who knew about accessible clinics, she had to bear (aguantar) the pain as well as the cost related to her treatment.

The cost of receiving health care experienced by participants made Güero hesitant to access services. He thought that he might not be able to afford paying for care, particularly because he had dependants in Mexico who relied on remittances:

> The moment I tried to go to the doctor, a specialist, with my own means, the consult cost $350. I said no thanks. I told my mom, "Let it be God's decision." ... I remember that one time a friend fainted, and she was very sick, and from the same fear (they started to call the ambulance) she had to get up to ask them to not call the ambulance because [when this happens] people think it's related to the police or immigration ... And it costs, it's money.

If someone earned minimum wage (fourteen dollars in 2018), then it would take twenty-five hours to make $350 (with no deductions, i.e. cash employment). Güero worked in the construction and landscaping industry, in which he was paid more than minimum wage. Yet even if he earned double minimum wage it would still take him over twelve hours to make enough money to pay for the specialist consultation, which he thought he could not afford, particularly given the rising costs of housing and food in Toronto.

Similarly, when Güero's friend fainted, the idea of paying for an ambulance, which in Toronto is billed at $240, made her get up (aguantar the pain) and beg her friends not to make the call (Toronto Paramedic Services

2014). She feared that the ambulance or hospital would relay her immigration status to the police or immigration authorities. And this fear circulated among those present, like Güero, who understood her reasons. Although the City of Toronto has a sanctuary policy, it applies only to municipal services, which in terms of health care involve only public health services. Other health-care services are organized provincially, and though the province provides Community Health Centres with funding for "uninsured" patients (homeless or mentally ill residents with lost cards or those without status), that funding is not always enough or evenly allocated (Community Health Centres of Greater Toronto 2008).

Aquetzalli also had to decide whether she should invest in her health and opted to do so despite the high cost:

> I first went to the gynecologist because I felt little needle pricks in my ovaries, and a friend started to put ideas in my head that maybe I had something wrong with me, and I wouldn't be able to have children, and blah blah blah. And so I went to the, I spent a lot of money on that, gynecologist . . . I spent like $1,000. For exams. Exams that I agreed to stupidly, well, not stupidly, it was good, right? But it was very expensive.

Aquetzalli illustrated health-care access as a gendered process. As the Toronto Board of Health (2013, 7) states, "gynaecological care is an ongoing need, particularly for undocumented women." In addition, Lebron et al. (2018) explain that, beyond reproduction, health-care access affects women differently given the types of work in which they engage more frequently, the potential for gender-based violence, and their disproportionate responsibility for family tasks.

Finally, an under-researched area involves access to mental health services. Research has demonstrated that immigration status is a social determinant of mental health (Asadbikli et al. 2016; Magalhaes, Carrasco, and Gastaldo 2010; Saad 2013; Simich, Wu, and Nerad 2007). However, accessing mental health services was even more difficult for participants given the stigma and limited availability of affordable services for all Toronto residents. Some participants were able to negotiate access. For instance, Leonel and Mexicano en Acción accessed depression medication during their refugee claims when they were enrolled in the

Interim Federal Health Benefits Plan. Aquetzalli and Leonel paid for counselling out of pocket.

Delaying Treatment

A strategy that participants used to avoid cost was to delay treatment. Research demonstrates that uninsured patients who delay care often experience worse health-care outcomes and cost the system because of emergency services and complications (Caulford and Vali 2006; Magalhaes, Carrasco, and Gastaldo 2010; Stanley 2014). For instance, according to a report by the Toronto Board of Health (2013, 9), "uninsured individuals may . . . experience injuries or develop serious health conditions (e.g., heart attack, stroke) requiring urgent care. People without health insurance are more likely to delay or forgo treatment until the circumstances are severe. Consequently, Toronto studies found that uninsured residents were twice as likely as insured residents to require resuscitation at acute care facilities." Like Emiliana Zapata, who based her treatment on teas and other plant-based medicines, participants often used home or over-the-counter treatments to avoid encounters with the health-care system and unregulated fees.

In addition to cost, participants worried about asking for time off work, fearing the loss of income as well as the possibility of losing their jobs. The latter has been documented for other immigrants who work in precarious conditions regardless of status (Hanley et al. 2014; Liladrie 2010). This produced a wait-it-out or suspended temporality that included living with pain for days, months, or long term (Griffiths 2014).

Maria Pérez's main mode of employment was working in restaurants. Her first job was as a dishwasher. However, the detergent used gave her a horrible rash: "It was very hard. For me, it was very hard because, since I was a girl, I had an allergy to detergent, so I couldn't use soap or any of that heavy-duty detergent." Maria Pérez did not seek medical services, opting to aguantarse. Her strategy was to wear gloves, which she thought hindered her ability to work in such a fast-paced, efficiency-driven environment. This meant that she sought care only when she felt very ill, putting up with pain on other occasions:

> MP: If I got sick, I put up with it [me aguantaba] because, because, in all the time I have been in Canada, seven years, I only went to the doctor

> once. And that time, it was really, I was dying. I had diarrhea for a week, and it wasn't going away. So I went to beg a doctor to give me medicine . . .
>
> P: So, when you went that time to the clinic, did you have to pay? Did you go to a walk-in clinic?
>
> MP: Yeah, I had to pay. It was sixty dollars plus the medicine, which at that time was a lot of money. Well, now as well.
>
> P: And did you have to miss work?
>
> MP: Yeah, I didn't work for two days. Which my boss did not like at all.

For Maria Pérez, going to the doctor meant having to miss work and face possible repercussions – "my boss did not like [it] at all." In contrast to Armando, she described going to the doctor as a process of "begging" as opposed to being a customer in the marketplace. This demonstrates how accessing care can be humiliating for precarious status migrants given their immigration status and the fact that a doctor could refuse care or treat patients with disdain.

For Berenice, treatment was not a matter of eligibility. She recounted that, as a refugee claimant (she subsequently applied for permanent residence through a sponsorship application), she had been eligible to receive care through the IFHP. However, when she renewed her health-care benefits, the processing time took longer than anticipated, forcing her coverage to lapse:

> Everywhere I went to seek out health-care services I took my brown paper.
>
> "What's that?" [they would ask].
>
> And I said, "My health permit," and I showed it to them . . .
>
> It turns out that refugee claimants, every year, you have to renew your health paper. I had sent in my renewal about three months before. But I didn't get it. I didn't get it, I didn't get it. At that time, I had an injury, and I didn't have the paper renewed. I couldn't go to a clinic, to any clinic, because they were going to charge me. So I couldn't go to the doctor. And then, because I couldn't go to the doctor, I couldn't give my workplace a letter saying that I had an injury . . . This led my workplace

> to question me about my status. They didn't tell me directly because it was illegal for the company to ask, because it was a company that respects workers' rights a lot and is anti-oppressive and anti-homophobic, anti, anti, anti, anti, anti, anti, anti [laughs]. Right? So, they didn't tell me, but they insinuated. So they told me "Why can't you go to the doctor?"
>
> And I said, "Because my health paper is expired."
>
> "And why should it have expired?" they accused me. They didn't understand the process that refugees face here. So, for them, it was suspicious that I didn't have papers and couldn't go to the doctor. And that led them to interrogate me.

Refugee claimants receive the "brown paper" to which Berenice referred, in Spanish *la hoja marron,* when they apply for protection. It includes a personal identification number that allows health-care providers to check eligibility for the Interim Federal Health Benefits Plan through a computer system (a surveillant assemblage). However, as has been documented, some health-care providers are not knowledgeable about services available for refugee claimants or do not want to go to the trouble, opting instead to turn them away (McKeary and Newbold 2010). Because of the backlog in renewing her health eligibility, and the associated cost of paying out of pocket, Berenice could not visit the doctor. She was not aware that clinics existed that could serve her regardless of her coverage.

Berenice also identified how her health status affected her working conditions. She had to explain the refugee determination process, and the movement in and out of health-care coverage produced through the backlog, to co-workers and managers. Her colleagues' lack of experience with being uninsured led to her illegalization by associating her temporary lack of access with being undocumented and extending that lack of eligibility to her work status.

Pathways to Information

Some participants did have information about accessible clinics. Such participants, in theory, were more likely to go to a doctor when they felt ill and could receive regular check-ups and preventative care, though work schedules also influenced those practices. For example, Güero explained why initially he did not seek services, which included his own sense of health as well as the cost associated with care:

> I think it's your age. At that age, you don't really have health problems. I came here when I was twenty-seven years old, so I looked really young, I played sports a lot, played American football, so physically I didn't have any problems. At that age, nothing hurts. Now that I'm thirty-six, it's not that I'm always in pain, but you start to think that you should take care of yourself . . . But before I was scared to even think about it and have to pay for all of that here.

In Toronto, Güero worked long hours and engaged in creative activities that prevented regular exercise. He also identified an affective aspect of delaying treatment: the fear that he could be sick. However, this changed when he discussed health-care services with a friend:

> I was here almost nine years [without health care]. You think, how are you going to have access to a doctor? But many times it's not knowing. Last year a friend . . . hurt his finger and said, "Well, I have to go to the doctor."
>
> So I said, "That's going to cost a lot of money."
>
> And he said, "No, there's a community centre."
>
> I said, "What do you mean?"
>
> "Oh, they have a program or a specialized area for people who do not have a health card."
>
> And I said, "What! How's that?"
>
> And he said, "Yeah," he says, "You go, and the only thing you have to show is that you live in the area, how long you've been here, and you have to take your passport, I'm not sure what they're going to check, and they're going to give you free medical services."
>
> I said, "Really?"
>
> "Yes!"
>
> So I went to this place and asked, "They told me that I can access medical services without a health card."

> They said, "Yes, yes, you can. Fill out this form, fill it out, and bring your passport. You do have to bring your passport."
>
> I don't know why they ask for a passport . . . That was when I was able to see a doctor.

When Güero asked himself "how are *you* going to have access to a doctor?" he referred to the fact that his legal status made access to health care seem to be insurmountable He later reflected on that aspect, stating that "many times it's not knowing." Yet accessing care is not always straightforward and often depends on where a person lives and the documents that he or she has. Güero was required to show proof of his address, a catchment requirement that prevented non-neighbourhood residents from accessing care at that specific clinic. Clinics did not exist throughout the city, sometimes making access contingent on one's housing situation. Güero also referred to showing a passport, which those without documents, or those who had their documents taken away during a refugee claim, are not able to provide.

Eduardo and Rebeca had a similar experience. He arrived in Toronto first and lived in the city for a few years before she and their children joined him. He explained that her arrival initiated the family's access to a thicker bundle of entitlements despite their legal status:

> Well, supposedly, people have access to health-care services, but when my wife arrived I didn't know anything about that. I, when you are here alone, the only thing you focus on is working, sending money, and that's it. When she came, I don't know how, . . . she went to some community centres, I don't know if someone took her . . . They told her that there were health-care services that we could access. She signed me and the children up. The children are covered completely; they have dental services, everything. She even found a dentist for me and for her. Not everything, but, yes, there is access . . . We have to pay for our medicine.

While living alone, Eduardo focused on working and sending remittances to his family. When Rebeca arrived, the family was reoriented toward their local context. She began to broaden their networks and find out information about services. Their case demonstrates the fact that seeking health care and other services is often a gendered process in families, whereby women have a disproportionate responsibility (Chavira-Prado 1992). This was particularly the case because when Rebeca arrived she had difficulty procuring employment and therefore had more time to seek out information.

Some specialized clinics also provide affordable access. For example, Aquetzalli mentioned that she knew of clinics that provided accessible sexual and reproductive care but found out about them only after having spent $1,000 on gynecological tests:

> A: I later found out about free clinics. And that's where I get my pap smear done and everything for free. And they treat you very well there. And everything is free. Well, if you want pills, to be careful, birth control, obviously they, they sell them, but they sell them cheaper because in the pharmacy they cost twenty dollars, and with them they cost five dollars. And everything is free . . . I lost a baby, and they did the delivery there.
>
> P: And who told you about such clinics?
>
> A: Who told me, let me see, I want to remember. I don't remember, but it was someone . . . who went in for a pap smear, and . . . I mentioned that I had paid a lot of money, and they told me "Oh, those clinics are free," . . . and they took me there. It was a woman who was *like me*, . . . and she told me, "Go, go, go." And she gave me a paper where they give you several addresses to see which one is near you and everything. You get there, and they ask you if you have official ID and if not so, so they don't know that you don't have status, but by default they do. But they're not so aggressive to tell you "Do you have your health card?" They ask you "What ID do you have?" And through that they know. You understand? . . . And they don't ask other questions. They don't. But they know that, well, you don't have status. They know.

Aquetzalli recounted that the person who shared the information was "like her," code for having precarious status. Extending the link between access and status, she also discussed the documentary practices employed at some clinics, which might not ask directly about status or eligibility but in reality still ask and potentially archive that information. Having had precarious status for eight years in Canada, I also encountered women's clinics. In my experience, such clinics did ask about status, which could make some migrants hesitant, but as Aquetzalli mentioned they were not aggressive in their questioning. Some clinics also had age cut-offs (e.g., only saw youth) but provided referrals to alternative care centres.

Given the potential for questions about status, several participants, including Juan Nadie, mentioned that they preferred not to access free clinics:

> JN: I have heard about, that there are [free clinics] in community centres. I have never had a reason to go. But I have heard that one, at, at one community centre that's here, that's called [says name] and another on [street name], I think there as well. But, no, I have never had the need to go. I don't think I would, I don't know. It causes certain, like paranoia, to try to go to those places. I would probably choose to go to a walk-in clinic first.
>
> P: Why?
>
> JN: I don't know, I don't know. It's like, I always have this fear that they might ask me something, or they might ask for ID or something. They have told me that they don't ask for anything. That it's free, I think. And that they don't ask for ID. They ask you your name, but I think you can say a fake name, no? But, yeah, perhaps if I need it I might go to a walk-in clinic first. Only because of lack of trust.

Juan Nadie renovated hotels for several years in Canada, regularly using his passport to fly to job sites across Canada. Yet he thought that not having a health card might identify him as not having status, signalling his fear of deportability, though he might also have to share that information at a walk-in clinic.

Treatment from Institutional Representatives/Health-Care Providers

The cost of health care can intersect with other forms of social exclusion, including health-care workers' negative attitudes and discretionary practices toward immigrants. In their study of health-care workers in Montreal,

Ruiz-Casares et al. (2013, 297) found "evidence that many support staff, often the first point of access, hold restrictive attitudes toward entitlement for undocumented migrants. Instances of refusal of care by health care staff with negative consequences for patients have been denounced." Similarly, in a review of access to health care for differently situated migrants, including precarious status migrants, Elgersma (2008, 8) found that "front-line workers, including doctors and emergency room personnel, do not always recognize the IFH [Interim Federal Health] benefit" that gave refugee claimants access to health-care services. This has led Aberman (2018) to refer to such workers as "civilian soldiers" who feel compelled to close off access and behave like deputized immigration authorities. Teresa referred to the actors and institutions that enforced an internal border after her application for permanent residence was refused: "The people or civil servants to whom I could go for my protection have become my enemies. No, there is no protection. None. When you want to be invisible, you can't, because it feels like they are looking for you."

A more specific example came from Johann, who sprained his wrist during a cycling accident while his refugee claim was under review. During a scheduled appointment at a hospital where he had to demonstrate health-care eligibility, which he had under the IFH program, the doctor ignored his presence for several hours. In fact, the doctor saw clients who arrived hours after Johann before telling him to return the next day. When Johann complained, the doctor begrudgingly saw him. Afterward, Johann received a bill: "For the five-minute [visit], I received a bill for about $300, for the bandage that he wrapped [on my wrist], which was not even new. He used the same one [I had on before]."

Libertad applied for refugee status and became pregnant while she was awaiting the resolution of her case. Her experience demonstrates the intersection among access to health care, visibility, and the role of institutional actors in augmenting precarious status migrants' deportability. Her unborn child's father was physically, financially, and emotionally abusive, and during one instance of abuse the police intervened and took her to the hospital:

> So I went to the hospital, and at the hospital they said, "Only because you are pregnant and because the police are bringing you, but you still have to pay." Ah, and everywhere they asked for your papers. So I learned

> that immigration status is a pass that allows you to survive and receive care. I don't know, I think that if, because they told me, "If it wasn't because a police officer brought you, we do not have to accept you."

Hospital workers assigned Libertad deservingness not because of her condition or status but because the police had brought her in, which might have affected her ability to remain in the country if she did not have an ongoing refugee claim. Put differently, someone with no status or with an open deportation order might have been detained by the police. Toronto police officers communicate and collaborate with the Canada Border Services Agency, in charge of enforcing removals and deportations (No One Is Illegal Toronto 2015). This puts precarious status migrants at risk, not only when the police are present but also when other actors, such as health-care workers, can put them in contact with the police or immigration officials, as in the case of criminal investigations.

Maria Nueva also visited a hospital. Although she did not interact with the police, she faced health-care workers who seemingly did not take her condition seriously. She said that they treated her "differently," she thought, perhaps because she had language difficulties:

> I took birth-control pills for many years, and one day I woke up with half my body asleep. So I got scared. I went to the doctor, to a walk-in clinic, . . . and they told me, "Miss, you are having a stroke. Go to the emergency room."
>
> . . . We took a taxi and went, and they asked me [at the emergency room], "What do you feel?"
>
> "I feel this part of my body is asleep, my leg is asleep."
>
> "Okay, wait a bit."
>
> We waited two hours. I went in, and they told me, "Well, you have to sign here because we are going to charge you because you don't have a health card." . . .
>
> And I said, "Yes, yes, anything, but please help me! I think it would be best if you see me now!" And I signed.
>
> "Your address please."
>
> Obviously, there's fear to give out your address, your name, everything. I went in, and they told me "Okay, turn to this side, turn to that

> side, lift one foot, your hand, no, no, you look okay. Maybe you slept wrong" [laughed].
>
> I said, "Wait, I take birth control, could it be causing this?"
>
> "No, I don't think so."
>
> "Is that it?"
>
> "Yes."
>
> "So you're not going to give me a candy or a star on my forehead or something?"
>
> "No, that's it, there's nothing wrong with you."
>
> "Geez!"
>
> "Go through there where you have to pay." Obviously, I didn't have the money. They told me "It doesn't matter, we can do a payment plan."
>
> "How much is it?"
>
> "It's $450."
>
> "Okay, send it to me please, send me the bill." Well, it was $450 for the scare. Obviously, I stopped taking birth-control pills just in case they were wrong.

Like Johann, Maria Nueva waited a long time to receive care, illustrating the temporal quality of aguantar, and had to face a lack of care from medical practitioners. Her account demonstrates the potential for institutions such as the health-care system that promote themselves as colour-blind to invest fewer resources on precarious status migrants (Dovidio and Fiske 2012).

Despite these examples, some participants found doctors whom they thought treated them with respect and dignity. For instance, Zyanya mentioned that

> with [my] doctor I've always felt very good . . . I know another friend who also goes to see him, and I always recommend him because he's a person who understands your situation without asking you. He only realizes because I think there's things that cannot be hidden, but he respects and finds the way to support you or to give you medicine for free.

Although she had to pay for services, Zyanya was reluctant to change doctors because she had developed a history with her doctor and knew him to be a decent person, demonstrating that good treatment can offset some of the negative effects of the cost of health care.

***

Access to health care for precarious status migrants is organized through an assembled internal border that contributes to migrant illegalization. One element of the assemblage involves the ways of knowing that health-care providers and other stakeholders internalize through their education and service provision. Another involves negative assumptions about precarious status migrants, including the idea that they "abuse" Canada's universal health-care system (Paloma Villegas 2013a), as well as racist and gendered framings of migrants. In addition to health-care providers, other actors participate in the production and negotiation of this internal border, including employers, co-workers, and friends. Institutions and the technologies that they employ, including databases of information that might never be erased, are another element. Finally, precarious status migrants experience contexts of fear, apprehension to use services, and the knowledge that not going to the doctor can entail long-term effects.

Given this internal border, health-care access for participants involved having appropriate information, eligibility, and/or ability to pay for services. Participants who did not know about affordable services often engaged in strategies to delay care, worried about missing work and paying prohibitive fees. This illustrates the temporal aspect of the internal border, which I have examined through the concept of aguantarse, bearing or putting up with the pain as well as the cost of receiving care. Those who could access affordable services did so given their expanding networks. Yet, despite knowing about affordable clinics, some participants were hesitant to visit them given their deportability and the fear that health-care workers would act like "civilian soldiers" and disclose their immigration status to officials (Aberman 2018). These factors interlock with other internal borders, including the labour market, which I turn to next.

7

At the Intersection of Precarious Work and Status

Toronto is a global city with a stratified labour market that assigns value according to socially constructed notions of skill and status (Goldring, Berinstein, and Bernhard 2009; Magalhaes, Carrasco, and Gastaldo 2010). Juan Nadie explained this status stratification during our interview in 2014 when he was working in the construction industry:

> I don't have papers, right? And if I go to a job, you can tell by the type of job, you know? If you work at a bank, it's obvious that you have status, right? That you have papers. But if you work in construction, or I don't know cleaning or things like that, it's more likely that you don't have status, right? Because if you did you wouldn't be a cleaner, right? You'd be working at the Tim Hortons or whatever is the lowest-paid job. Minimum wage. But I'd prefer to work at the Tim Hortons than cleaning, for example, [though] there's nothing wrong with cleaning.

The value accorded to workers determines how bodies are read, exploited, and discarded in the marketplace. Emiliana Zapata described this process:

> You have to work in the chambas [slang word for jobs/work] that no one wants to do, right? So they give you more hours, so they give you more work, so you break your back, because you have to break it, right? And fuck up your back. And fuck up your knees and fuck up your arms, right? So that they can collect on everything, right? Because like everything we're talking about your value.

Emiliana Zapata illustrated the physical (embodied) manifestation of a race to the bottom for extracting value from workers. This process involves precarious work, a move away from a standard employment relationship (SRE) that provides permanent employment with benefits and protections. Precarious work has grown globally as well as in the Greater Toronto Area in recent years (Lewchuk et al. 2015). Although differently situated people – including those racialized or disabled, women, and immigrants – historically have had differential access to the SRE, in recent years the increased flexibilization of markets has downloaded more risk onto workers. This has led to non-standard precarious relationships that create limited control over one's schedule, limited access to benefits, labour unions, and labour protections, as well as (often) low wages (Cranford, Vosko, and Zukewich 2003; Fudge 2012; Kalleberg 2009; Vosko 2003). Furthermore, as Strauss and Fudge (2013, 5) note, we are also seeing a move toward increased intermediation or the process that brings together "institutions, mechanisms or actors that intervene between job seekers and employers." Intermediaries include employment agencies and recruiters.

Given this embodied and precarious context, participants experienced an internal border assembled via limited protections, difficulty finding work, physically and mentally demanding conditions, and the threat of deportability. These conditions were produced through the intersection of labour and immigration policies: *ways of knowing* that influenced employers' and other stakeholders' behaviours, particularly given the lack of documentation such as work permits. Judith Butler (2009, ii) elaborates on this multilayered precarity:

> "Precarity" designates that politically induced condition in which certain populations suffer from failing social and economic networks of support and become differentially exposed to injury, violence, and death. Such populations are at heightened risk of disease, poverty, starvation, displacement, and . . . exposure to violence without protection. Precarity also characterizes that politically induced condition of maximized vulnerability and exposure for populations exposed to arbitrary state violence and to other forms of aggression that are not enacted by states and against which states do not offer adequate protection.

Furthermore, because working under the table makes precarious status migrants less legible to technologies of surveillance, they are also less likely to have access to formal mechanisms for making complaints. This makes workers put up with bad conditions or aguantarse, an example of *ways of feeling* that circulate in and through workplaces. Finally, participants' experiences of precarious work were organized temporally: they measured the time that it took for them to look for and find work, their work experiences, and how they put up with conditions across time.

Protections and Information

Although anyone employed in Canada is entitled to labour protections, immigration status affects a person's ability to access such protections. According to the Workers' Action Centre (2014), a worker-based support organization in Toronto,

> even if a person is undocumented, without status or a valid work permit[,] they are still covered under Ontario's Employment Standards Act (ESA). They can seek unpaid wages and other entitlements through a claim at the Ministry of Labour. However, the greatest risk in fighting for unpaid wages or filing a complaint as an undocumented worker is the threat of retaliation by an employer. In many cases this means a threat to call immigration to get the worker deported rather than follow the law and pay all statutory entitlements.

Similarly, the Law Commission of Ontario (2012, 25) states that "non-status or undocumented workers do not have immigration status to be in Canada. These workers are highly vulnerable to exploitation by employers since they are often unable or unwilling to enforce employment standards or health and safety protections." Finally, a City of Toronto (2012, 6) report outlines eligibility for entitlements: "They have no access to Employment Insurance, Ontario Works, or the Ontario Disability Support Program."

Another barrier emerges in relation to outreach and support in making complaints. First, information about support organizations might not reach all workers, making access complicated. Second, organizations might not be able to provide extensive support. For instance, when one of Leonel's friends was not paid by his employer, Leonel reached out to a support organization that recommended he organize with other workers to carry out a public campaign against the employer. Working together to enact social change can be an empowering practice. However, Leonel did not have experience with labour organizing, nor did he or his friends feel comfortable participating in a public campaign, leading them to do nothing.

Transnational Employers/Intermediaries

The clock to find work can begin ticking before migrants leave their countries of origin. Some migrants organize employment through their networks. Others might seek additional help through intermediaries or look for information on the internet or social media. However, information online can be limited given the legality of employing migrants without employment eligibility. The government of Canada has also identified scams in which recruiters promise migration and employment facilitation but do not comply (Immigration, Refugees and Citizenship Canada 2018).

Participants had varying experiences with such "services." For instance, Zyanya's boyfriend and Eduardo encountered migration facilitators in Mexico. Eduardo did not pay for their services but found the information provided a helpful start for planning his migration to Canada. Zyanya's boyfriend elected to pay for their services, as Zyanya described during our interview: "He arrived before [me]. So he, yes, he contacted the agency, an agency that supposedly found work for you." Zyanya referred to the facilitators/intermediaries as an agency, alluding to their transnational organizational structure and role as intermediaries. The agency did not promise a job but did provide one month's accommodation in Toronto and information about employment agencies in the city. However, Zyanya explained that the apartment where her boyfriend stayed was crowded, housing seven people. The service was therefore expensive and did not provide a competitive advantage since he was sent to the same employment agencies that other participants frequented upon arrival without paying intermediary fees.

Another example came from Armando, whom I interviewed in his apartment in 2015. He was the only participant who did not immediately live in Toronto, having arrived in Montreal and worked in eastern Ontario first. Because of limited networks and information, he had a hard time finding work. He therefore decided to accept employment from co-nationals who provided a service that also brought Mexicans to Canada. This "service" did guarantee employment and housing upon arrival:

> The guy, he had a business, he went to Mexico and brought people from there. He told them "Look, you're going to earn dollars, and everything is going to be great, the government gives you money . . . I'm going to pay you eight dollars an hour." And you think of the exchange [rate], and you say, "Wow! Eighty pesos an hour!" . . . And they would bring a lot of people . . . Those guys had a complete business, . . . [and] they provided housing, gave you food, gave you everything. And, if you didn't have money, they lent it to you. They would say, "No problem, I'll sponsor you [economically]. You'll work and pay me back and make your own money." . . . But they did underpay, . . . [and] they had [workers] apply for refugee status . . . They told them "No, no, no, you ask for refugee status, do it, the government will give you money, and then what you make from your job will be extra."

Armando's account demonstrates the intricate and networked transnational business scheme organized by employers, who were able – by providing housing, food, and loans – to control their workers as well as, from Armando's point of view, facilitate their migration. This is an important point. The employers underpaid, overworked, and might have led migrants astray in relation to refugee applications, meaning that they participated in the transnational production of migrant illegalization. However, they also provided a service that allowed migrants to procure work, at least initially, which Armando appreciated. Therefore, though transnational migration facilitators engage in questionable practices, they also fill an important role for migrants who seek opportunities abroad.

Armando described the encounter during which his employers offered him a job. At that point, he had been living in Montreal for a month and had only worked three days:

> One day my friends who owned that company arrived to see how we [Armando and his roommates] were. They brought beer, and we sat down to talk, and they said, "You know we have work. Are you working?"

> "No, no, nothing." . . .
>
> "Well, we have chamba [work]. Do you want chamba? We have chamba."
>
> And we were like "Of course we'll sign up."
>
> "Okay, but the chamba is not here."
>
> And we said, "Ohhh, where is it?"
>
> "Well, we have the same company in [two other cities, one in Quebec and one in eastern Ontario]. So you could go to one of those places." . . .
>
> I said, "I don't have work, I'm pulling my hair out. I don't have money anymore, I don't have money to pay for food, I don't have anything anymore." . . . I said, "I can't stay here anymore, if they give me stable work, I'm going to take it."

Armando selected the eastern Ontario site because, in a less metropolitan area, he thought that he could at least communicate better in English, despite his dream of learning French. However, he thought that being in a smaller town allowed his employers to control him more extensively.

Internal Borders: The Effects of Precarious Work/Precarious Status

Internal borders related to work sometimes manifest themselves in relation to time: waiting for and tolerating (*aguantando*) not finding work. At other times, having to stay at a job to make ends meet entails physical and emotional violence. Most participants faced difficult working conditions at some point in Canada, taking what can be referred to as 3D jobs (dirty, difficult/dangerous, and degrading/demeaning). In addition to the physical and emotional impacts of 3D jobs, participants believed that their bodies, lives, and time were constantly controlled and surveilled. And, after such arduous work, precarious status migrants can experience wage theft and other vulnerabilities when they demand their wages and rights, a facet of the downloading of risk to precarious status workers. This demonstrates the links between racial capitalism (Robinson 1983) and migrant illegalization as they subordinate workers in global cities. Put differently, precarious status migrant workers enter Canada's labour market with the disadvantage of their legal status, which predisposes them to exploitation. Being Mexican exacerbates these conditions given the representation of the labouring Mexican body in North America (Urquijo-Ruiz 2012).

The Temporality of Looking for Work

Unless they applied for refugee protection, participants did not have the opportunity to apply for work eligibility. This meant that most worked under the table and therefore relied on their contacts or employment agencies and other intermediaries to procure work for them. Those who did not know anyone in Toronto experienced an additional difficulty looking for work because they had to discern the places and situations that lead to employment while also navigating a new city on their own. For example, when I interviewed Maria Nueva in 2015, she recounted how she and her boyfriend would leave their hostel in downtown Toronto early in the morning in search of work, walking around the city all day, only to return at the end of the day without success and with the stress of seeing their money slowly running out:

> My feet hurt . . . I remember that everything hurt, tired, walking obviously, it was to see if we found some, some work, some place to stay. Something. Something. It was like the third day. I remember that we were walking. I now know that it's by [a downtown street] that we were walking. Imagine. And there was a restaurant . . .
>
> So my boyfriend told me "Okay, it's time. Prepare yourself. Breathe deeply and go in, ask for the owner or the manager, and tell them you want a job."
>
> I said, "Okay, how do you say owner or manager?"
>
> He said, "Just ask for 'owner' okay?" . . .
>
> So I went in very confident that I, that I could do something [laughs] . . . So I get to the bar and say, "Hello, can I speak to the manager [and repeats in English] can I speak to the manager?"
>
> Oh, by the way, before coming to Canada, they told me, "If you are going to Canada, you have to know how to ask for work. You have to say [says in English], 'I am looking for a job, do you need some help?'" So, for a month, before going to sleep, I repeated "I am looking for a job, do you need some help?" . . . Like that, in the mirror. "I am looking for a job, do you need some help?" When I woke up, "I am looking for a job,

> do you need some help?" On the plane, "I am looking for a job, do you need some help?"
>
> So now was my moment, right? [laughs] So I get there, they tell me "Okay," and a man walks toward me, a man this tall [points high above her with her arm], with blue eyes and grey hair, enormous, and he stares at me. And I stood there looking up [looks up], he intimidated me so, so, so, so much that I started to cry [laughs]. And I began to run and left. Imagine! . . . The man probably thought, he probably said, "Oh, it's my long-lost daughter." [laughs] . . .
>
> And my boyfriend asked me "What happened? Did you find work?"
>
> And I said, "No, I can't, I can't, it's too difficult."

Maria Nueva's account demonstrates the effort involved in procuring work in a new city, including the role of language proficiency as illustrated by her mantra "I am looking for a job, do you need some help?" Luck changed for the couple when they encountered a man who spoke Spanish. Being able to communicate with someone in their own language brought some relief. In addition, the man offered Maria Nueva's boyfriend a job and the couple a room to rent. Although hesitant because they did not know his intentions, the couple accepted the offers, alleviating their fear of spending all their money on temporary housing.

Like Maria Nueva, Eduardo arrived in Toronto without knowing anyone except his co-traveller. They also walked around the city looking for housing and work: "We walked long distances because we couldn't afford public transportation." Unable to procure a job that way, Eduardo met someone who provided vital information: "I found a person at a store that recommended a newspaper where I could find information about where to rent and find work. We waited for the newspaper to be printed." The newspaper, *El Compra y Venta,* was a Spanish-language classifieds publication. Thus, meeting well-intentioned people who provided good tips or actual accommodations and jobs changed the course of Eduardo's and Maria Nueva's stays in Canada.

Initial experiences of finding work ranged from a few days to months. For example, Zyanya found work days after landing in Canada through the same employment agency as her boyfriend: "It was an employment agency where they sent you to factories . . . I arrived straight to work.

It was like ugh! I arrived . . . [on] a Thursday or Friday, and by Monday I was working. At the agency." Güero and Aquetzalli also sought work right away to pay for their living expenses. Güero worked in construction, hoping to transition quickly out of his cramped quarters:

> The first days . . . I felt like [I was in] an immigrant movie [laughs] because my cousin lived with roommates. They rented the house, a room for each of them. They had their way of life, but then my cousin decided to bring his family [including Güero] . . . So [then] we were six people living in the living room, almost like sardines . . . A week later they found me work. My cousin's friends, his roommates.

Aquetzalli arranged to rent a room from a friend's friend in Toronto while she got her bearings. Her second day in Canada he showed her how to use public transportation and directed her toward an employment agency:

> He said, "If you want to look for work, you take such and such bus and go to such and such [employment] agency. There you can apply, and they'll tell you if there's work." . . .
>
> So I went there and applied, and right away I started to work at a bread factory. Very difficult [laughs]. But since they said it was long term, I said, "Well, I'm here now, and I need money now, right?"

Aquetzalli's and Güero's urgency was manifest through a need to pay for their living situations and to save enough money to move quickly. Aquetzalli later discovered that her roommate charged her an exorbitant rent (much more than the going rate for a room). Therefore, though some co-nationals and Latinx migrants facilitated participants' adaptation to and integration into the labour market, others made things more difficult.

Alternatively, friends of Maria Pérez preceded her in Canada and went through the process of looking for work, which they shared with her. However, it still took her six weeks to find a job:

> I think that I was depressed the first three [weeks]. Completely, because to start we didn't have a lot to eat. Everything was so expensive. It was a shock to see that a lime cost, three limes cost two dollars. Or milk cost

> six dollars. I started to look for work reading the *El Compra y Venta* [Spanish-language classified newspaper] . . . That's where I found a job, my first job, washing dishes.

Facing her financial reality affected her mental health and diet. Maria Pérez elected not to work in construction given the physical labour involved. Furthermore, though her friends worked washing dishes, she was reluctant to do so because of an allergy to detergent. Yet her desperation forced her to put up (aguantar) with the physical effects and accept the job.

Table 7.1 outlines participants' work trajectories, which varied across time, including during shifts, seasons, and years. Although participants

TABLE 7.1
Work trajectories

Leonel	Cleaning → factory work → construction, landscaping → construction, sales, art/creative work
Rebeca	Cleaning, sales (catalogue products), bathroom attendant (club)
Eduardo	Construction
Sergio	Construction
Manolo	Factory work, construction → art/creative work
Berenice	Factory work → construction → cleaning, art/creative work
Libertad	Cleaning, construction, communications, volunteer work → cleaning, volunteer work
Emiliana Zapata	Factory work, cleaning
Mexicano en Acción	Food industry, volunteer, administrative services → settlement services
Teresa	Service sector
Johann	Construction → telemarketing, sales
Arne Saknussemm	Interpretation, immigration consultant
Lencho	Construction → cleaning, art/creative work
Maria Nueva	Server → factory work → art/creative work
Juan Nadie	Construction, art/creative work
Liz	Cook, hostess → server, restaurant bookkeeper
Aquetzalli	Factory work → construction and cleaning (alternating depending on the availability of work) → house cleaner (self-employed), art/creative work
Armando	Construction → cleaning → construction
Güero	Construction (framing) → meatpacking → landscaping, art/creative work
Zyanya	Factory work → cleaning, art/creative work
Maria Pérez	Dishwasher, house cleaner → server

initially found work through agencies, by the time I interviewed them in 2009–10 and 2014–15 no one was using them to find employment, having developed more robust networks in which friends and acquaintances circulated job information. This did not protect them from the difficulties and dangers of precarious work and the possibility of being cheated by employers. However, their increased experience did produce better opportunities and higher wages. Female participants regularly worked as janitors or in factories and restaurants, whereas male participants worked more often in construction and landscaping. Most participants also worked in several industries across time, trying a specific type of work and deciding whether the benefits outweighed the costs. For instance, some participants worked in construction and then decided that it was too physically demanding, opting instead to work in cleaning (businesses, buildings, houses, etc.) despite the lower wages. Other participants decided to shift to construction work because of the better wages, particularly if they had accrued experience in it. Finally, some patchworked different types of work at the same time to make ends meet, selling products on the side or supplementing their artistic work with subsistence jobs.

Asking for Papers

Canadian employers are required to ask potential employees for their work eligibility documents, namely a social insurance number (SIN). However, given a large informal sector, participants knew that they could find work under the table if they could not furnish a work permit and SIN. This entailed knowing which employers would agree to hire them, a tricky endeavour given that, if they were not recommended from trusted sources, participants had to disclose their immigration status in a potentially dangerous context.

Before Armando moved to eastern Ontario and eventually Toronto, he had difficulty providing work eligibility documentation to potential employers in Montreal:

> They had just imposed the visa, and they were all crazy [about asking for status] . . . [For] those who were already here, jobs started to shut down. My friend . . . worked for a cleaning company, and at her work they stopped hiring. I would call, and sometimes jobs would come up,

> agencies and everything, and the first thing they said was "Do you have a work permit?"
>
> "No."
>
> "Refugee paper? Brown paper?"
>
> "No."
>
> "Okay, well, we'll write your name down, but we'll see." . . .
>
> They even made me get out of a van one time [at a day labour pickup site]. I got on, and . . . I was already seated, and they [asked] me "Do you have a work permit?"
>
> "No." . . .
>
> And they said, "No, you know what, we can't right now, because the migra [immigration authorities] [are] really annoying, and if they fine us it's a lot of money, we can't risk it."

Employers can lean toward more conservative hiring practices after raids or punitive immigration policies (Bloch, Kumarappan, and Mckay 2015). Armando and other participants described such a shift in immigration policing, whereby employers, even those that hired day labourers in the past, were afraid to hire those without work eligibility. Armando linked this policing to the 2009 visa policy.

Eduardo also faced questions about his immigration status. One example occurred when he arrived in Canada. He and his co-traveller walked for hours to reach an employment agency. When they finally got there, they were asked

> "Do you have papers?"
>
> We said, "Papers?"
>
> [In English] "Yes, do you have your [social insurance] number?"
>
> And I said, "No."
>
> "We don't accept applications without a social [insurance number]."
>
> "Okay, thanks." We weren't there two minutes and had to walk back.

Juan Nadie experienced a similar interaction. He was turned away from an employment agency that his father had used. However, Juan Nadie later returned and was offered work, demonstrating the flexibility of internal borders given changes in personnel, labour demands, or political context.

Even when employers did not ask about immigration status, they likely knew who had status given the questions about cash wages and type of work and the lack of documentation.

Co-workers also asked "uncomfortable questions" about status. Juan Nadie discussed one encounter:

> A woman began to work with us . . . No one knew her, right? And we worked during the week, and during our break she started to talk – "I used to work at another company with Mexicans" and whatnot – and how she'd had a difficult time. And she, she like, she asked us if we had status: "Do you guys have papers?"
>
> And we were like, "Well, yeah." Everyone always says that, right? Or we say, "Yeah, I'm waiting" [on the outcome of an application]. You know.
>
> "Well, I have my papers," she said.
>
> And we were like, nobody asked her, it came out of nowhere, but I think she wanted to show that she supposedly had papers, although you know that she shouldn't be asking those questions. It's not relevant. But she wanted it known that she had papers because she mentioned that in her previous work they tried to take advantage of her and pay her less and things like that because they thought she didn't have status.

Juan Nadie's co-worker asked about status as a strategy to assert herself given the gendered aspects of construction work and incidence of harassment (Antecol and Cobb-Clark 2001; Brunner and Dever 2014; Lafontaine and Tredeau 1986; Paloma Villegas 2019b). However, to assert herself, she made her co-workers uncomfortable without convincing them that she had secure status.

Control over One's Time

Participants also experienced difficulties controlling their schedules, a key aspect of precarious work (Goldring and Landolt 2011). For instance, participants who worked in construction, including Eduardo, Sergio, and Juan Nadie, were continuously "on call." Their work depended on the availability of job sites, the weather, the number of workers needed, and whether their employers were happy with them. This created anxiety among workers who never knew when they would work next (Paloma Villegas 2014).

During the workday, participants also did not have control over their time. Maria Nueva, Zyanya, and Aquetzalli, who worked in factories early on, commented on the control of their movements, breaks, and ability to socialize with co-workers. For instance, Aquetzalli stated,

> I got really depressed . . . because they didn't let me listen to music, they forced me to take my earrings off. You couldn't eat, you couldn't talk to your co-workers, and we wore caps, it was really cold, and we stood for ten hours. They only gave us a fifteen-minute break and then an hour for lunch and then another fifteen-minute break. But in the factories they count the time. You can't go over five minutes or take forty. Unless the machines failed. Those were happy times. But regularly it was, oh, horrible. So I started to be depressed because I said, "This is worse than being in jail." At first, you put up with it [te aguantas] because . . . you don't know if there's other possibilities, right? And so I put up with it [me aguanté], and I said, "Oh, well, here I'm earning, I know that I'll make so much money during a pay period, right?" That's why I didn't quit. But it's horrible to work in factories.

Journalist Sara Mojtehedzadeh went undercover at a bread factory and described the work in very similar ways:

> The pace on the production line is crushing. Men feed dough into machines running alongside us, which spit out partially-formed pastries. Half of the women on the line pinch the ends together to form circles. The rest of us scoop up as many clumps of dough as we can between our fingers, packing them as quickly as possible into plastic trays. We need to ensure they are placed the right way, or they deform in the oven and are wasted. Work that is too slow elicits shouting. Work that is too sloppy elicits more shouting. Our lead hand fires out a salvo of shrill commands to push the tempo. (Mojtehedzadeh and Kennedy 2017)

Because of this disciplining, a number of participants commented that they felt like robots. Yet they chose to aguantar their factory jobs, many of them for years, because they were afraid of the time that it would take to get a new job, whether they would be able to keep that job, and whether the conditions would be worse.

Embodied Precarity

In addition to controlling their time, participants' working conditions controlled their bodies. This was another facet that they had to aguantar. As Aquetzalli mentioned, participants often worked in food factories that had extreme temperatures, including those that focused on baked goods. This meant tolerating the cold temperatures involved in cooling and freezing the goods. Manolo, who faced a deportation order when I interviewed him in 2010, after his refugee claim was denied, explained this experience:

> I'm now at a factory that pays cash because of my legal situation and [the fact] that I don't have a work permit. They took away my papers. I don't even have a passport. Nothing . . . I can't get another job, so I'm in this factory and have to bear the cold. I have to wear a bunch of latex gloves and keep working.

Although tolerating the cold did not lead to specific injuries, it had detrimental health effects. Participants were cognizant of the link between bad conditions and well-being. However, their inability to connect ill health directly to the cold or repetitive tasks made it difficult for them to argue for better conditions, particularly because they were reluctant to lose their jobs.

When repetitive work leads to specific injuries, it is difficult to take time off work to visit a doctor. Before working at the warehouse that promised to sponsor her, Zyanya worked in another job at which she had to carry heavy boxes. She woke up one day and could not turn her body. Nevertheless, she went to work, where she lost feeling in her legs. Her co-workers told her that her condition was common, and therefore systemic, given the heavy lifting and the fact that workers received little training. This normalization shocked Zyanya, who began to look for a different job despite the precarity that doing so entailed.

Maria Nueva discussed this slow deterioration of bodies that occurs through precarious work: "Generally, you can see, in I think 90 percent of women that I know, . . . we have problems with our hands. Almost all of us . . . And obviously you can't go to the doctor because it's super expensive." Her observation also alluded to the gendered division of labour of precarious work, in which women are often hired to do detailed work with their hands under the "nimble fingers" trope. Maria Nueva asked her employer for time off work to visit the doctor. During the visit, she was told that a specialist consultation would cost $400 and surgery $5,000. She opted to ask her boss to change her work tasks instead:

> I said to my boss, "You know what? No, make me do something else because my hand hurts." . . .
>
> "No, that's your job"
>
> . . . I told him "Look, you need me more than I need you . . . It's good for you to take care of me. I'm a good worker, and you're exploiting me. I'm able to do a lot of work, but I'm not going to do it, you know why? Because you take advantage [of me], . . . and you do that because they demand a lot from you upstairs, and you take it out on me. I can't. I can't do it. What are you going to do? Fire me? Fire me already. But don't torture me like this."
>
> And he said, "Don't talk to me like that," and he was acting crazy. So the next day I went to work, [and] he fired me.

Although precarious status migrants are often assumed not to know their rights, Maria Nueva's account demonstrates why they might hesitate in bringing up health-related issues to employers, who might retaliate given a hostile work environment and difficult conditions. Her public firing worked to police other workers, sending a message about what would happen to them if they asked for better conditions.

Wage Theft

Given such conditions, participants were careful with their money, having to pay for their rent, food, and transportation and often sending remittances to Mexico. One common practice that affected their ability to make ends meet was wage theft. It includes "employer practices that result in employees taking home less than they are legally entitled to . . . [These practices include] paying below the legal minimum[;] not paying for time worked by having workers work 'off the clock' before checking in, after clocking out, or by requiring work during break time; not paying for overtime work[;] . . . or just not paying at all" (Finkin 2015, 851). A *Toronto Star* article noted in 2016 that wage theft is rampant in Ontario given that "just $19 million of the $47.5 million stolen from out-of-pocket workers since 2009 has ever been recovered" (Mojtehedzadeh 2016a). A problem with enforcement exists for those with secure status who can launch a complaint. When we add precarious immigration status, recuperating lost wages becomes even more difficult. Participants described the different versions of wage theft – below minimum wage pay, unpaid hours, wage deductions, and fees for services – demonstrating wage theft as part of an assemblage of precarious and exploitative work that incorporates employers, intermediaries, friends, family members, employment policies, and enforcement, as well as the circulation of emotions.

Both Leonel and Armando experienced wage theft while cleaning movie theatres when they first arrived in Canada. Leonel was paid per day, amounting to three dollars an hour. When he complained to his sister, who referred him for the job, she warned him that he should not make the family look bad. Without his family's support, he was left to fend for himself as he looked for alternative work. Armando cleaned movie theatres at night in a small eastern Ontario town and slept little during the day. He lived with his employer, the father of the two migration facilitators who had offered the job and who expected Armando to drive their father around and do errands after work. He recounted the first month at the job, which he spent in Quebec and eastern Ontario to decide which site he preferred:

A: I didn't get any money that month. All month, yes, they gave me food every day, very good, chicken, potatoes, cookies, they fed me well.

P: But had that been the deal?

A: There was no deal. Yes, we agreed that they would pay me eight dollars an hour, but, I don't know, we were supposedly on trial. People help you, and you say, "Wow, these are really nice people, great heart." . . . The first two weeks [in eastern Ontario] we worked every day . . . There was no rest. Every day, seven days a week. The

> movie theatre doesn't close . . . Later we took turns so we each had a night to rest . . .
>
> [After two weeks,] they said, . . . "Let's settle up."
>
> And we said, "Okay." . . . Our pay was the last straw. After those two weeks, they gave me eighty dollars.

Armando was charged for everything that he thought his employers were generously providing during the "trial" period, including food, transportation, and car maintenance. The calculations did not account for his low wages (eight dollars per hour), the fact that he did not have control over his accommodations, food, and time off work.

Participants discussed other arithmetic that employers used to deduct fees or "lose" hours, including rounding down wages, shaving off hours, and making multiple deductions. For instance, Manolo stated that

> they took money away for time that I had already worked. That is, they told me, I would work ten hours, and they only paid me seven. Details that didn't make sense, like, if they had to pay me $780, not counting the hours that were stolen, . . . he told me "I'm only going to pay you $700, I'll pay you the eighty dollars later." Things like that, that you say, "I'm really here to work for peanuts [*pepitas*]," and you go work somewhere else and the same thing and someone else and the same thing.

Güero described other deductions that his employers used to reduce his paycheque:

> It's a business. It's a mafia, their agencies. Actually, one of those agencies said "worker rentals." Yes, on the truck that they used to pick you up and take you to work to those businesses, they work for big businesses . . . They took you there and brought you back. And charged you ten dollars a day . . . When you first get here, you don't know anything, and everything seems so far, and you're afraid to travel, so you pay for everything. So then they tell you, "We're going to pay you $11.50 when the company pays, $14, $15," for example. They have a way for them, the company pays them a lot. So many workers, so many hours . . . They supposedly write you a cheque that they cash for you, but they charge you 3 percent.

> And you say, "How?" So, when you go to get paid, you realize they give you an envelope with cash. They supposedly cashed your cheque right there and charged you the 3 percent of what you earned to cash it . . . So it's not a lot, its twenty dollars, but twenty dollars from all the workers plus what they stole from you, so that's how it works . . . There was always one or two hours missing . . . They said, "No, I did send your hours, look, but that's all they paid me." And you would say, "Well, I'm not going to get in a fight for two hours," but it's two hours from everyone. It's a big business these men have, without doing anything.

Participants used employer services, such as cheque-cashing and ride-sharing, because they had no access to a bank account, had limited knowledge of public transportation, or worked in areas outside the city where transportation was slow or non-existent. Manolo and Güero described brazen forms of stealing by employers, perhaps informed and encouraged by the low success rate of complaints and the knowledge of employees' immigration status. As Güero explained, these thefts had an additive effect as they occurred multiple times among multiple workers.

Several participants commented about the conundrum in which they had outstanding wages but thought that if they quit they would never recuperate their money. Maria Nueva explained this process: "I've known that many people don't get paid, a lot of money, a lot of money. They have them tied up. You can't leave the job because they haven't paid you. You can't quit because then they're not going to pay you, and you can't complain. They intimidate you by saying 'I'm going to call immigration.'" Similarly, Manolo explained his rationale for not quitting jobs in which his wages were stolen:

> Why? Because they tell you "The cheque's coming, don't worry." But you're in the position of, if I quit right now, they're not going to pay me. I better wait. So you wait. And they don't pay you for that month. They say, "No, no, no, now you're getting paid." So at the end they say, "Guess what? The houses turned out bad, and they didn't pay me. They stopped payment. I'm going to go to court, and when I win I'll pay you." What a coincidence.

Given this trend, participants whose employers were behind on payments had to calculate whether they were likely to pay them. For instance, Leonel had an employer with financial difficulties, meaning that he was always behind on his payments, and his cheques regularly bounced, but he always paid Leonel. Yet being patient with employers, as he was, is still a way that risk is downloaded onto precariously situated workers who have time-sensitive financial responsibilities.

It also took time and resources to track down missing wages. Although Eduardo did not remember losing wages outright, he did remember tracking down an employer:

> One time I worked with an Argentinian, painting, and I had to follow him around like three weeks for him to pay me, but he paid me at the end ... [Following people around] is to a certain extent normal because as time passes one finds out so many things, and you know people who, I mean it's rare that I didn't experience it. Almost all the people I know who work here and are immigrants, all of them, at one time or another, have not been paid, whether it is $100 or $1,000 to $1,500, there's people whom I know that have worked almost a month, two months, and haven't been paid.

Eduardo referred to tracking down employers as a normal occurrence. Thus, similar to the general insecuritization that participants experienced in Mexico, their precarity also became normalized in Canada.

And, as in Manolo's account above, employers often made up excuses. Maria Nueva described another instance:

> They robbed me several times, saying "I'll give you the cheque later" or "Come get it" or "But you didn't tell me, come earlier, come later, come wearing pink, you didn't put your hair up": that is, they had a thousand excuses. A Mexican ... stole like $700 ... He had me going from here to there, here to there, and never paid me, until I got tired and said, "He surely needs it more than me." Mexican. And then a Portuguese woman also, where I worked cleaning offices, the same thing.

Given her inability to complain to the authorities, Maria Nueva rationalized her situation by thinking that her employer needed the money more than she did.

Alternatively, his experiences with wage theft led Güero to conclude that employers were racially profiling him: "They're smart because these fuckers always profile. For example, this happens a lot to Mexicans. Those people look for Mexicans because they work fast, and they know that a lot of us don't have papers, and they don't pay you." Güero's wage theft, like that of other participants, was a systemic problem related to immigration status, occupation, and in some cases how employers linked Mexicanness with status precarity.

Sergio had a similar response. Given that he had participated with the Ejercito Zapatista de Liberación Nacional in Mexico, he recognized his rights as a person and a worker, but he also understood how dominant society marginalized vulnerable groups (Indigenous people in Mexico and precarious status migrants in Canada):

> At work, they don't pay me. It's been difficult. Some time ago, I worked with a man who also ended up owing me ten days. And he didn't pay me because I don't have papers; he knows I can't do anything, and that's how it is . . . One feels very sad to face that. Because the reality is we work, but we work to be paid, so I'm thinking my work is a sacrifice [that I endure] to support my family, send a bit of money to my family in Mexico . . . Like him, my boss, we also need to eat. His kids need to eat and shit. That's how I speak. So my kids also need to eat and shit.

For Sergio, losing ten days of wages, which probably involved more than eighty hours of work, meant an affront to himself and to his family in Mexico, demonstrating a transnational outcome to precarious working conditions.

Finally, those who had some form of status but sought cash employment were also vulnerable. Although Berenice had had access to social assistance and work eligibility as a refugee claimant, her experience was similar to non-status participants because she sometimes worked for cash to supplement the limited social assistance funds that she received from the government. As Berenice related,

> another job I had for two days was at a bread-making factory. We went, the agency took us, to work at the factory, and the next day we had to

> get there ourselves, and we got lost. So we didn't make it ... The first day we went we worked ten hours. The agency called us and asked, "Why didn't you go?"
>
> "We got lost." ...
>
> "Well, I'm sorry, but I'm not going to pay you for the day you worked."
>
> I asked, "Why?"
>
> "Because that's how they are. If you don't work the following day, they don't pay you anything."
>
> They did not pay us anything ... We didn't fight it. We didn't know who to go to or anything. We didn't do anything; the only thing we got out of it was our anger ... And why is it so common? Because everyone works without a social [insurance number], you think that you have everything to lose and that of course you can't complain because they're going to ... accuse you of working without a social [insurance number]. So the fear makes you say, "No, no, no, because if I say something they are going to tell ... immigration, and then ahhh!" And you think of the worst and feel that you are going to lose out on everything, right?

Legally, the employer and the agency were required to pay Berenice even though she did not show up the next day. Although she was not facing immediate deportation, she was afraid that the government would find out that she worked under the table, so she did not report the incident.

***

Precarious work is a systemic and growing issue. It affects precarious status migrants specifically because of the disconnect between what might seem to be protective employment policies and exclusionary immigration policies. Although protective employment policies exist, they are not carried out in practice. This means that working without authorization or with temporally limited authorization renders migrants more exploitable and deportable, demonstrating an internal border similar to that of health care.

Precarity and deportability occur during the work tenure as migrants experience exploitation in 3D jobs that physically and mentally cause injuries. They also affect workers economically through their experiences of wage theft, which affect not only their ability to subsist but also the transnational circulation of remittances. Finally, precarious work is also an affective process in which fear of deportation, anger at exploitation, embodied experiences of precarity, and feelings of not being able to speak out (having to bear the situation) emerge. As I discuss in the next chapter, though participants welcomed specific types of work (particularly creative and artistic projects in which they felt more valued and productive), this work did not protect them from instances of deportability, wage theft, and overall precarity.

8

Creative Practices amid Internal Borders

In 2016, the short film *Canciones* premiered in Toronto (Casas 2016). It was shown twice, once in a local bar and then at a "Hispanic" art and literature festival based at a university (*Latinos Magazine* 2016). *Canciones,* directed by Jeronimo Casas, is based on a poem by Jesús Maya (2012), both Mexican nationals. It depicts the story of a Mexican migrant living in Toronto and navigating precarious work, transnational memories of pain and violence, and engagement with art. The film begins with Martín, a construction worker, painting a mechanical room. At the end of the day, Martín and his co-worker receive a ride from their boss. During the trip, Martín asks his boss to let him know whether there will be work the next day, something not always guaranteed in the employment sector (Paloma Villegas 2014). This representation of Mexican migrants working in precarious 3D jobs in North America is familiar. And, though the film does not discuss immigration status, given Martín's employment and his dependence on a ride to get to and from work, the audience might also associate Martín with precarious status. This is particularly the case given Maya's other poetry and political work, which explicitly speaks to migrant illegalization in Canada (Maya 2012, 2013; Paloma Villegas 2013b).

Yet *Canciones* does not end with the representation of an abject precarious status migrant. During the drive from work, Martín sees a painting through a gallery window and spontaneously asks his boss to drop him off. He then enters the gallery and purchases the painting. This scene and the painting, depicting food on a brightly coloured table, facilitate a childhood memory. Martín recollects his family gathered around a table and the discord and violence that can ensue in such intimate encounters. However, the scene also disrupts a one-dimensional view of migrants as abject cogs in a capitalist machine, devoid of time or energy for other endeavours. Martín not only enjoys art but also has the will and ability to purchase it. He takes the painting home to show it to his partner, a dancer.

I use *Canciones* as a point of departure to think through how working-class migrants with precarious status appreciate and participate in artistic/creative expressions, broadly defined. Some of the participants in my study saw themselves as artists, whereas others saw themselves as participating in occasional creative work. Despite this, I understand all their creative work as work. That is, the time, effort, and care put into their creative expressions warrant the label of work. I also understand their activities as generative practices, producing a sense of community and identity as well as challenging assembled elements of precarity.

As multidisciplinary artists, participants engaged in various forms of artistic expression at one time or over time. Given their visibility in the Latinx community in Toronto, during some interviews participants decided not to name their specific artistic/creative expressions. Pseudonyms can protect participants from being identified via their names, but their experiences and abilities were unique, making them identifiable despite their pseudonyms. Although this might take away some of the texture of their stories, it is an important trade-off. Broadly, participants engaged in visual art, dance, literary art, music, theatre, film and digital media, photography, and work related to Mexican culture and Indigenous peoples.

In her work with Salvadoran and Guatemalan immigrants in the United States, Menjívar (2006, 1027–28) argues that "liminal legality is . . . prominently reflected in . . . immigrants' artistic expressions, especially among those who emigrated as adults (the immigrant generation), and thus shapes these immigrants' particular forms of participation in society." Those who arrive as children or the 1.5 generation, as in the case of Dreamers in the United States, also utilize their artistic skills to visibilize their experiences. For instance, the artwork of Julio Salgado, an undocuqueer activist, has circulated widely in migrant justice solidarity circles (Seif 2014). In Toronto, these artistic practices are also prevalent. A community holiday party organized by Jesús Maya in 2007 addressed the problem of wage theft in the Latinx migrant community. The invitation stated

> ¡Gran fiesta decembrina Latinoamericana! [Great Latin American December Party!] Diviértete y conoce nuevos amigos . . . [Enjoy and meet new friends . . .] Habrá ponche, rica comida, música, poesía y baile, piñatas y ¡mucha diversión! [We'll have punch, good food, music, poetry and dance, piñatas and lots of fun!] No te pierdas la pelea a un round entre los mortales enemigos: [Don't miss the fight between the mortal enemies:] Súper Ilegal vs El Patrón Ladrón (personal communication, December 2, 2007)

The event featured a skit that included Mexican Lucha Libre (wrestling) that pitted the protagonist-hero Súper Illegal against the villain El Patrón Ladrón (the thief employer). Súper Ilegal overcame El Patrón Ladrón and forced him to pay his unpaid employees. The name Súper Ilegal was chosen as a way to disrupt and appropriate illegalizing terminology regarding migrants and to visibilize their problems with wage theft. The event also included a presentation from a community organization about migrant workers' rights.

Although many participants did not address their immigration status in their artistic/creative expressions, possibly to "pass" as having status or to move away from being identified only through their status, it affected how they carried out their work. In fact, participants' engagement with creative/artistic work was complex. On the one hand, they saw how their creative expressions facilitated their embeddedness in social and creative networks and improved their quality of life given their precarious status and work. Through their creative practices, they resisted exploitation and alienation. They also practised citizenship and belonging, disrupting assumptions of legal status as a necessary prerequisite for these forms of participation, what Yuval Davis (2006) refers to as the politics of belonging. On the other hand, some used their work to draw boundaries between them and other migrants with precarious status who did not have the will or ability to work on similar projects. Thus, their generative practices produced and articulated power relations that sometimes policed and devalued other migrants.

Finally, participating in creative work had its limitations. Participants experienced internal borders that affected their ability to grow their practices, and they had to aguantar negative comments, rejection, and the threat of deportation.

Given this complicated process, we can understand precarious status migrants' artistic/creative expressions as assembled. Participants negotiated different ways of knowing in order to engage in creative work: legal frameworks dictating their immigration and work eligibility as well as their existing and growing knowledge base of creative work, which often manifested itself through a precarious creativity (Grant and Buckwold 2013). These ways of knowing limited how participants saw themselves as artists or creatives, but they also allowed them to disrupt structures of power that associated them with abject subjectivity. In addition to participants, other actors involved in this process included artists/creatives, migrants, teachers, and facilitators. These actors created and policed the boundaries of access to creative work, sometimes opening access and other times closing it. Art/creative institutions and funding agencies with eligibility criteria were another element of the assemblage. They drew on technologies of documentation to identify entitlement.

Finally, in terms of affect, I extend my discussions of yearning and aguantar from previous chapters (Burman 2010). Yearning involves the aspirations of migrants and diasporic subjects in relation to improving their lives and creating a more equitable or just world/future. Legal status affected some participants' aspirations of becoming full-time artists or opening their own businesses, studios, and so on, making them have to bear or tolerate their conditions and wait for the appropriate time to participate in creative projects. In sum, participants' experiences were part of a continuous process of *becoming* as artists, creators, and cultural producers, one marked by successes, failures, and the everydayness of being an immigrant and having precarious status.

Precarious Creativity

Creative/artistic work often involves what Grant and Buckwold (2013) refer to as a "precarious creativity" and Bain and McLean (2013) term the "artistic precariat." Both sets of scholars draw from critiques of Florida's (2002) romanticized understanding of the "creative class" as an innovative group of flexible workers who drive new economic sectors as well as urban development through 3Ts: technology, talent, and tolerance. Scholars have critiqued this understanding of creativity as a masculinist, neoliberalized operation of arts and city planning that ignores the roles of unpaid work and social reproduction and exacerbates gender and racial inequalities (Bain and McLean 2013; Leslie and Catungal 2012; Li 1994). Precarity is key in this conceptualization given that "creatives" often engage in precarious working situations, even if their employment is not low waged. Creative workers also often patchwork artistic/creative and survival jobs in order to subsist (Grant and Buckwold 2013). Thus, the 3Ts intersect with precarious work's 3D jobs, particularly for precarious status migrants.

The term "artistic precariat" describes the situation in which risk is downloaded to creative workers seen as "infinitely adaptable and already *accustomed to assuming risk* and, thus, somehow better able to withstand fluctuations in the economy" (Bain and McLean 2013, 98). This is not the case of course. In the Canadian context, Grant and Buckwold (2013, 115) tell us that

> the stereotype of the struggling artist reflects some of the challenges of labour in the cause of creative engagement . . . In Canada, the typical cultural worker earns about 75% of an average worker's income . . . The 20% of Canadian artists who are immigrants earn slightly below the average artist's income. Cultural workers have high educational levels. A higher than average proportion is female. Half of Canadian artists hold multiple jobs, only one-third work full time and one-fifth offer educational services.

Similarly, an Ontario report notes that 57.7 percent of employment in the arts, recreation, and entertainment sectors is precarious, "temporary, contract, casual, or 'non-standard'" work (Mojtehedzadeh 2016b). Artists are at the forefront of disrupting assumptions about their inherent flexibility and creating strategies to alleviate this system of precarity. For instance, the 2017 theme of the Toronto Mayworks festival, a "festival of working people and the arts," was "Art against Precarity" (Global News Wire 2017).

Less closely examined is the experience of precarious status migrants who engage in artistic/creative expressions. Grant and Buckwold's (2013) work on immigrants to Halifax, Nova Scotia, is important in demonstrating the deskilling, racism, language barriers, and social exclusion experienced by immigrant artists in a new context. However, their participants were mobile in ways that precarious status migrants are not, spending some of their time abroad, framing themselves as cosmopolitan, and holding multiple passports.

Disrupting "Illegality" and Precarity

Participants understood their artistic work as an avenue to disrupt their wholesale exploitation and illegalization, linking my discussions of precarious work, deportability, and well-being from previous chapters. They often framed their engagement with art/creative expressions as a coping mechanism, or a way for their lives in Canada to have meaning, as well as an opportunity to meet new people and increase their social networks.

The Social Benefits of Working in/with Communities

According to the Canadian Index of Wellbeing (2016), well-being involves "the presence of the highest possible quality of life in its full breadth of expression focused on but not necessarily exclusive to: good living standards, robust health, a sustainable environment, vital communities, an educated populace, balanced time use, high levels of democratic participation, and access to and participation in leisure and culture." Similarly, Lai and Hynie (2010) tell us that community engagement is an important factor in immigrant well-being. Whereas in previous chapters I focused on the effects of precarious status and internal borders on living standards, health, and time use, here I focus on "vital communities" and "participation in leisure and culture" as ways to counteract the negative effects of precarious status and work.

Several participants discussed the impacts of their artistic/creative work on their social lives. This was not only an individual process of accumulating more contacts but also involved participating and becoming embedded in communities. For instance, Aquetzalli reflected on the multidisciplinary artistic and cultural practices in which she engaged in Canada: "Well, yeah, to do this type of work [names multiple creative expressions] makes me feel very, like a part of Mexico, right? Like I'm close to my family. Pride to represent my country in a country that is not mine.

To show my roots, right? It's like, it's my passion." For Aquetzalli, participating in cultural work involved being part of an emerging Mexican community in Canada. Many US cities have long-standing Mexican communities with deeply rooted cultural and artistic practices given US imperialism and extensive in-migration from Mexico. However, Mexicans in Canada have had to create such practices from scratch in recent years (*Latinos Magazine* 2015; Portal Politico 2017).

Through her artistic/creative work, Aquetzalli mobilized a nationalist affect. Her pride was not directed toward the Mexican state per se. She was in fact critical of that state's participation in a generalized violence through fraudulent elections and forced disappearances. She was also critical of nationalist performances during events such as the World Cup. Instead, her pride related to her own definition of Mexicanness, its relationship to her cultural work, her peers who participated in that work, and the link created among her, her family in Mexico, and a transnational Mexican community, despite living in a country that she thought was "not hers" because of her immigration status.

Güero also experienced a yearning for social connection. He enjoyed the contacts that he made as he became more embedded in the different expressions of his artistic/creative work:

> A friend and I started a Spanish radio [station], . . . and from there I found out about a theatre group. And I began to connect with people. I went everywhere to meet people . . . I was bored. I began to get involved with people . . . When I found out that there was something happening here, that there were other people in my situation, well, who were also migrants who also worked and who were also doing something related to the arts, I said, "I want to be with those fuckers," and I have until today.

Throughout our interview, Güero articulated an aversion to the stereotypical representation of an "immigrant life": an abject existence of precarious work and suffering. His creative work and associated social networks were manifestations of a transition from such a life and into a well-rounded existence. The connections that he made produced in him a sense of solidarity. Although forging networks outside one's immigrant/ethnic network is beneficial in terms of finding work and generating upward mobility, finding people with similar experiences and tastes also lessens alienation.

Leonel found a sense of connection and meaning through his public creative practice:

L: I like to . . . visit my family and to [perform artistic work] . . . I love the applause [laughs].
P: So you go to [community] events?
L: Of course.
P: What types of people go to these activities?
L: All kinds.
P: Yeah?
L: Yes. You have working-class people, one time even a politician attended [laughs]. Politicians, journalists . . .
P: And do you [perform] in Spanish?
L: Yes.
P: So the people who go to these activities speak Spanish?
L: Yes, they speak Spanish.
P: . . . And does your immigration status affect your activities?
L: Absolutely not. People think I have status. Some time ago, I was invited to go to Chile.
P: So you feel safe at these activities?
L: Yes, I feel safe.

Leonel described an affective aspect of performing in public: the connection between the audience and himself. This was exhibited through the act of applauding, a bodily response of appreciation. Leonel felt comfortable participating in events because they occurred in Spanish and because "all types of people" attended them. As a working-class Mexican, without formal training, Leonel found a way to work through his feelings of intimidation in public spaces. As Bain and McLean (2013, 94) state, "in many art forms, formal arts training, while advantageous, is not a prerequisite for a sustained and successful career." And this was facilitated by the fact that he could use his artistic persona to quell any doubts about his immigration status. As Francisco Villegas (2006) has argued in relation to undocumented university students, having a classed position (e.g., as a university student) can facilitate passing as documented. In her research on undocumented migrants in California, Garcia (2019, 134) uses the concept of "legal passing," a "strategic presentation of self to the outside world that takes on characteristics associated with mainstream, U.S.-born groups to mask unauthorized immigration status" to signal to the embodied and internalized practices in which migrants engage strategically to avoid detection and deportation. I propose that legal passing can also be achieved in some contexts through artistic engagement. Because the illegal immigrant trope is so imbued with ideas of abject poverty (economic, artistic, etc.), those who do not fit that trope can disrupt, to an extent, their identification with precarious status. However, the persona must be carefully crafted and maintained.

Rebeca also discussed the social effects of engaging in artistic/creative expressions. Although she was not a trained artist, she participated in a public, collaborative artistic project linked to a community centre and programming for immigrant women. Through that community centre, she also found things to do with her children:

> We look for places, museums, through the library, places we know we can attend for free. We look for ways, because definitely the money is not there, but here you have an advantage, you have an opportunity if you look for [activities] through community centres . . . And you don't need to spend money, especially because the winter is difficult emotionally, being cooped up is terrible. So you have to look.

Mcleod and Ricketts (2013) argue that community arts projects such as the ones in which Rebeca participated should be seen as dialogical processes between different sets of artists or creative peoples, in this case migrants and non-migrants, as well as counterhegemonic practices. In Rebeca's case, her participation countered migrant illegalization, the stress that it produced, and its effects on her children. Rebeca thus sought to expose them to art exhibits in the city.

Finally, Zyanya, who also engaged in various artistic/creative expressions (including dancing and visual arts), noted that, once she began to participate in projects, "the artistic part started to grow and grow and demand more time, and I began to have more benefits [from that work]."

For her, the benefits came from obtaining opportunities to present her work, learn more skills, and teach those skills to others, all of which contributed to her community's vitality.

Attenuating the Effects of Precarious Status/Work and Providing Life with More Meaning

Lewchuck et al. (2015, 8) note that "employment precarity increases the stress on households and limits community participation." When coupled with precarious status, it can become a heavy burden. However, participants found ways to engage in their artistic/creative work despite engaging in difficult paid employment and dealing with difficult immigration cases. In fact, their artistic/creative work became a welcome activity away from their difficulties.

For instance, Güero noted the beneficial effects of participating in creative work:

> G: I was very tired, but I went [to work] very tired on the bus and slept on the bus on the way back. It's difficult, but you can do it, you can do such things. You just have to organize your time . . . I'm working, but I'm thinking of writing a script, I'm thinking of lines for a play. I'm thinking what I'm going to play with my band . . . Those are the types of things that break up your day, break up your work, break up monotony; they make it better, easier. It's difficult, very difficult.
>
> P: And how has that changed your life?
>
> G: It made it less flat . . . The monotonous aspect of an immigrant's life, which is to be always working. To always be worrying about bills. It's a vicious cycle, no? You come here for a better life, and when you have a better life you have to pay for that better life . . . So what it has given me is that, it gave me the opportunity to feel alive, to feel creative, to feel like a person, not like a worker. Not like an immigrant. That's it. It awakens creativity, the day changes.

Güero engaged in several different creative practices, including playing music, writing, and acting. In addition to a spatial description of his experience (dimension versus flatness), Güero thought that his activities disrupted the dehumanization caused by an immigrant's life, read here as a precarious status immigrant's life. Disrupting that representation, he depicted himself as working on both his paid employment and his artistic/creative work simultaneously. Doing so provided not only a respite from the difficult physical labour but also an incentive to finish that labour to pursue his creative interests.

During her refugee claim, Libertad was encouraged to engage in volunteer activities to improve her application's chance for approval, something that many migrants/refugee claimants are advised to do. The recommendation has been problematized since it can be a way to use refugee claimants' (and other im/migrants who want to seem "respectable" for the purpose of obtaining status) unpaid labour in the NGO sector. Although potentially exploitative, volunteering can also be fulfilling. For example, one of Libertad's volunteer efforts had to do with news reporting – "reading the news, making news, and reporting, synthesizing information," as well as sometimes taking photographs. Libertad explained the feeling that she received from doing that work, which she compared to being an artist:

> It is what I was born to do, it was my refuge. I could be having a really bad time, but as well I had that, even if it was unpaid, doing what I like, and also I think of it as my art. I was very happy, and I forgot everything. I could ... funnily, it was moments of stress, because I had to do the news at 7 a.m., 9 [a.m.], and 12 [p.m.], but it was those moments where I pampered myself.

Libertad understood herself as crafting and becoming embedded in the news, a way to engage in self-care given the stresses in her life, including her refused refugee claim, the criminal case against her child's father, and the barriers that her child experienced being in a mixed status family (limited eligibility for social services despite being a Canadian citizen and issues at school that could not be easily resolved because of Libertad's immigration status).

Aquetzalli also understood her work as providing meaning to her life, which she thought that she did not experience in Mexico:

> It gave my life a lot of meaning in terms of, yes, yes, it really gave it meaning to be here, alone ... I was always going from work, home, home,

> work. I had friends or whatever but nothing more. I suddenly found [artistic/creative work], and I was like, wow! I'm doing something I like, I'm devoting my time, I'm doing something that's beneficial, I'm interacting with people, with co-nationals. My passion therefore changed my life. It changed my life here . . . It's something I wanted to do my whole life. This made me cling to Canada even more. To want to stay here . . . because I have created that community and because I'm doing things that in Mexico I could have done but I was not allowed.

Aquetzalli described the significance of her cultural work as "hacer un bien [to do good/to do something that is beneficial]." The yearning "to do good" operated at different scales. At the individual level, she meant to do good for herself, giving her life meaning through her creative practices. This had transnational dimensions. Aquetzalli sought to resist her family's earlier expectation for her to study something that would lead to a good job (which she was unable to procure in Mexico) instead of pursuing her creative interests. In Canada, she also sought to resist the alienation of being a single immigrant woman by building community ties with other Mexicans and non-Mexicans.

When I first met Aquetzalli, she mentioned that she participated in many different activities because she did not want to be home alone. She felt depressed with the monotony of working in factories (and subsequently cleaning offices and houses). Thus, another dimension of artistic/creative work is the mental health effects that it produced in participants, who, because of the meaning that it provided to their lives, felt happier. I asked Aquetzalli how her engagement in artistic/creative work helped her to balance her precarious working conditions and their effects on her health:

> I arrive [to participate in artistic/creative practice] super tired sometimes, but being there it's like I get energy from I don't know where. I feel happy, I don't think about having to pay the phone bill or rent. It's my time, my space, it's my [sense of] being. I forget everything from the outside. Personal problems, money, work, blah, blah, blah. I used to get off work stressed and would say, "But I'm going to [do that cultural work]." And I forgot everything. I haven't been depressed for a long time . . . It's not

> like going to the gym, but, well, I also do that. But it's not the same . . . to do something about which I'm passionate.

Participating in activities that made her happy disrupted, albeit partially, the worries and responsibilities associated with her everyday life: having to pay her bills and worrying about her immigration status.

Other participants also experienced an improvement in their social networks and connections despite their continued engagement in precarious work. Lencho did not work when he first arrived in Canada. He was lucky that his family supported him while he went to school to learn English. There he met a number of other students, mainly international students from other parts of the world, with whom he forged relationships. Although Lencho subsequently began to work in precarious jobs, he was able to use his new contacts to engage in artistic/creative activities. His English helped in this process since it allowed him to work within and beyond the Latinx community. Lencho played music in Mexico and extended that practice to Canada as well as engaging in other creative visual practices.

Similarly, Juan Nadie travelled a lot renovating hotels his first years in Canada, making it difficult for him to put down roots in Toronto. However, he quit his stable and good-paying job because he feared that his co-worker, with whom he had a fight, would report him to immigration authorities. Finding construction work in Toronto was not always easy, but being present in the city was the silver lining of a lower salary, for he could participate in community practices related to his interest in music.

Maria Nueva experienced not only the effects of precarious work and deportability but also, like Libertad, domestic violence when she first arrived in Canada (Villegas 2019b). She described how she sought to heal from that experience by doing something creative:

> So I said, "Well, I want to learn art, right? Or to dance or something." Because I felt completely torn up. I had been used too much. I couldn't anymore . . . So I began to look for an activity that would give me, that would make me live again. So I said, "I'm going to learn to dance tango, well, no, I'm going to learn to do [artistic work]." . . . I began to look on

> the internet how and where to learn. But no, there was no way. So I went to different studios and asked, "Hey, can you teach me?"
>
> "No."

This account explains Maria Nueva's choice of pseudonym. Maria is a common name in Mexico, and her choosing it was related to her wanting to remain anonymous. However, Nueva means new, alluding to the change that she experienced after leaving the violent relationship and recreating her life and profession through her participation in artistic/creative work. The process was not easy. After she chose the artistic/creative practice that she wanted to learn, Maria Nueva faced rejection from experts in the field, who refused to allow her to apprentice with them. She eventually found a course, but it was in Spain, and its cost was prohibitive, even if she found a way there. Then her friend recommended a place where she could learn:

> He took me to the studio. I said, "Hi, can you teach me?" No, I said, "Can I talk to the owner?"
>
> "He's busy, he'll be back at the end of the year."
>
> So I said, "That's surely a no."
>
> But I always rode my bike because I didn't have money to buy a metropass [Toronto transit pass]. So, in January, I was passing on my bike. Imagine, I earned forty dollars per day cleaning offices. I said, "I'm going to stop, and at least I'll get warm [laughs]." . . . So I go in and say, "Can I talk to the owner?"
>
> And they say, "Yeah, he's coming."
>
> He comes, big with blue eyes, and looks at me, and I say, "Hi, I want to learn [artistic work]."
>
> And he says, "Do you know [artistic work]?"
>
> I said, "I think so, a little, I don't know." Very insecure, very insecure.
>
> And he says, "But you have to buy [materials]."
>
> I said, "I already bought them."
>
> . . . "Well," he said, "I want to teach someone, but the idea is that they'll work here."
>
> [Maria Nueva moved her hands as if weighing two sides] "Clean offices or do [artistic/creative work]? Clean offices or do [artistic/creative work]?" I said, "That would be great. Yes, I'm good enough, I would like to do it of course."

> He said, "Okay, I'll teach you."
> I said, "But there's a problem. I can't work legally in the country."
> He said, "Who cares? Change your name."
> I said, "Okay." And that's what I did.

The scene that Maria Nueva described mirrored and contrasted with her experience looking for work for the first time in Canada. However, this time, instead of running away, she stayed. Although it is important to disrupt a meritocratic explanation that might depict the "new" Maria as having worked hard enough and being "deserving," for Maria Nueva the shift was significant and life changing, not only because it provided an entry point into an artistic practice but also because it allowed her to move away from non-creative precarious work.

Boundary Making

Although participants rationalized their engagement in artistic/creative work as a strategy to disrupt the effects of precarious work and status, in doing so they sometimes, perhaps inadvertently, mobilized critiques of their peers who did not engage in such practices. This demonstrates the employment of boundary work (Lamont and Molnár 2002) to create a division between themselves and other precarious status migrants. Boundary work involves symbolic and social boundaries. Symbolic boundaries are "conceptual distinctions made by social actors to categorize objects, people, practices, and even time and space" (Lamont and Molnár 2002, 168). Once those boundaries become rigid and affect access to resources and opportunities, they become social boundaries. Although perhaps not deliberately, this boundary work operated to create a hierarchy of value. It reflected the positioning of some participants who saw their creative work as highly beneficial to society (Florida 2002) and reproduced discourses that reward productivity and resourcefulness.

For instance, Zyanya explained how she saw herself and her peers who engaged in precarious work:

> I remember that I was like, I saw people who, people who, I don't know, had certain neglect. So . . . there comes a point when you kind of see it as normal, it becomes habitual, and you don't see that line where you can see yourself as a cleaner and that you look down on yourself instead of

> thinking that you can be a worker but also do other things. And see it [cleaning] as a job that allows you to pay your bills. But it's such a fine line that many people are unable to separate it. So I saw that I was hurting myself emotionally. Because I saw millions of people who became depressed, and they went back, . . . and they were always crying, and I said, "I don't want to be like that." So I said, "No, I have to change this."

Zyanya discussed the normalization of her exploitation in the workplace and the flattening of her life, reduced to her work cleaning. We see here the extension of the normalization of exploitation and insecuritization from Mexico to Canada. Zyanya was also critical of the "neglect" of her co-workers and peers who did not have the energy to participate in activities after work. Although understanding that cleaning was a dignified profession, she did not want it to be something that defined her whole existence. This meant toeing a fine line between recognizing the difficult conditions that led her and her peers to engage in such work and the fact that she wanted something more. That yearning for status here manifested itself in terms of participating in creative work and the meaningful effects that it had for participants. Yet the fact that Zyanya sought something else and thought that others did not led her to create boundaries. Those who did not manifest that yearning were depicted as not having the capacity to face the different barriers presented to them ("unable," "crying," "depressed," and "went back"). Zyanya recognized the effects that precarious status and work had on mental health and quality of life. Yet, in her comment, there is a lack of recognition that going to work and returning safely home or being able to pay bills might be enough for some migrants.

Emiliana Zapata participated in creative activities related to her academic/activist interests: the recuperation of Indigenous languages and cultures in Mexico. Although this was difficult to do in Canada given her status, Emiliana Zapata broadened her knowledge base by participating in activities with local Indigenous communities. In describing her experience, she also engaged in boundary work, outlining a typology of "workers" whom she saw while in Canada:

> There's some that are, that already have papers here, . . . but they don't leave cleaning, and there are others who, who just arrived, or there's people who are just trying, like hunting jobs, and they say, "Well, let's try

> cleaning" [laughs]. And there's others who, like everything, are out to see what they can get out of it, no? And there's other people who have similar reasons, [but] they want to do something, want to participate in projects, and in the meantime we work.

In Emiliana Zapata's list, we see a diversity of workers and their reasons for doing their work. First, there are those who have papers and are often imagined to have access to other work but who often do not given classed, gendered, and racialized labour market stratification (Wilson et al. 2011). Second, there are those who change jobs and try everything, whom Emiliana Zapata described as somewhat fickle. Third, there are those who have just arrived and are more likely to engage in low-paid, hyper-precarious work. And fourth, there are those who, like Emiliana Zapata herself, use their work as a means to pursue other projects. Like Zyanya, in offering this list, Emiliana Zapata depicted a boundary between herself and other workers, one that attributed value to her endeavour to "do something" besides subsist. She returned to Mexico soon after our interview because of a family issue. Upon her return to Mexico, she was also able to pick up her social and cultural interests and pursue postgraduate work.

Aguantando Internal Borders

Although participants created symbolic borders with those of similar legal status, they also experienced internal borders in the pursuit of their creative work. This occurred when they sought training or other opportunities or when there was the possibility of receiving payment for their work. These internal borders attenuated the beneficial effects of participating in creative work given that participants had to aguantar (bear or tolerate) exclusions to continue and grow their work.

As I stated above, Maria Nueva faced difficulties when she decided to pursue her artistic/creative work. She found limited opportunities for training until she became an apprentice and changed her name. Similarly, Zyanya, who participated in different visual and performance arts, described receiving what she referred to as a *beca,* a scholarship or grant that paid for courses to learn film-editing techniques. She explained that, whenever she participated in such training, she always expected to be asked for proof of her status: "I've had three becas doing this, and they haven't asked me for anything. But I'm always afraid when I go. At what point will I have to tell them that I can't? So there's always that fear. I learned to say, 'Stop being afraid, stop being afraid.' If it's for you, you're going to get it." Zyanya rationalized a "positive thinking" approach to her deportability. Although this strategy can be useful to explain barriers or shortcomings, it has its limits given that it individualizes deportability, ignoring systemic migrant illegalization that excludes specific persons because of their status. Zyanya experienced one such moment when it was "not for her":

> So I said, "You have to be more, the more authentic you are, you are going to show what you want and what you can give." So . . . I started to do well, . . . and they [the organization that granted the *beca*] asked me to be part of their board . . . I was going to start by taking notes and everything, so I said, "Ah, like a secretary." But I never saw what it was really, I always think that things will be easy. That's why I say yes to things. And then, when I'm in the middle of it, I say, "Oh, I don't think it was that easy," and then I think of how to fix it. So then I saw that they were asking for more, that they started to send me information, and I was like "Why are they sending me this?"

Although Zyanya reflected on her decision by stating that she always thought things were easy, and when they were not she would fix them, her discussion of fearing that she would be asked for proof of her legal status disrupted that idea, demonstrating that she was always aware that her status might affect her, even if it had not up to that moment. Her uncertainty, she went on to explain, involved internalized feelings of migrant illegalization, which manifested themselves "as a personal devaluation" and "the sense of being less than a person" (Abrego 2016, 10):

> Because you have something inside you that follows you. You can't remove it while your status is no good. That idea of why are they trusting me? Why are they sending me this? Because I know that I'm not good, but they don't know that I'm not, so they trust you as if you are part of the team. So it was like "Wow, I think this is more than what I thought, I don't think it's just about taking notes." . . . They asked me to send them information, . . . and I was like "Oh, no," and I felt bad because this woman

> supported me a lot, and I said, "I didn't know this was going to grow." So I got there and told her I wanted to speak with her, and I needed to tell her some things, and then I told her. I didn't tell her everything, I told her that I couldn't work because I was in the process . . . But since she's very honest, it was like, it was like, even more because they receive government assistance, so it was like, I felt bad . . . I think that was the first time that I felt that they closed the doors because of my status. But I said, . . . "It's not that I can't do it, it's that my status is stopping me right now." I know that I can find something and not a cleaning job, I can aspire to something else. Now that doors are opening in that regard, it's my status that begins to stop me.

Zyanya was resourceful by not disclosing her immigration status completely and instead telling the organization the she was "in the process." Given that, as she stated, the board member was "very honest," this was still a dangerous move since the woman could have felt compelled to act like a "civilian soldier" and turn her in to immigration officials (Aberman 2018; Orr 2004). The result was that Zyanya lost an important strand of her artistic network, one that provided her with important training and contacts, because of her legal status.

Aquetzalli faced a similar barrier when her peers received a grant to engage in creative work (in which she was also engaged). Although she could not include her name on the grant, initially her peers agreed to share the money with her. However, there were subsequent discussions among the group, and they decided that they could not pay her for fear of getting in trouble with the funders/government. The decision parallels Zyanya's discussion of the board member's following the rules. It is also unclear how funders/the government would have found out if her peers gave Aquetzalli money out of pocket. The about-face hurt her both emotionally and financially and can be conceptualized as wage theft given the unpaid work that she engaged in to contribute to the project. Eventually, some of her peers did give her money, but the experience demonstrates how immigrants/co-nationals also enforce the social boundaries of legal status.

Creative work also influenced how participants related and reacted to their immigration status. Aquetzalli thought that her creative activities would provide evidence of her incorporation into Canada and improve her chances of obtaining legal status. Her hope was to apply through a humanitarian and compassionate (H&C) application. However, given her legal status, she also could not travel with her peers during international trips to promote their work, which ironically would have improved her chances of obtaining secure status as an artist.

In contrast, Leonel initially mentioned that he felt safe participating in cultural events given that he was identified as an artist and not a precarious status migrant. However, when his H&C application was denied, his outlook changed. He no longer felt safe attending activities given that his public persona might alert immigration authorities to his whereabouts. This made him withdraw socially, which also affected his self-esteem.

Finally, Manolo described a temporal border that occurred when he received a removal order from immigration authorities. When I asked him how this change in status would alter his life, he explained it by referring to living "under someone's shadow": "For example, I can't open my tattoo business, as I hoped. Why? Because I don't have status. I can't open a company, I can't open my own tattoo shop. I now have to live under someone's shadow. And hopefully no one sees my name." Doing tattoo work can involve health and safety oversight from the state in ways that other artistic/creative work might not. This prevented Manolo from opening the shop, fearing that he would be further illegalized through the process.

***

Creativity brings additional layers of meaning to migrants' lives, redirecting their association with exploitation and precarity. Participants became embedded in different ways of knowing through their creative work. It nudged them toward institutions and organizations that they previously had not encountered, including artistic organizations and funding institutions. This broadened their networks and opportunities to grow their creative practices. They also encountered other artists/creatives, migrants, teachers, and facilitators who upheld, policed, and sometimes challenged the boundaries of access to creative work. For participants who engaged in precarious work, creative practices involved negotiating schedules, energy levels, and other barriers produced through the internal borders of migrant illegalization. These barriers included exclusion from teachers, organizations, and peers, through technologies of documentation that sought to grant opportunities only to eligible artists, as well as wage theft and invisibility. In these cases, participants had to bear exclusions and limited inclusions in order to continue their creative work, yearning for a time when they could engage in their artistic work more freely. Finally, some participants also engaged in the drawing of boundaries, judging those who chose not to or were unable to engage in similar work.

Conclusion

Although much research on Mexican migration has focused on undocumented migrants to the United States, several factors have led Mexican emigrants to look for alternative migration sites, such as Canada. First, increased militarization at the US-Mexico border in recent decades rerouted entry points to the Arizona desert, leading to increased apprehensions and transit fatalities. Second, the growth of the immigration industrial complex and "crimmigration" in the United States makes it a less palatable migration site even if migrants make it there safely. Third, increased insecuritization in Mexico, including economic instability because of the growth of neoliberal policies in the country, lack of police protection, impunity of perpetrators, and specified threats given gender, race, and sexual orientation, produced an increased need to emigrate.

The route discussed here therefore complicates assumptions about the migration trajectories of Mexicans in three ways. First, though some research exists on Mexican skilled migration to Canada (Lujan 2017), as well as on the experiences of exploitation and precarity of temporary migrant workers (Basok 2003; McLaughlin 2010; Preibisch and Encalada Grez 2010), little research exists on how Mexican precarious status migrants experience their lives in urban contexts such as Toronto. Second, it also disrupts assumptions about Mexican migrants as only or always "economic" migrants, differentiated from "deserving" refugee claimants, and works to problematize the economic migrant/refugee binary. Third, it disrupts assumptions about the Canadian context as less violent and xenophobic than the US context.

Assemblage is an important framework to understand migration and immigration status trajectories, how they are produced and structured, and how they shape the lived experiences of Mexican precarious status migrants. Foregrounding *ways of knowing, actors, institutions/organizations, technologies,* and *ways of feeling* in this framework allows the consistent analysis of social phenomena as contingent and emergent. Ways of knowing include government policies, civil society reports, media stories, and other discursive circulations. For example, lack of knowledge about Canada as a migration site influenced participants' experiences during transit and upon arrival. Ways of knowing also influenced experiences during the refugee determination system and encounters with immigration representatives. Immigration policies, such as the 2009 visa requirement, redrew the ways in which Mexican migrants encountered the refugee determination system and entry into Canada, producing and reinforcing borders. The public visibility associated with "bogus refugee" discourses circulating in the media and from politicians placed a spotlight onto Mexican migrants regardless of their status. The circulation of tropes depicting migrants as "swarms," irresponsible, and entering through the "backdoor" challenged nation-building narratives of Canada "welcoming immigrants" and facilitated the development of policies and practices to ensure the maintenance of physical and ideological borders. Other policy frameworks, though not always specifically about migration and migrant illegalization, shaped participants' experiences of illegalization. For instance, health-care and employment standards in theory provide certain protections for all residents of Canada. In practice, they can operate as non-performatives (Ahmed 2004b) and contribute to the exclusion of migrants.

Ways of knowing also influence the actions of actors – border officials, employers, health-care providers, lawyers, creative workers, and other migrants – opening up access or encouraging them to act as gatekeepers or "civilian soldiers" (Aberman 2018; Orr 2004). Institutions/organizations are made up of actors who put into practice ways of knowing. Citizenship and Immigration Canada (now Immigration, Refugees and Citizenship Canada) and Canada Border Services Agency are important state examples. They produce and store information through technologies of documentation on migrants and make decisions about their ability to stay in Canada. Other organizations, including settlement services, health-care clinics, workers' centres, and artistic organizations, do not have the power to deport claimants, but they can influence the material conditions that migrants experience through the denial of services. Finally, ways of feeling, or affective circulations, also influence the enforcement and experience of borders.

In addition to the application of assemblage as a conceptual lens, the book makes five contributions to the existing literature that can be applied beyond the Toronto/Canada context to other sites that produce precarious immigration statuses. First, the book contributes to framings of citizenship and membership, focusing on how precarious status migrants make citizenship claims in order to achieve secure status through immigration applications (Chapters 4 and 5). Although the latter aligns precarious status migrants with a project that legitimizes sovereignty claims and Canada's white settler nation building, as demonstrated by some of the participants, a yearning for status can coexist with a critical engagement of the power relations that structure it.

Second, the book extends existing knowledge on migrant illegalization by illustrating the contingent and flexible process whereby precarious statuses are produced and multiplied. In addition to disrupting binary framings of undocumented/documented and legal/illegal, and challenging discourses of illegality as an inherent condition of migrants, I tracked the legal status transitions (Goldring and Landolt 2013) that participants underwent as they sought secure status, as well as the formal and informal barriers (internal borders) that they experienced in the process. Specifically, I used assemblage to think through the process of navigating the refugee determination system, which involves encounters with institutions and their representatives, information that circulates about a person's country of origin and level of "safety," and affective responses from applicants and non-migrants. Similarly, applying for secure status through other means – sponsorship or the humanitarian and compassionate application – requires navigating discourses of deservingness and legitimacy (e.g., marriages of convenience) and the different types of entitlements associated with each.

Third, the book focuses on how the temporality of migrant illegalization operates both locally and transnationally through the imposition of precarity/insecurity of internal and external borders. Participants narrated their experiences before migration through time: living hand to mouth, experiencing everyday risks, and enduring deteriorating conditions. As a result, processes that occurred pre-migration influenced experiences during transit. Some participants accrued class benefits as they crossed borders because of their previous migration experiences and educational/professional attainments, whereas others used their existing networks to find information about the best times, routes, and strategies to enter Canada (Chapter 2).

Participants described their experiences once in Canada procuring work and housing through time, referring to economic situations of precarity similar to those in Mexico. Some had existing knowledge of Canada, having travelled there before. Others drew on transnational facilitators who provided housing and employment information. Finally, others spent a lot of time getting a lay of the land through trial and error. Although most thought that Canada was more secure in terms of physical safety, the temporal limbo produced through "dead," "sticky," and "suspended" times affected participants' abilities to make plans (Dow 2007; Griffiths 2014). "Ruptured" times, such as when refugee claims were refused, led to stress and anxiety (Griffiths 2014). Finally, time also mediated the experience of internal borders – learning to access social services as well as to navigate and sometimes bear working conditions and shifts.

Internal borders, enforced through the requirement of documents such as passports, driver's licences, work permits, and health cards, were also experienced temporally. Although documents are socially produced, they allow a number of privileges, including the right to mobility (internally and externally) as well as access to health care and employment. When they arrived in Canada, many participants experienced difficulties finding jobs, particularly those that provided them with sufficient earnings given limited access to work permits (Chapter 7). Through the process of networking and building friendships, participants obtained access to less precarious work, though for those with no status this was never guaranteed. Similarly, accessing health-care services was also influenced by participants' access to quality information about accessible clinics and eligibility requirements and often luck in terms of friendly health-care providers (Chapter 6). Finally, access to opportunities for creative expression also improved over time and as participants became acquainted with Toronto and its citizens. Thus, outlooks, possibilities, and aspirations shifted or became reassembled over time as participants navigated their work, their well-being, and Toronto itself.

Fourth, the book contributes to research on how creative/artistic practice interlocks with precarious status. Creative work is precarious (Grant and Buckwold 2013) regardless of legal status. However, internal borders (engaging the workplace, accessing health care and other public goods, as well as being in public spaces) augment or at least contribute to precarious creativity. However, engaging in artistic/creative practices provided meaning to participants' difficult lives. For some, it also provided (limited) protection in terms of "legal passing" (Garcia 2019) as artists, which allowed them to avoid "uncomfortable questions" about their status (Bernhard et al. 2007).

And fifth, the book focuses on affect. Participants recounted having to bear specific violence associated with internal borders. The concepts of yearning (Burman 2002, 2010) and aguantarse are useful in thinking through this affective process. Yearning refers to a forward-looking process, a hopeful desire for improved conditions, security, and social justice (Burman 2002). Aguantar refers to bearing, tolerating, or enduring difficult situations. I understood participants' use of the term as a strategy to attenuate present difficulties and wait for opportunities to improve them (securing status, more decent work, better health-care coverage, improved opportunities to express themselves creatively). Although it is important to think about migrants' resourcefulness in light of their situations, I do not want to romanticize the term. Bearing is an action that assumes that something is *bearable*. Yet bearing means undergoing a process by which we might be left *bare*. In her analysis of refugee camps, Woldemikael (2017) alludes to the limits of bearing when she proposes that it does not imply consent to violence for those who enact it or that conditions should be bearable: "Because refugees have no choice but to bear the conditions of the refugee camps, we as Westerners . . . wrongly think that they're bearable. This is partially due to an unconscious assumption that refugees from developing countries are all poor or at least accustomed to squalor and discomfort." Similar framings of abjectivity are imposed on precarious status migrants. As Güero reflected in Chapter 7, discourses on abject precarious status migrants circulate widely in film and popular discourse. Thus, they might make audiences assume that the limited options and resources of migrants make them especially adept at bearing difficulties. Concrete examples and case studies of precarious status migrants help to dispel the idea that having the potential to aguantar means that one should have to be resilient and resourceful.

Appendix

PARTICIPANT INFORMATION AT A GLANCE

Pseudonym	Age	Gender	Context of departure	Arrived in Canada	Status trajectory	Work experiences
Leonel	40s	M	Estado de Mexico	2001	Tourist → expired visa → refugee claim several years after arrival → negative decision → humanitarian and compassionate application → negative decision	Cleaning, factory, construction
Rebeca	30s	F	Mexico City	2008	Tourist → expired visa → refugee claimant → negative decision → deported	Cleaning, sales, bathroom attendant
Eduardo	30s	M	Mexico City	2005–07	Tourist → returned to Mexico → tourist → expired visa → refugee claimant → negative decision → deported	Construction
Sergio	20s	M	Chiapas	2007–09	Tourist → expired visa → voluntary departure → later migrated to United States	Construction
Manolo	20s–30s	M	Mexico City	2007	Refugee Claimant → negative decision	Factory, construction, artist/tattooist

Pseudonym	Age	Gender	Context of departure	Arrived in Canada	Status trajectory	Work experiences
Berenice	30s	F	Leon, Guanajuato	2005	Tourist → refugee claim → negative decision → sponsorship claim → permanent residence	Factory work, construction, cleaning
Libertad	30s	F	Mexico City/ Acapulco	2005	Tourist → refugee claim → negative decision → humanitarian and compassionate application → negative decision → contemplating sponsorship	Cleaning, journalism, construction
Emiliana Zapata	20s	F	Mexico City	2008	Tourist → expired visa → Voluntary departure	Factory work, cleaning
Mexicano en Acción	20s	M	Aguascalientes	2004	Refugee claimant → negative decision → humanitarian and compassionate application → permanent residence	Settlement worker, volunteer, administrative services, food industry
Teresa	20s	F	Northern Mexico	2004–05	Applied for status (declined to specify) → received negative decision	Service sector
Johann	30s	M	Monterrey	2007	Refugee claimant → negative decision → sponsorship application approved	Telemarketing, construction
Arne Saknussemm	40s	M	Mexico City	2008	Refugee claimant	Services, interpretation, immigration consultant
Lencho	20s	M	Estado de Mexico	2009	Tourist → expired visa	Services, cleaning, construction
Maria Nueva	30s	F	Mexico City	Mid-2000s	Tourist → expired visa → sponsored spouse	Service sector (restaurants), factory work, art/creative work

Pseudonym	Age	Gender	Context of departure	Arrived in Canada	Status trajectory	Work experiences
Juan Nadie	30s	M	Queretaro	Mid- to late 2000s	Tourist → expired visa → contemplating sponsorship or H&C application	Construction
Liz	30s	F	Mexico City	2009	Tourist → expired visa	Cook, hostess, server
Aquetzalli	30s	F	Mexico City	2007	Tourist → expired visa → contemplating sponsorship	Factory work, construction, cleaning (self-employed)
Armando	20s	M	Puebla	2009	Tourist → expired visa → refugee claimant → negative decision	Cleaning, construction
Güero	30s	M	Mexico City	2006	Tourist → expired visa → beginning sponsorship application	Construction
Zyanya	20s	F	Mexico City	2006–09	Tourist → returned to Mexico → tourist → expired visa	Factory work, cleaning
Maria Pérez	30s	F	Mexico City	2008	Tourist → expired visa → sponsored spouse	Server

References

Aberman, Tanya. 2018. "'It Actually Made Me Feel like I Didn't Even Want to Stay Here': Experiences of 'Voluntary Return' in a Sanctuary City." PhD diss., York University.

Abrego, Leisy J. 2014. *Sacrificing Families: Navigating Laws, Labor, and Love across Borders*. Stanford, CA: Stanford University Press.

–. 2016. "Illegality as a Source of Solidarity and Tension in Latino Families." *Journal of Latino/Latin American Studies* 8 (1): 5–21. https://doi.org/10.18085/1549-9502-8.1.5.

Ahmed, Azam, and Nicole Perlroth. 2017. "Using Texts as Lures, Government Spyware Targets Mexican Journalists and Their Families." *New York Times*, June 19, 2017. https://www.nytimes.com/2017/06/19/world/americas/mexico-spyware-anticrime.html.

Ahmed, Sara. 2004a. "Affective Economies." *Social Text* 22 (2): 117–39. https://doi.org/10.1215/01642472-22-2_79-117.

–. 2004b. "Declarations of Whiteness: The Non-Performativity of Anti-Racism." *Borderlands* 3 (2): http://www.borderlands.net.au/vol3no2_2004/ahmed_declarations.htm.

–. 2016. "Evidence." *feministkilljoys* (blog), July 12, 2016. https://feministkilljoys.com/2016/07/12/evidence/.

Alba, Francisco. 2010. "Mexico: A Crucial Crossroads." *Migration Information Source*, February 25, 2010. https://www.migrationpolicy.org/article/mexico-crucial-crossroads.

Anderson, Ben, Matthew Kearnes, and Colin McFarlane. 2012. "On Assemblages and Geography." *Dialogues in Human Geography* 2 (2): 171–89. https://doi.org/10.1177/2043820612449261.

Anderson, Bridget. 2013. *Us and Them? The Dangerous Politics of Immigration Control*. Oxford: Oxford University Press.

Andersson, Ruben. 2014. "Time and the Migrant Other: European Border Controls and the Temporal Economics of Illegality." *American Ethnologist* 116 (4): 795–809. https://doi.org/10.1111/aman.12148.

Antecol, Heather, and Deborah Cobb-Clark. 2001. "Men, Women, and Sexual Harassment in the US Military." *Gender Issues* 19 (1): 3–18. https://doi.org/10.1007/s12147-001-0001-1.

Arat-Koc, Sedef. 2010. "Whose Transnationalism? Canada, 'Clash of Civilizations' Discourse, and Arab and Muslim Canadians." In *Colonialism and Racism in Canada: Historical Traces and Contemporary Issues*, edited by Maria A. Wallis, Lina Sunseri, and Grace-Edward Galabuzi, 266–83. Toronto: Nelson Education.

Arce, Dwyer. 2010. "Mexico High Court Upholds Mexico City Same-Sex Marriage Law." *Jurist Legal News and Research*, August 6, 2010. http://www.jurist.org/paperchase/2010/08/mexico-supreme-court-upholds-same-sex-marriage-law.php.

Aristegui Noticias. 2017. "Se dispara número de peticionarios mexicanos de refugio en Canadá." *Aristegui*, October 24, 2017. http://aristeguinoticias.com/2410/mundo/se-dispara-numero-de-peticionarios-mexicanos-de-refugio-en-canada/.

Asadbikli, Paria, Tyler Dzingala, Kunal Mishra, and Yvonne Ruan. 2016. "Mental Health and Immigration Status: Let's Talk Mental Health." University of Toronto Scarborough. http://www.utsc.utoronto.ca/immigrantscarborough/mental-health-and-immigration-status.

Ashutosh, Ishan, and Alison Mountz. 2011. "Managing Migration for the Benefit of Whom? Interrogating the Work of the IOM." *Citizenship Studies* 15 (1): 21–38. https://doi.org/10.1080/13621025.2011.534914.

Atungo, Simone, Richard Edwards, Linda Gardner, Sarah Hobbs, Anthony Mohamed, and Angela Robertson. 2010. "Connecting Services to the Uninsured: Collaboration between CHCs and Hospitals." Paper presented at the AOHC 2010 Conference, Niagara Falls, ON, June 2010.

Bacon, David. 2008. *Illegal People: How Globalization Creates Migration and Criminalizes Immigrants*. Boston: Beacon Press.

Bailey, Adrian J. 2001. "Turning Transnational: Notes on the Theorisation of International Migration." *International Journal of Population Geography* 7 (6): 413–28. https://doi.org/10.1002/ijpg.239.

–. 2013. "Migration, Recession and an Emerging Transnational Biopolitics across Europe." *Geoforum* 44: 202–10. https://doi.org/10.1016/j.geoforum.2012.09.006.

Bailey, Adrian J., Richard A. Wright, Alison Mountz, and Ines M. Miyares. 2002. "(Re)producing Salvadoran Transnational Geographies." *Annals of the Association of American Geographers* 92 (1): 125–44. https://doi.org/10.1111/1467-8306.00283.

Bain, Alison, and Heather McLean. 2013. "The Artistic Precariat." *Cambridge Journal of Regions, Economy and Society* 6 (1): 93–111. https://doi.org/10.1093/cjres/rss020.

Bannerji, Himani. 2000. *The Dark Side of the Nation: Essays on Multiculturalism, Nationalism and Gender*. Toronto: Canadian Scholars' Press.

Basch, Linda G., Nina Glick Schiller, and Cristina Szanton Blanc. 1994. *Nations Unbound: Transnational Projects, Postcolonial Predicaments, and Deterritorialized Nation-States*. Basel: Gordon and Breach.

Basok, Tanya. 2000. "He Came, He Saw, He . . . Stayed: Guest Worker Programmes and the Issue of Non-Return." *International Migration* 38 (2): 215–38. https://doi.org/10.1111/1468-2435.00108.

–. 2003. *Tortillas and Tomatoes: Transmigrant Mexican Harvesters in Canada*. Montreal and Kingston: McGill-Queen's University Press.

Basulto, Cynthia. 2016. "Eliminación de visa canadiense para mexicanos incrementará la residencia illegal." *W Radio*, December 1, 2016. http://play.wradio.com.mx/audio/111RD380000000042725/.

Batiz, Martha. 2017. "Talk to a Legitimate Mexican Refugee and You'll See: Canada Is a Friend." *Globe and Mail*, April 1, 2017. https://www.theglobeandmail.com/opinion/talk-to-a-legitimate-mexican-refugee-and-youll-see-canada-is-a-friend/article34552701/.

Becklumb, Penny. 2008. *Canada's Inland Refugee Protection System*. Background paper BP-185E. Ottawa: Parliament of Canada, Law and Government Division. http://publications.gc.ca/collections/collection_2016/bdp-lop/bp/YM32-2-2008-185-eng.pdf.

Bell, Stewart. 2013. "Czech Tourists Will No Longer Need Visas, but Mexican Travellers Out of Luck as 'Serious' Security Concerns Remain." *National Post*, October 16, 2013. http://nationalpost.com/news/canada/czech-tourists-will-no-longer-need-visas-but-mexican-travellers-out-of-luck-as-serious-security-concerns-remain.

Berinstein, Carolina, Peter Nyers, Cynthia Wright, and Sima Zeheri. 2006. "Access not Fear: Non-Status Immigrants and City Services." Report prepared for the "Don't Ask, Don't Tell" campaign. Toronto. https://we.riseup.net/assets/17034/Access%20Not%20Fear%20Report%20(Feb%202006).pdf.

Bernhard, Judith, Luin Goldring, Julie Young, Carolina Berinstein, and Beth Wilson. 2007. "Living with Precarious Legal Status in Canada: Implications for the Well-Being of Children and Families." *Refuge: Canada's Periodical on Refugees* 24 (2): 101–14.

Bhuyan, Rupaleem, Daphne Jeyapal, Jane Ku, Izumi Sakamoto, and Elena Chou. 2017. "Branding 'Canadian Experience' in Immigration Policy: Nation Building in a Neoliberal Era." *Journal of International Migration and Integration* 18 (1): 47–62. https://doi.org/10.1007/s12134-015-0467-4.

Blanchfield, Mike. 2013. "Mexican Ambassador Wants 'Road Map' for End of Visa Rules." *Globe and Mail*, September 15, 2013, modified May 11, 2018. https://www.

theglobeandmail.com/news/world/were-really-mad-at-canada-over-visa-restrictions-mexico/article14326868/.

Bloch, Alice, Leena Kumarappan, and Sonia Mckay. 2015. "Employer Sanctions: The Impact of Workplace Raids and Fines on Undocumented Migrants and Ethnic Enclave Employers." *Critical Social Policy* 35 (1): 132–51. https://doi.org/10.1177/0261018314545600.

Bohaker, Heidi, and Franca Iacovetta. 2009. "Making Aboriginal People 'Immigrants Too': A Comparison of Citizenship Programs for Newcomers and Indigenous Peoples in Postwar Canada, 1940s–1960s." *Canadian Historical Review* 90 (3): 427–61. https://doi.org/10.3138/chr.90.3.427.

Boyd, Monica. 1989. "Family and Personal Networks in International Migration: Recent Developments and New Agendas." *International Migration Review* 23 (3): 638–70. https://doi.org/10.2307/2546433.

Breslow, Jason M. 2015. "The Staggering Death Toll of Mexico's Drug War." *Frontline*, PBS, July 27, 2015. http://www.pbs.org/wgbh/frontline/article/the-staggering-death-toll-of-mexicos-drug-war/.

Brown, Michael, and Larry Knopp. 2003. "Queer Cultural Geographies: We're Here! We're Queer! We're Over There Too!" In *Handbook of Cultural Geography*, edited by Kay Anderson, 313–24. London: Sage.

Brunner, Laura K., and Maryanne Dever. 2014. "Work, Bodies and Boundaries: Talking Sexual Harassment in the New Economy." *Gender, Work and Organization* 21 (5): 460–71. https://doi.org/10.1111/gwao.12048.

Buahene, Bediako. 2004. *A Guide to Humanitarian and Compassionate Applications (H&C)*. Vancouver: MOSAIC. https://www.mosaicbc.org/wp-content/uploads/2016/10/A-Guide-to-Humanitarian-and-Compassionate-Applications-English.pdf.

Burman, Jenny. 2002. "Remittance; Or, Diasporic Economies of Yearning." *Small Axe* 12: 49–71. https://doi.org/10.1353/smx.2002.0017.

–. 2010. *Transnational Yearnings: Tourism, Migration, and the Diasporic City*. Vancouver: UBC Press.

Butler, Don. 2011. "Findings Raise Questions about Immigration Rulings: Judges Appointed by Conservatives Less Likely to Overturn Denied Refugee Claims." *Vancouver Sun*, November 25, 2011. http://www.canada.com/Findings+raise+questions+about+immigration+rulings/5771959/story.html#ixzz1f1Vzy51p.

Butler, Judith. 2009. "Performativity, Precarity and Sexual Politics" *AIBR: Revista de Antropología Iberoamericana* 4 (3): i–xiii. https://doi.org/10.11156/aibr.040303e.

Cabra, Eduardo, and René Pérez. 2014. "El Aguante [Recorded by Calle 13]." In *MultiViral*. Woodland Hills, CA: El Abismo.

Canada Border Services Agency. 2013. "Arriving by Air." Last modified December 11, 2013. http://www.cbsa-asfc.gc.ca/travel-voyage/aba-apa-eng.html.

–. 2017. Freedom of Information Request (A-2017-00414/SS).

Canada Newswire. 2009. "It Is Time Parliament Called 'Strike Three' on Immigration and Refugee Board Appointment Practices, Staff Union Says." October 22, 2009. http://www.newswire.ca/en/releases/archive/October2009/22/c9364.html.

–. 2010. "CJFE Reports that 87 Journalists Were Killed Worldwide in 2010." December 30, 2010. http://www.newswire.ca/en/releases/archive/December2010/30/c8115.html.

Canadian Council for Refugees. 2013. "Refugee Health Care: Impacts of Recent Cuts." https://ccrweb.ca/sites/ccrweb.ca/files/ifhreporten.pdf.

–. 2015. "Court Strikes Down Appeal Bar for Nationals of Designated Countries of Origin." July 24, 2015. http://ccrweb.ca/en/court-strikes-down-RAD-bar-DCOs.

Canadian Healthcare Association. 2012. "Changes to the Interim Federal Health Program: Position Statement." November 2012. http://www.healthcarecan.ca/wp-content/uploads/2012/11/IFHP-reform-policy-statement-November-2012.pdf.

Canadian Index of Wellbeing. 2016. "What Is Wellbeing?" https://uwaterloo.ca/canadian-index-wellbeing/reports/2016-canadian-index-wellbeing-national-report/what-wellbeing.

Cantú, Lionel, Nancy A. Naples, and Salvador Vidal-Ortiz. 2009. *The Sexuality of Migration: Border Crossings and Mexican Immigrant Men, Intersections*. New York: New York University Press.

Carlsen, Laura. 2008. "Armoring NAFTA: The Battleground for Mexico's Future." *NACLA*, August 27, 2008. https://nacla.org/node/4958.

Casas, Jeronimo. 2016. *Canciones*. https://www.youtube.com/watch?v=Nh6GlVdwuuU.

Casswell, Donald G. 1996. *Lesbians, Gay Men and Canadian Law*. Toronto: Emond Montgomery Publications.

Caulford, Paul, and Yasmin Vali. 2006. "Providing Health Care to Medically Uninsured Immigrants and Refugees." *Canadian Medical Association Journal* 174 (9): 1253–54. https://doi.org/10.1503/cmaj.051206. Medline:16636321.

CBC News. 2009a. "Canada Defends Visa Change for Mexicans, Czechs." *CBC News*, July 14, 2009. http://www.cbc.ca/world/story/2009/07/14/czech-visas-mexico.html.

–. 2009b. "Mexicans Trying to Immigrate 'through the Back Door,' Says Kenney." *CBC News*, April 15, 2009. https://www.cbc.ca/news/canada/calgary/mexicans-trying-to-immigrate-through-the-back-door-says-kenney-1.792456.

–. 2017. "Canada Has Detained More Mexicans in 2 Months than in All of 2016." *CBC News*, March 18, 2017. http://www.cbc.ca/news/politics/mexican-refugees-canada-detained-1.4031389.

Chadwick, Andrew, and Philip N. Howard. 2009. *Routledge Handbook of Internet Politics*. London: Routledge.

Chase, Liana E., Janet Cleveland, Jesse Beatson, and Cécile Rousseau. 2017. "The Gap between Entitlement and Access to Healthcare: An Analysis of 'Candidacy' in the Help-Seeking Trajectories of Asylum Seekers in Montreal." *Social Science and Medicine* 182: 52–59. http://doi.org/10.1016/j.socscimed.2017.03.038.

Chatterjee, Soma. 2015. "Skills to Build the Nation: The Ideology of 'Canadian Experience' and Nationalism in Global Knowledge Regime." *Ethnicities* 15 (4): 544–67. https://doi.org/10.1177/1468796815577702.

Chavez, Leo R. 2001. *Covering Immigration: Popular Images and the Politics of the Nation*. Berkeley: University of California Press.

Chavira-Prado, Alicia. 1992. "Work, Health, and the Family: Gender Structure and Women's Status in an Undocumented Migrant Population." *Human Organization* 51 (1): 53–64. https://doi.org/10.17730/humo.51.1.2qq68v3p70l10848.

Cisneros, Josue David. 2012. "Looking 'Illegal': Affect, Rhetoric, and Performativity in Arizona's Senate Bill 1070." In *Border Rhetorics: Citizenship and Identity on the US-Mexico Frontier*, edited by D. Robert DeChaine, 133–50. Tuscaloosa: University of Alabama Press.

Citizenship and Immigration Canada. 2008. "True or False?" http://www.cic.gc.ca/English/department/media/facts/workers.asp.

–. 2009a. "Backgrounder: The Visa Requirement for Mexico." http://www.cic.gc.ca/english/department/media/backgrounders/2009/2009-07-13.asp.

–. 2009b. "Canada Imposes a Visa on Mexico." http://www.cic.gc.ca/english/department/media/releases/2009/2009-07-13.asp.

–. 2009c. "Formative Evaluation of the Pre-Removal Risk Assessment Program." Modified June 26, 2009. http://www.cic.gc.ca/english/resources/evaluation/prra/section4.asp.

–. 2009d. "Apply to the Federal Court of Canada for Judicial Review." Modified December 3, 2019. http://www.cic.gc.ca/english/refugees/inside/appeals-review.asp.

–. 2010. "Pre-Removal Risk Assessment." Modified May 25, 2010. http://www.cic.gc.ca/english/refugees/inside/prra.asp.

–. 2011a. "Changes to the Humanitarian and Compassionate and Temporary Resident Permit Provisions." Modified August 18, 2011. http://www.cic.gc.ca/english/refugees/reform-changes.asp.

–. 2011b. "Refugee Appeal Division." Modified February 13, 2011. http://www.cic.gc.ca/english/refugees/reform-rad.asp.

–. 2012a. "Backgrounder – Conditional Permanent Resident Status." Modified October 26, 2012. http://www.cic.gc.ca/english/department/media/backgrounders/2012/2012-10-26a.asp.

–. 2012b. "Backgrounder – Summary of Changes to Canada's Refugee System." Modified January 12, 2016. http://www.cic.gc.ca/english/department/media/backgrounders/2012/2012-06-29b.asp.

–. 2012c. "Notice – Notice of Regulatory Changes to Applications for Permanent Resident Status and Changes on Accessing a Pre-Removal Risk Assessment." Modified August 15, 2012. http://www.cic.gc.ca/english/department/media/notices/notice-prra.asp.

–. 2013. "Designated Countries of Origin." Modified June 17, 2013. http://www.cic.gc.ca/english/refugees/reform-safe.asp.

–. 2014. "Facts and Figures 2013 – Immigration Overview: Temporary Residents." Modified December 31, 2014. http://www.cic.gc.ca/english/resources/statistics/facts2013/temporary/index.asp.

–. 2015. "Facts and Figures 2014 – Immigration Overview: Permanent Residents." Modified August 1, 2015. http://www.cic.gc.ca/english/resources/statistics/facts2014/index.asp.

–. 2016a. "Changes at the Immigration and Refugee Board of Canada (IRB)." Modified June 16, 2016.

–. 2016b. "Humanitarian and Compassionate Assessment: Best Interests of a Child." Modified March 2, 2016. http://www.cic.gc.ca/english/resources/tools/perm/hc/processing/child.asp.

–. 2017. "Express Entry Year-End Report 2015." Modified March 15, 2017. http://www.cic.gc.ca/english/resources/reports/ee-year-end-2015.asp.

City of Toronto. 2007. "Access to Services for Toronto Residents: Information and Identification Requirements." Toronto: City of Toronto.

–. 2012. "Undocumented Workers in Toronto." Staff report, AFS #15467, October 22, 2012. http://www.toronto.ca/legdocs/mmis/2013/cd/bgrd/backgroundfile-55291.pdf.

–. 2015. "Access to City Services for Undocumented Torontonians: Progress of the Access T.O. Initiative." Staff report, AFT #20866, November 10, 2015. http://www.toronto.ca/legdocs/mmis/2015/cd/bgrd/backgroundfile-85779.pdf.

–. 2018. "Equity, Diversity and Inclusion." https://www.toronto.ca/city-government/accessibility-human-rights/equity-diversity-inclusion/.

Coffman, Maren J., Marcia A. Shobe, and Beth O'Connell. 2008. "Self-Prescription Practices in Recent Latino Immigrants." *Public Health Nursing* 25 (3): 203–11. https://doi.org/10.1111/j.1525-1446.2008.00697.x.

Colaiacovo, Innessa. 2013. "Not Just the Facts: Adjudicator Bias and Decisions of the Immigration and Refugee Board of Canada (2006–2011)." *Journal on Migration and Human Security* 1 (4): 122–47. https://doi.org/10.14240/jmhs.v1i4.17.

Coll, Kathleen M. 2010. *Remaking Citizenship: Latina Immigrants and New American Politics*. Stanford, CA: Stanford University Press.

Collyer, M. 2007. "In-Between Places: Trans-Saharan Transit Migrants in Morocco and the Fragmented Journey to Europe." *Antipode* 39 (4): 668–90. https://doi.org/10.1111/j.1467-8330.2007.00546.x.

Colour of Poverty Campaign. 2007. "Fact Sheet # 6: Understanding the Racialization of Poverty in Ontario in Income Levels and Social Assistance in 2007." http://www.colourofpoverty.ca/.

Committee to Protect Journalists. 2020. "52 Journalists Killed in Mexico between 1992 and 2020/Motive Confirmed." https://cpj.org/killed/americas/mexico/.

Community Health Centres of Greater Toronto. 2008. "Community Health Centres, Hospitals and People without Health Insurance." Report. Toronto.

–. 2011. *Health Equity Plan: Building on Potential/Driving Action*. Toronto: Wellesley Institute. http://www.wellesleyinstitute.com/wp-content/uploads/2012/04/Community-Health-Centres-of-Greater-Toronto-Health-Equity-Plan-final.pdf.

Community Legal Education Ontario. 2008. "Pre-Removal Risk Assessment (PRRA)." http://www.settlement.org/sys/faqs_detail.asp?faq_id=4000569.

Connell, Robert William, and Raewyn Connell. 2000. *The Men and the Boys*. Berkeley: University of California Press.

Consejos Gratis. 2011. "Trabajar de ilegal en Canada." http://www.consejosgratis.es/trabajar-de-ilegal-en-canada/.

Consulate General of Mexico in Toronto. 2009. "Mexico's Position on Canadian Authorities' Decision to Impose Visas on Mexican Nationals." http://www.consulmex.com/eng/pressrelease.asp?169.

Coutin, Susan Bibler. 2000. *Legalizing Moves: Salvadoran Immigrants' Struggle for U.S. Residency*. Ann Arbor: University of Michigan Press.

–. 2003. "Illegality, Borderlands, and the Space of Nonexistence." In *Globalization under Construction: Governmentality, Law, and Identity*, edited by Richard Warren Perry and Bill Maurer, 171–202. Minneapolis: University of Minnesota Press.

–. 2007. *Nations of Emigrants: Shifting Boundaries of Citizenship in El Salvador and the United States*. Ithaca, NY: Cornell University Press.

–. 2015. "Deportation Studies: Origins, Themes and Directions." *Journal of Ethnic and Migration Studies* 41 (4): 671–81. https://doi.org/10.1080/1369183x.2014.957175.

Cranford, Cynthia J., Leah F. Vosko, and Nancy Zukewich. 2003. "Precarious Employment in the Canadian Labour Market: A Statistical Portrait." *Just Labour* 3: 6–22. https://doi.org/10.25071/1705-1436.164.

Cruz, José Miguel. 2009. "Public Insecurity in Central America and Mexico." *Americas Barometer Insights* 28: 1–7.

CTV News. 2018. "Embassy Angered by Conservative MP Linking Mexican Visitors to Drug Trade." *CTV News.ca*, June 15, 2018. https://www.ctvnews.ca/politics/embassy-angered-by-conservative-mp-linking-mexican-visitors-to-drug-trade-1.3974643.

Cypher, James M., and Mateo Crossa. 2019. "T-MEC en el espejo del TLCAN: Engañosas ilusiones, brutales realidades | USMCA in the NAFTA mirror: Deceptive illusions, brutal realities." *Ola Financiera*, 34 (12): 56–87.

Daniel, Drew. 2013. *The Melancholy Assemblage: Affect and Epistemology in the English Renaissance*. New York: Fordham University Press.

De Genova, Nicholas. 2002. "Migrant 'Illegality' and Deportability in Everyday Life." *Annual Review of Anthropology* 31: 419–47. https://doi.org/10.1146/annurev.anthro.31.040402.085432.

–. 2005. *Working the Boundaries: Race, Space, and "Illegality" in Mexican Chicago*. Durham, NC: Duke University Press.

De Genova, Nicholas, and Nathalie Mae Peutz. 2010. *The Deportation Regime: Sovereignty, Space, and the Freedom of Movement*. Durham, NC: Duke University Press.

DeLanda, Manuel. 2006. *A New Philosophy of Society: Assemblage Theory and Social Complexity*. London: Continuum.

Delcorto, Elysa. 2007. "Illegals Flocking to Canada on Promise of Legalization." *Naples Daily News*, September 21, 2007. http://archive.naplesnews.com/news/local/illegals-flocking-to-canada-on-promise-of-legalization-ep-403436742-345135372.html/.

Deleuze, Gilles, and Felix Guattari. 1987. *A Thousand Plateaus: Capitalism and Schizophrenia*. Translated by Brian Massumi. Minneapolis: University of Minnesota Press.

Delgado Wise, Raúl. 2015. "Unravelling Highly Skilled Migration from Mexico in the Context of Neoliberal Globalization." In *Social Transformation and Migration: National and Local Experiences in South Korea, Turkey, Mexico and Australia*, edited by Stephen Castles, Derya Ozkul, and Magdalena Arias Cubas, 201–17. London: Palgrave Macmillan.

Dittmer, Jason. 2014. "Geopolitical Assemblages and Complexity." *Progress in Human Geography* 38 (3): 385–401. https://doi.org/10.1177/0309132513501405.

Dovidio, John F., and Susan T. Fiske. 2012. "Under the Radar: How Unexamined Biases in Decision-Making Processes in Clinical Interactions Can Contribute to

Health Care Disparities." *American Journal of Public Health* 102 (5): 945–52. https://doi.org/10.2105/ajph.2011.300601.

Dow, Mark. 2007. "Designed to Punish: Immigrant Detention and Deportation." *Social Research* 74 (2): 533–46.

Drachman, Edward R., and Alan Shank. 2003. *You Decide! Controversial Global Issues*. Lanham, MD: Rowman and Littlefield.

Dua, Enakshi. 2007. "Exclusion through Inclusion: Female Asian Migration in the Making of Canada as a White Settler Nation." *Gender, Place and Culture* 14 (4): 445–66. https://doi.org/10.1080/09663690701439751.

Dzenovska, Dace. 2014. "Bordering Encounters, Sociality and Distribution of the Ability to Live a 'Normal Life.'" *Social Anthropology* 22 (3): 271–87. https://doi.org/10.1111/1469-8676.12075.

Edwards, Steven. 2009. "Refugee Claims Spike by 30%: UN Figures; Minister Calls It Abuse of Canada's Generosity." *National Post*, March 25, 2009. http://www.nationalpost.com/todays-paper/story.html?id=1424202.

Eggebø, Helga. 2013. "'With a Heavy Heart': Ethics, Emotions and Rationality in Norwegian Immigration Administration." *Sociology* 47 (2): 301–17. https://doi.org/10.1177/0038038512437895.

El Espectador. 2014. "Calle 13 estrena la canción 'El Aguante.'" *El Espectador*, February 18, 2014. http://www.elespectador.com/entretenimiento/agenda/musica/calle-13-estrena-cancion-el-aguante-articulo-475737.

El Universal. 2017. "A casi un año de que Canadá eliminara su visa para mexicanos." *El Universal*, November 29, 2017. https://www.informador.mx/mexico/A-casi-un-ano-de-que-Canada-eliminara-su-visa-para-mexicanos-20171129-0089.html.

Elgersma, Sandra. 2008. *Immigration Status and Legal Entitlement to Insured Health Services*. PRB 08-28E. Ottawa: Library of Parliament, Political and Social Affairs Division.

Elliott, Louise. 2014. "Decisions by Refugee Appeal Division Members Vary Widely." *CBC News*, December 15, 2014. http://www.cbc.ca/news/politics/decisions-by-refugee-appeal-division-members-vary-widely-1.2867191.

Enriquez, Laura E. 2015. "Multigenerational Punishment: Shared Experiences of Undocumented Immigration Status within Mixed-Status Families." *Journal of Marriage and Family* 77 (4): 939–53. https://doi.org/10.1111/jomf.12196.

Escalante, Sebastian. 2004. "Disrupting Mexican Refugee Constructs: Women, Gays and Lesbians in 1990s Canada." In *Canadian Migration Patterns from Britain and North America*, edited by Barbara Jane Messamore, 207–28. Ottawa: University of Ottawa Press.

Espiritu, Yen Le. 2003. *Home Bound: Filipino American Lives across Cultures, Communities, and Countries*. Berkeley: University of California Press.

Fekete, Jason. 2009. "Citizenship Program Needs to Focus on Canadian 'Values': Kenney." *National Post*, April 14, 2009. http://www.nationalpost.com/news/story.html?id=1496639#ixzz0veuNHWWI.

Fife, Robert, and Shawn McCarthy. 2016. "Ottawa Seeks Assurances from Mexico in Lifting Visa Restrictions." *Globe and Mail*, June 22, 2016. https://www.theglobeandmail.com/news/politics/ottawa-seeks-assurances-from-mexico-in-lifting-visa-restrictions/article30570640/?ord=1.

Finkin, Matthew W. 2015. "From Weight Checking to Wage Checking: Arming Workers to Combat Wage Theft." *Indiana Law Journal* 90 (2): 851–77.

Florida, Richard L. 2002. *The Rise of the Creative Class: And How It's Transforming Work, Leisure, Community and Everyday Life*. New York: Basic Books.

Flynn, Matthew. 2015. "Bureaucratic Capitalism and the Immigration Detention Complex." Global Detention Project Working Paper No. 9, Geneva, June 2015. https://www.globaldetentionproject.org/wp-content/uploads/2015/06/matt_flynn_gdp_paper_2015-1.pdf.

Fong, Petti. 2009. "Majority of Canadians Back Visa Rules, Poll Finds." *Toronto Star*, July 18, 2009. http://www.thestar.com/news/canada/article/668272.

Foreign Affairs and International Trade Canada. 2011. "International Trade: Fast Facts on Canada-Mexico Commercial Relations." *Canada.ca*. http://www.international.gc.ca/commerce/facts-infos/mexico-mexique-2009.aspx?view=d.

Forrest, Maura. 2017. "'Dreamers' Unlikely to Rush to Claim Asylum in Canada, Immigration Experts Say." *National Post*, September 6, 2017. http://nationalpost.com/news/politics/dreamers-unlikely-to-rush-to-claim-asylum-in-canada-immigration-experts-say.

Foucault, Michel. 1995. *Discipline and Punish: The Birth of the Prison*. 2nd ed. New York: Vintage Books.

Frelick, Bill, Ian M. Kysel, and Jennifer Podkul. 2016. "The Impact of Externalization of Migration Controls on the Rights of Asylum Seekers and Other Migrants." *Journal on Migration and Human Security* 4 (4): 190–220. https://doi.org/10.14240/jmhs.v4i4.68.

French, Laurence, and Magdaleno Manzanárez. 2004. *NAFTA and Neocolonialism: Comparative Criminal, Human and Social Justice*. Lanham, MD: University Press of America.

Friedman, Sara L. 2010. "Determining 'Truth' at the Border: Immigration Interviews, Chinese Marital Migrants, and Taiwan's Sovereignty Dilemmas." *Citizenship Studies* 14 (2): 167–83. https://doi.org/10.1080/13621021003594817.

Friesen, Joe, and Campbell Clark. 2010. "Minister Promises Crackdown on Immigration Consultants Who Counsel Fraud." *Globe and Mail*, February 2, 2010. http://www.theglobeandmail.com/news/politics/minister-promises-crackdown-on-immigration-consultants-who-counsel-fraud/article1208100/.

Fudge, Judy. 2012. "Precarious Migrant Status and Precarious Employment: The Paradox of International Rights for Migrant Workers." *Comparative Labor Law and Policy Journal* 34 (1): 95–131. https://doi.org/10.2139/ssrn.1958360.

Gallo Farias v. Canada (Citizenship and Immigration). 2008. FC 1035. http://decisions.fct-cf.gc.ca/en/2008/2008fc1035/2008fc1035.html.

Galloway, Gloria. 2007. "Flood of Mexicans Delays Other Refuge-Seekers." *Globe and Mail*, December 4, 2007, A10.

Garcia, Angela S. 2019. *Legal Passing: Navigating Undocumented Life and Local Immigration Law*. Oakland: University of California Press.

Gaucher, Megan. 2014. "Attack of the Marriage Fraudsters! An Examination of the Harper Government's Antimarriage Fraud Campaign." *International Journal of Canadian Studies* 50: 187–205. https://doi.org/10.3138/ijcs.2014.011.

George, Usha, and Julie Young. 2006. *Immigration to Canada: The Case of Mexicans*. Report prepared for MIGSYS (Immigrants, Policies and Migration Systems: An Ethnographic Comparative Approach). Toronto: Metropolis Network and the Foundation for Population, Migration and Environment. http://www.eliamep.gr/wp-content/uploads/en/2009/04/migsys_canada_mexicans_july_06.pdf.

Gibney, Matthew J. 2006. "'A Thousand Little Guantanamos': Western States and Measures to Prevent the Arrival of Refugees." In *Displacement, Asylum, Migration*, edited by K. Tunstall, 137–69. Oxford: Oxford University Press.

Global News Wire. 2017. "32nd Annual Mayworks Festival Opens on April 28th and Features 'Art Against Precarity'". http://www.globenewswire.com/news-release/2017/04/28/1105811/0/en/32nd-annual-Mayworks-Festival-opens-on-April-28th-and-features-Art-Against-Precarity.html.

Godenau, Dirk. 2014. "Irregular Maritime Immigration in the Canary Islands: Externalization and Communautarisation in the Social Construction of Borders." *Journal of Immigrant and Refugee Studies* 12 (2): 123–42. https://doi.org/10.1080/15562948.2014.893384.

Godoy, Emilio. 2011. "Mexico: Deadly Cocktail of Sexual Violence and Impunity." *InterPress Service*, November 23, 2011. http://www.ipsnews.net/2011/11/mexico-deadly-cocktail-of-sexual-violence-and-impunity/.

Goldring, Luin, Carolina Berinstein, and Judith Bernhard. 2009. "Institutionalizing Precarious Migratory Status in Canada." *Citizenship Studies* 13 (3): 239–65. https://doi.org/10.1080/13621020902850643.

Goldring, Luin, and Patricia Landolt. 2011. "Caught in the Work-Citizenship Matrix: The Lasting Effects of Precarious Legal Status on Work for Toronto Immigrants." *Globalizations* 8 (3): 325–41. https://doi.org/10.1080/14747731.2011.576850.

–. 2012. "The Impact of Precarious Legal Status on Immigrants' Economic Outcomes." IRPP Study 35. https://irpp.org/wp-content/uploads/assets/research/diversity

-immigration-and-integration/the-impact-of-precarious-legal-status-on-immigrants-economic-outcomes/IRPP-Study-no35.pdf.

–. 2013. "The Conditionality of Legal Rights and Status: Conceptualizing Precarious Non-Citizenship." In *Producing and Negotiating Non-Citizenship: Precarious Legal Status in Canada*, edited by Luin Goldring and Patricia Landolt, 3–27. Toronto: University of Toronto Press.

Gomez Cruz, Manuel Angel, and Rita Schwentesius Rindermann. 2009. "NAFTA's Impact on Mexican Agriculture: An Overview." In *NAFTA and the Campesinos: The Impact of NAFTA on Small-Scale Agricultural Producers in Mexico and the Prospects for Change*, edited by Juan M. Rivera, Scott Whiteford, and Manuel Chávez Márquez, 1–20. Scranton, PA: University of Scranton Press.

González, F.E. 2009. "Mexico's Drug Wars Get Brutal." *Current History* 108 (715): 72–76.

Gonzalez, Gilbert G., and Raul A. Fernandez. 2003. *A Century of Chicano History: Empire, Nations, and Migration*. New York: Routledge.

Gonzalez, Maria de la Luz. 2010. "Tepito vende bases de datos oficiales." *El Universal*, April 19, 2010. http://www.eluniversal.com.mx/primera/34792.html.

Gonzales, Roberto G. 2008. "Left Out but Not Shut Down: Political Activism and the Undocumented Latino Student Movement." *Northwestern Journal of Law and Social Policy* 3 (2): 1–22.

Gould, Jon B., Colleen Sheppard, and Johannes Wheeldon. 2010. "A Refugee from Justice? Disparate Treatment in the Federal Court of Canada." *Law and Policy* 32 (4): 454–86. https://doi.org/10.1111/j.1467-9930.2010.00325.x.

Government of Canada. 2009. "Statutory Instruments 2009 SOR/2009-207 to 211 and SI/2009-63 and 64." *Canada Gazette Part II* 143 (16): 1447–88. http://canadagazetteducanada.gc.ca/rp-pr/p2/2009/2009-08-05/pdf/g2-14316.pdf.

–. 2015a. "Facts and Figures 2015: Immigration Overview – Permanent Residents – Annual IRCC Updates." July 31, 2015. https://open.canada.ca/data/en/dataset/2fbb56bd-eae7-4582-af7d-a197d185fc93?_ga=2.49243823.842472763.1528227510-196492561.1517265268.

–. 2015b. "Facts and Figures 2015: Immigration Overview – Temporary Residents – Annual IRCC Updates." July 31, 2015. https://open.canada.ca/data/en/dataset/052642bb-3fd9-4828-b608-c81dff7e539c?_ga=2.241060746.842472763.1528227510-196492561.1517265268.

–. 2016. "Regulations Amending the Immigration and Refugee Protection Regulations (Temporary Resident Visa) P.C. 2016-981." *Canada Gazette Part II* 150 (24): 4242–4250. http://www.gazette.gc.ca/rp-pr/p2/2016/2016-11-30/pdf/g2-15024.pdf.

–. 2017a. "Detail by Organization for Supplementary Estimates (C), 2016–17." February 13, 2017. https://www.canada.ca/en/treasury-board-secretariat/services/

planned-government-spending/supplementary-estimates/c-2016-17/detail-organization.html#toc1-14.

–. 2017b. "Notice – Government of Canada Eliminates Conditional Permanent Residence." April 28, 2017. https://www.canada.ca/en/immigration-refugees-citizenship/news/notices/elminating-conditional-pr.html.

–. 2018a. "Facts and Figures 2016: Immigration Overview – Permanent Residents – Annual IRCC Updates." June 6, 2018. https://open.canada.ca/data/en/dataset/1d3963d6-eea9-4a4b-8e4a-5c7f2deb7f29.

–. 2018b. "Facts and Figures 2016: Immigration Overview – Temporary Residents – Annual IRCC Updates." April 13, 2018. https://open.canada.ca/data/en/dataset/6609320b-ac9e-4737-8e9c-304e6e843c17.

Grant, Jill L., and Benjamin Buckwold. 2013. "Precarious Creativity: Immigrant Cultural Workers." *Cambridge Journal of Regions, Economy and Society* 6 (1): 113–26. https://doi.org/10.1093/cjres/rss008.

Griffiths, Melanie B.E. 2014. "Out of Time: The Temporal Uncertainties of Refused Asylum Seekers and Immigration Detainees." *Journal of Ethnic and Migration Studies* 40 (12): 1991–2009. https://doi.org/10.1080/1369183x.2014.907737.

Gutierrez Garza, Ana. 2018. "The Temporality of Illegality: Experiences of Undocumented Latin American Migrants in London." *Focaal: Journal of Global and Historical Anthropology* 81: 86–98. https://doi.org/10.3167/fcl.2018.810107.

Gutiérrez-Haces, Maria Teresa. 2015. *Los Vecinos del Vecino: La continentalizacion de Mexico y Canada en America del Norte*. Mexico City: Universidad Nacional Autonoma de Mexico.

Hacker, Karen, Maria Anies, Barbara L. Folb, and Leah Zallman. 2015. "Barriers to Health Care for Undocumented Immigrants: A Literature Review." *Risk Management and Healthcare Policy* 8: 175–83. https://doi.org/10.2147/rmhp.s70173.

Haggerty, Kevin D., and Richard V. Ericson. 2000. "The Surveillant Assemblage." *British Journal of Sociology* 51 (4): 605–22. https://doi.org/10.1080/00071310020015280.

Hall, Rachel. 2015. *The Transparent Traveler: The Perfornmance and Culture of Airport Security*. Durham, NC: Duke University Press.

Hanley, Jill, Sylvie Gravel, Katherine Lippel, and Jah-Hon Koo. 2014. "Pathways to Healthcare for Migrant Workers: How Can Health Entitlement Influence Occupational Health Trajectories?" *Perspectives interdisciplinaires sur le travail et la santé* 16 (2): 1–22. https://doi.org/10.4000/pistes.3980.

Hansen, Darah. 2009. "Mexican Refugees Flee to Canada as Gang Wars Get Deadlier." *Vancouver Sun*, March 28, 2009. http://www.vancouversun.com/news/Mexican+refugees+flee+Canada+gang+wars+deadlier/1437399/story.html.

Harris, Kathleen. 2016a. "Canadian Officials Preparing for Potential Flood of Mexican Migrants after Trump Wins Presidency." *CBC News*, November 10, 2016.

–. 2016b. "John McCallum Says Mexican Visa Could Be 'Reimposed' if Refugee Claims Spike." *CBC News*, November 15, 2016. http://www.cbc.ca/news/politics/mexico-visa-refugee-canada-trump-1.3851904.

–. 2016c. "Mexican Visa Lift Expected to Cost Canada $262M over a Decade." *CBC News*, December 1, 2016. http://www.cbc.ca/news/politics/mexico-visa-immigration-canada-mccallum-1.3875483.

–. 2017. "Mexican Refugee Claims Jump after Visa Requirement Dropped." *CBC News*, January 10, 2017. http://www.cbc.ca/news/politics/mexican-refugee-claims-canada-1.3927178.

Harvey, David. 1989. *The Condition of Postmodernity: An Enquiry into the Origins of Cultural Change*. Cambridge, MA: Blackwell.

Henry, Frances, and Carol Tator. 2002. *Discourses of Domination: Racial Bias in the Canadian English-Language Press*. Toronto: University of Toronto Press.

Henton, Darcy. 2009. "Stelmach Urges Ottawa to Reconsider Mexican Visa Changes." *Calgary Herald*, July 22, 2009. http://www.calgaryherald.com/travel/Stelmach+urges+Ottowa+reconsider+Mexican+visa+changes/181779/story.html.

Hier, Sean P. , and Joshua L. Greenberg. 2002. "Constructing a Discursive Crisis: Risk, Problematization and Illegal Chinese in Canada." *Ethnic and Racial Studies* 25 (3): 490–513. https://doi.org/10.1080/01419870020036701.

Hing, Bill Ong. 2010. *Ethical Borders: NAFTA, Globalization, and Mexican Migration*. Philadelphia: Temple University Press.

Hoffman, Andy, and Gloria Galloway. 2009. "Mexican Authorities Shut Down Blackfire Mine." *Globe and Mail*, December 9, 2009, B5.

Hondagneu-Sotelo, Pierrette. 1994. *Gendered Transitions: Mexican Experiences of Immigration*. Berkeley: University of California Press.

Hong, Amy. 2014. "Advocacy Strategies to Defend France's Sans-Papiers: Contradictions and Complexities." *International Journal of Human Rights* 18 (1): 20–44. https://doi.org/10.1080/13642987.2013.862617.

Hook, Derek. 2001. "Discourse, Knowledge, Materiality, History: Foucault and Discourse Analysis." *Theory Psychology* 11 (4): 521–47. https://doi.org/10.1177/0959354301114006.

Hulchanski, J. David. 2010. *The Three Cities within Toronto: Income Polarization among Toronto's Neighbourhoods, 1970–2005*. Toronto: Cities Centre, University of Toronto. http://www.urbancentre.utoronto.ca/pdfs/curp/tnrn/Three-Cities-Within-Toronto-2010-Final.pdf.

Human Resources and Social Development Canada. 2006. "A Profile of Latin Americans in Canada." http://www.hrsdc.gc.ca/eng/lp/lo/lswe/we/ee_tools/data/eedr/annual/2001/DGProfiles/LatinAmericansProfile.shtml.

Huot, Suzanne, Andrea Bobadilla, Antoine Baillard, and Debbie L. Rudman. 2016. "Constructing Undesirables: A Critical Discourse Analysis of 'Othering' within the Protecting Canada's Immigration System Act." *International Migration* 54 (2): 131–43. https://doi.org/10.1111/imig.12210.

Ibarra, Maria De La Luz. 2003. "Buscando la vida: Mexican Immigrant Women's Memories of Home, Yearning, and Border Crossings." *Frontiers: A Journal of Women's Studies* 24 (2–3): 261–83. https://doi.org/10.1353/fro.2004.0018.

Ibrahim, Maggie. 2005. "The Securitization of Migration: A Racial Discourse." *International Migration* 43 (5): 163–87. https://doi.org/10.1111/j.1468-2435.2005.00345.x.

Immigration and Refugee Board of Canada. 2001. "Mexico: Whether 'Madrinas' Are Available for Hire by Influential or Wealthy People." MEX36942.E, June 21, 2001. http://www.unhcr.org/refworld/docid/3df4be6cc.html.

–. 2009. Access to Information Request (A-2009-00024/de).

–. 2016. "Refugee Appeal Division." December 22, 2016. http://www.irb-cisr.gc.ca/eng/refapp/pages/radsar.aspx.

–. 2019. "Canada Removes All Countries from the Designated Country of Origin List." May 17, 2019. https://irb-cisr.gc.ca/en/news/2019/Pages/remove-designated-country-list.aspx.

Immigration, Refugees and Citizenship Canada. 2016. *Evaluation of the Pre-Removal Risk Assessment Program*. Evaluation report. cic.gc.ca/english/resources/evaluation/prra.asp#4-6.

–. 2017a. "Ad Hoc Intergovernmental Task Force on Irregular Migration Met Yesterday in Montréal." News release, August 24, 2017. https://www.canada.ca/en/immigration-refugees-citizenship/news/2017/08/ad_hoc_intergovernmentaltaskforceonirregularmigrationmetyesterda.html.

–. 2017b. "Humanitarian and Compassionate Assesment: Establishment in Canada." February 3, 2017. www.cic.gc.ca/english/resources/tools/perm/hc/processing/establishment.asp.

–. 2018. Access to Information Request (A201776696).

Inda, Jonathan Xavier. 2006. *Targeting Immigrants: Government, Technology, and Ethics*. Malden, MA: Blackwell.

Infante, Cesar, Sandra G. Sosa-Rubi, and Silvia Magali Cuadra. 2009. "Sex Work in Mexico: Vulnerability of Male, Travesti, Transgender and Transsexual Sex Workers." *Culture, Health and Sexuality* 11 (2): 125–37. https://doi.org/10.1080/13691050802431314.

Instituto de los Mexicanos en el Exterior. 2016. "Mexicanos en el mundo: Estadística de la población mexicana en el mundo 2016." Secretaria de Relaciones Exteriores. http://www.ime.gob.mx/gob/estadisticas/2016/mundo/estadistica_poblacion.html.

IRB Communications Directorate. 2006. "Immigration and Refugee Board of Canada: An Overview." http://www.irb-cisr.gc.ca/eng/brdcom/publications/Pages/OverAper.aspx (accesssed May 9, 2011).

Isin, Engin F., and Greg M. Nielsen, eds. 2008. *Acts of Citizenship*. New York: Zed Books.

Isin, Engin F., and Patricia K. Wood. 1999. *Citizenship and Identity*. London: Sage.

Jimenez, Marina. 2003. "200,000 Illegal Immigrants Toiling in Canada's Underground Economy." *Globe and Mail*, November 15, 2003, A1.

–. 2010. "Felipe Calderon: The Man Who Took on the Drug Cartels." *Globe and Mail*, May 28, 2010. https://www.theglobeandmail.com/news/world/felipe-calderon-the-man-who-took-on-the-drug-cartels/article4353244/.

Johnson, Kevin R. 2001. "Immigration Politics, Popular Democracy and California's Proposition 187." In *The Latino/a Condition: A Critical Reader*, edited by Richard Delgado and Jean Stefanic, 110–17. New York: New York University Press.

Joynes-Burgess, Kate. 2009. "Mexico's Rural Mennonites Feel Impact of Drug Violence." *BBC News*, November 23, 2009. http://news.bbc.co.uk/2/hi/8369200.stm.

Kalleberg, Arne L. 2009. "Precarious Work, Insecure Workers: Employment Relations in Transition." *American Sociological Review* 74: 1–22. https://doi.org/10.1177/000312240907400101.

Kaufman, Joyce P., and Kristen P. Williams. 2010. *Women and War: Gender Identity and Activism in Times of Conflict*. Sterling, VA: Kumarian Press.

Kendall, Christopher N. 2003. "Lesbian and Gay Refugees in Australia: Now that 'Acting Discreetly' Is No Longer an Option, Will Equality Be Forthcoming?" *International Journal of Refugee Law* 15 (4): 715–49. https://doi.org/10.1093/ijrl/15.4.715.

Keung, Nicholas. 2007. "Mexican Refugee Requests Skyrocket." *Toronto Star*, August 5, 2007. http://www.thestar.com/News/article/243329.

–. 2010. "New Watchdog to Regulate Immigration Consultants." *Toronto Star*, June 8, 2010. https://www.thestar.com/news/canada/2010/06/08/new_watchdog_to_regulate_immigration_consultants.html.

–. 2013a. "City Declared a 'Sanctuary': Historic Move Means Non-Status Migrants Can Use Key Services without Fear of Deportation." *Toronto Star*, February 22, 2013, A1.

–. 2013b. "Cuts to Leave Refugees Lawyerless: Plan Would Stop Legal Aid from Representing Asylum Seekers Who Come from 'Safe' Countries." *Toronto Star*, April 5, 2013, GT1.

–. 2015. "Canada's Refugee Acceptance Rate up Despite Asylum Restrictions." *Toronto Star*, March 1, 2015. https://www.thestar.com/news/immigration/2015/03/01/canadas-refugee-acceptance-rate-up-despite-asylum-restrictions.html.

–. 2016a. "Legal Aid Faces Financial Crunch in Serving Refugee Claimants." *Toronto Star*, November 12, 2016. https://www.thestar.com/news/immigration/2016/11/12/legal-aid-faces-financial-crunch-in-serving-refugee-claimants.html.

–. 2016b. "Liberals Announce Changes to Spousal Sponsorship Rules." *Toronto Star*, October 31, 2016. https://www.thestar.com/news/immigration/2016/10/31/liberals-announce-changes-to-spousal-sponsorship-rules.html.

Khosravi, Shahram. 2014. "Waiting: Keeping Time." In *Migration: The COMPAS Anthology*, edited by Bridget Anderson and Michael Keith, 66–67. Oxford: COMPAS.

Koehl, Albert. 2007. "Unlocking the School Door: Immigration Status and the Right to Learn." *Education Canada* 47 (3): 58–61.

Kolossov, Vladimir, and James Scott. 2013. "Selected Conceptual Issues in Border Studies." *Belgeo: Revue belge de géographie* 1. https://doi.org/10.4000/belgeo.10532.

Kyle, David. 2000. *Transnational Peasants: Migrations, Networks, and Ethnicity in Andean Ecuador*. Baltimore: Johns Hopkins University Press.

Lafontaine, Edward , and Leslie Tredeau. 1986. "The Frequency, Sources, and Correlates of Sexual Harassment among Women in Traditional Male Occupations." *Sex Roles* 15 (7–8): 433–42. https://doi.org/10.1007/bf00287982.

Lahav, Gallya. 2000. "The Rise of Nonstate Actors in Immigration Regulation in the United States and Europe: Changing the Gatekeepers or Bringing Back the State?" In *Immigration Research for a New Century: Multidisciplinary Perspectives*, edited by Nancy Foner, Rubén G. Rumbaut, and Steven J. Gold, 215–41. New York: Russell Sage Foundation.

Lai, Yvonne, and Michaela Hynie. 2010. "Community Engagement and Well-Being of Immigrants: The Role of Knowledge." *Canadian Issues*, Summer 2010, 93–97.

Lamont, Michèle, and Virág Molnár. 2002. "The Study of Boundaries in the Social Sciences." *Annual Review of Sociology* 28: 168–95. https://doi.org/10.1146/annurev.soc.28.110601.141107.

Landolt, Patricia, and Luin Goldring. 2015. "Assembling Noncitizenship through the Work of Conditionality." *Citizenship Studies* 19 (8): 853–69. https://doi.org/10.1080/13621025.2015.1110280.

Larchanché, Stéphanie. 2012. "Intangible Obstacles: Health Implications of Stigmatization, Structural Violence, and Fear among Undocumented Immigrants in France." *Social Science and Medicine* 74: 858–63. https://doi.org/10.1016/j.socscimed.2011.08.016.

Latinos Magazine. 2015. "Top 10 Most Successful Mexicans in Canada 2015." December 31, 2015. https://issuu.com/latinosmagazine/docs/top_10_most_successful_mexicans_in_.

–. 2016. "25 Festival de la Imagen y Palabra presenta el Cortometraje CANCIONES." http://latinosmag.com/25-festival-de-la-imagen-y-palabra-presenta-el-cortometraje-canciones/.

Law Commission of Ontario. 2012. *Vulnerable Workers and Precarious Work Final Report*. Toronto: Osgoode Law School, York University.

Law, Stephanie. 2012. "Mexican Journalist Launches Last-Ditch Bid to Fight Deportation." *Globe and Mail*, January 16, 2012. https://www.theglobeandmail.com/news/british-columbia/mexican-journalist-launches-last-ditch-bid-to-fight-deportation/article4241448/.

LeBrón, Alana M.W., Amy J. Schulz, Cindy Gamboa, Angela Reyes, Edna A. Viruell-Fuentes, and Barbara A. Israel. 2018. "'They Are Clipping Our Wings': Health Implications of Restrictive Immigrant Policies for Mexican-Origin Women in a Northern Border Community." *Race and Social Problems* 10: 174–92. https://doi.org/10.1007/s12552-018-9238-0.

Ledesma, Alberto. 2017. *Diary of a Reluctant Dreamer: Undocumented Vignettes from a Pre-American Life*. Columbus, OH: Mad Creek Books.

Leerkes, Arjen, James D. Bachmeier, and Mark A. Leach. 2013. "When the Border Is 'Everywhere': State-Level Variation in Migration Control and Changing Settlement Patterns of the Unauthorized Immigrant Population in the United States." *International Migration Review* 47 (4): 910–43. https://doi.org/10.1111/imre.12047.

Leitner, Helga, and Christopher Strunk. 2014. "Assembling Insurgent Citizenship: Immigrant Advocacy Struggles in the Washington DC Metropolitan Area." *Urban Geography* 35 (7): 943–64. https://doi.org/10.1080/02723638.2014.943582.

Leslie, Deborah, and John Paul Catungal. 2012. "Social Justice and the Creative City: Class, Gender and Racial Inequalities." *Geography Compass* 6 (3): 111–22. https://doi.org/10.1111/j.1749-8198.2011.00472.x.

Levitz, Stephanie. 2017. "Number of Asylum Claims Lodged in Canada from Mexico Rose Again in March – Highest Yet in 2017." *National Post*, April 16, 2017. http://news.nationalpost.com/news/canada/canadian-politics/number-of-asylum-claims-lodged-in-canada-from-mexico-rose-again-in-march-highest-yet-in-2017.

Lewchuk, Wayne, et al. 2015. *The Precarity Penalty: The Impact of Employment Precarity on Individuals, Households and Communities – And What to Do about It*. Toronto: Poverty and Employment Precarity in Southern Ontario (PEPSO). https://pepso.ca/documents/precarity-penalty.pdf.

Lewis, Rachel. 2013. "Deportable Subjects: Lesbians and Political Asylum." *Feminist Formations* 25 (2): 174–94. https://doi.org/10.1353/ff.2013.0027.

Li, Peter S. 1994. "A World Apart: The Multicultural World of Visible Minorities and the Art World of Canada." *Canadian Review of Sociology* 31 (4): 365–91. https://doi.org/10.1111/j.1755-618x.1994.tb00827.x.

–. 2001. "The Racial Subtext in Canada's Immigration Discourse." *Journal of International Migration and Integration* 2 (1): 77–97. https://doi.org/10.1007/s12134-001-1020-1.

Liladrie, Sirena. 2010. "'Do Not Disturb/Please Clean Room': Hotel Housekeepers in Greater Toronto." *Race and Class* 52 (1): 57–69. https://doi.org/10.1177/0306396809354177.

Lindquist, Johan. 2018. "Reassembling Indonesian Migration: Biometric Technology and the Licensing of Informal Labour Brokers." *Ethnos* 83 (5): 832–49. https://doi.org/10.1080/00141844.2017.1364780.

Ljunggren, David. 2020. "Canadian Parliament Rushes through Ratification of USMCA Trade Pact." *Reuters*, March 13, 2020. https://www.reuters.com/article/us-usa-trade-usmca-canada/canadian-parliament-rushes-through-ratification-of-usmca-trade-pact-idUSKBN2102I5.

Luibhéid, Eithne. 2004. "Heteronormativity and Immigration Scholarship: A Call for Change." *GLQ: A Journal of Lesbian and Gay Studies* 10 (2): 227–35. https://doi.org/10.1215/10642684-10-2-227.

–. 2008. "Sexuality, Migration and the Shifting Line between Legal and Illegal Status." *GLQ: A Journal of Lesbian and Gay Studies* 14 (2–3): 289–315. https://doi.org/10.1215/10642684-2007-034.

Luibhéid, Eithne, and Lionel Cantú. 2005. *Queer Migrations: Sexuality, U.S. Citizenship, and Border Crossings*. Minneapolis: University of Minnesota Press.

Lujan, Omar. 2017. "The 'Other' Mexicans: Transnational Citizenship and Mexican Middle Class Migration in Toronto, Canada." PhD diss., Ryerson University.

MacLaren, Barbara. 2010. *A Policy Seminar: Managing Undocumented Migration in North America*. Ottawa: Metropolis North America.

Magalhaes, Lilian, Christine Carrasco, and Denise Gastaldo. 2010. "Undocumented Migrants in Canada: A Scope Literature Review on Health, Access to Services, and Working Conditions." *Journal of Immigrant Minority Health* 12 (1): 132–51. https://doi.org/10.1007/s10903-009-9280-5.

Mahler, Sarah J. 1995. *American Dreaming: Immigrant Life on the Margins*. Princeton, NJ: Princeton University Press.

Mahtani, Minelle. 2008. "How Are Immigrations Seen and What Do They Want to See? Contemporary Research on the Representation of Immigrants in the Canadian English-Language Media." In *Immigration and Integration in Canada in the Twenty-First Century*, edited by John Biles, Meyer Burstein, and James Frideres, 231–52. Montreal and Kingston: McGill-Queen's University Press.

Malcolm, Candice. 2016. "Scrapping Mexican Visa a Mistake." *Toronto Sun*, June 29, 2016. http://www.torontosun.com/2016/06/29/scrapping-mexican-visa-a-mistake.

Marcos, Subcomandante, and Ejército Zapatista de Liberación Nacional. 2006. *The Other Campaign/La otra campaña*. Bilingual ed. San Francisco: City Lights.

Marcus, George E., and Erkan Saka. 2006. "Assemblage." *Theory, Culture and Society* 23 (2–3): 101–6. https://doi.org/10.1177/0263276406062573.

Marsden, Sarah. 2012. "The New Precariousness: Temporary Migrants and the Law in Canada." *Canadian Journal of Law and Society* 27 (2): 209–29. https://doi.org/10.3138/cjls.27.2.209.

Mas, Susana. 2016. "Canada Drops Mexican Visa Requirement, Mexico Lifts Beef Ban." *CBC News*, June 28, 2016. http://www.cbc.ca/news/politics/trudeau-pena-nieto-bilateral-visas-beef-1.3655746.

Massey, Douglas S., Rafael Alarcon, Jorge Durand, and Humberto Gonzalez. 1987. *Return to Aztlan: The Social Process of International Migration from Western Mexico*. Berkeley: University of California Press.

Massey, Douglas S., Joaquin Arango, Graeme Hugo, Ali Kouaouci, Adela Pellegrino, and J. Edward Taylor. 1993. "Theories of International Migration: A Review and Appraisal." *Population and Development Review* 19 (3): 431–66. https://doi.org/10.2307/2938462.

Mattingly, Doreen J. 1997. "'Working Men' and 'Dependent Wives': Gender, 'Race,' and the Regulation of Migration from Mexico." In *Women Transforming Politics: An Alternative Reader*, edited by Cathy J. Cohen, Kathleen B. Jones, and Joan C. Tronto, 47–61. New York: New York University Press.

Maya, Jesús. 2012. *La Tolvanera*. Toronto: Latin American Researchers of Ontario.

–. 2013. "Pancho." In *Lumbre y Relumbre: Antologia de la poesia hispano canadiense*, edited by Julio Torres-Recinos and Margarita Feliciano, 82. Toronto: Antares.

Mayeda, Andrew. 2009. "Harper Unlikely to Bend on Visas: Official; Mexico Sore Spot." *National Post*, August 8, 2009, A6.

McGregor, Janyce. 2016a. "Beef Industry Celebrates 'Symbolic' Re-Opening of Mexican Market." *CBC News*, June 28, 2016. http://www.cbc.ca/news/politics/beef-canada-mexico-reopen-1.3656466.

–. 2016b. "Lifting Mexican Visa Rules Runs Counter to Official Advice." *CBC News*, June 23, 2016. http://www.cbc.ca/news/politics/mexico-visa-restrictions-lifting-three-amigos-1.3648757.

McKeary, Marie, and Bruce Newbold. 2010. "Barriers to Care: The Challenges for Canadian Refugees and Their Health Care Providers." *Journal of Refugee Studies* 23 (4): 523–45. https://doi.org/10.1093/jrs/feq038.

McLaughlin, Janet. 2010. "Classifying the 'Ideal Migrant Worker': Mexican and Jamaican Transnational Farmworkers in Canada." *Focaal: Journal of Global and*

Historical Anthropology 57: 79–94. https://doi.org/10.3167/fcl.2010.570106.

Mcleod, Heather, and Kathryn Ricketts. 2013. "'In Between the Fireflies': Community Art with Senior Women of Chinese Heritage around Issues of Culture, Language and Storytelling." *International Journal of Education through Art* 9 (1): 23–39. https://doi.org/10.1386/eta.9.1.23_1.

McRuer, Robert. 2006. "Introduction: Compulsory Able-Bodiedness and Queer/Disabled Existence." In *Crip Theory: Cultural Signs of Queerness and Disability*, 1–32. New York: New York University Press.

Meloni, Francesca, Cécile Rousseau, Catherine Montgomery, and Toby Measham. 2014. "Children of Exception: Redefining Categories of Illegality and Citizenship in Canada." *Children and Society* 28 (4): 305–15. https://doi.org/10.1111/chso.12006.

Méndez Pineda, Martín. 2017. "I'm a Reporter in Mexico. My Life Is in Danger. The United States Wouldn't Give Me Asylum." *Washington Post*, May 25, 2017. https://www.washingtonpost.com/posteverything/wp/2017/05/25/im-a-reporter-in-mexico-my-life-is-in-danger-the-u-s-wouldnt-give-me-asylum/?tid=ss_tw&utm_term=.4a360b665ff5.

Meng, Yunliang. 2017. "Profiling Minorities: Police Stop and Search Practices in Toronto, Canada." *Human Geographies* 11 (1): 5–23. https://doi.org/10.5719/hgeo.2017.111.1.

Menjívar, Cecilia. 2000. *Fragmented Ties: Salvadoran Immigrant Networks in America*. Berkeley: University of California Press.

–. 2006. "Liminal Legality: Salvadoran and Guatemalan Immigrants' Lives in the United States." *American Journal of Sociology* 111 (4): 999–1037. https://doi.org/10.1086/499509.

Meurrens, Steven. 2016. "Supreme Court of Canada Expands Humanitarian and Compassionate Grounds." *Canadian Immigrant*, January 6, 2016. http://canadianimmigrant.ca/news-and-views/news/supreme-court-of-canada-expands-humanitarian-and-compassionate-grounds.

Mezzadra, Sandro, and Brett Neilson. 2013. *Border as Method: Or, The Multiplication of Labor*. Durham, NC: Duke University Press.

Mojtehedzadeh, Sara. 2016a. "Wage-Theft Victims Lost $28M to Poor Enforcement, Statistics Show." *Toronto Star*, August 2, 2016. https://www.thestar.com/news/gta/2016/08/02/wage-theft-victims-lost-28m-to-poor-enforcement-statistics-show.html.

–. 2016b. "Workplace Violations Widespread in Ontario, Government Report Says." *Toronto Star*, July 27, 2016. https://www.thestar.com/news/gta/2016/07/27/workplace-violations-widespread-in-ontario-government-report-says.html.

Mojtehedzadeh, Sara, and Brendan Kennedy. 2017. "Undercover in Temp Nation." *Toronto Star*, September 8, 2017. http://projects.thestar.com/temp-employment-agencies/.

Mongia, Radhika V. 2003. "Race, Nationality, Mobility: A History of the Passport." In *After the Imperial Turn: Thinking with and through the Nation*, edited by Antoinette Burton, 196–214. Durham, NC: Duke University Press.

Morris, Carolyn. 2009. "Your Money or Your Life." *This Magazine*, April 28, 2009. https://this.org/2009/04/28/your-money-or-your-life/.

Mountz, Alison. 2004. "Embodying the Nation-State: Canada's Response to Human Smuggling." *Political Geography* 23 (3): 323–45. https://doi.org/10.1016/j.polgeo.2003.12.017.

Mueller, Richard E. 2005. "Mexican Immigrants and Temporary Residents in Canada: Current Knowledge and Future Research." *Migraciones internacionales* 3 (1): 32–56.

Mukherjee, Alok. 2008. *Victims and Witnesses without Legal Status Policy*. Toronto: Toronto Police Services Board.

Munro, Kimberly, Catherine Jarvis, Ling Yuan Kong, Vinita D'Souza, and Lisa Graves. 2013. "Perspectives of Family Physicians on the Care of Uninsured Pregnant Women." *Journal of Obstetrics and Gynaecology Canada* 35 (7): 599–605. https://doi.org/10.1016/s1701-2163(15)30880-x.

Murray, David A.B. 2015. *Real Queer? Sexual Orientation and Gender Identity Refugees in the Canadian Refugee Apparatus*. London: Rowman and Littlefield.

Mutsaers, Paul. 2014. "An Ethnographic Study of the Policing of Internal Borders of the Netherlands." *British Journal of Criminology* 54 (5): 831–48. https://doi.org/10.1093/bjc/azu033.

NACLA. 2005. "Mexican Workers since NAFTA." *NACLA Report on the Americas* 39 (1): 15. https://doi.org/10.1080/10714839.2005.11725300.

Nakache, Delphine. 2013. "The Canadian Temporary Foreign Worker Program: Regulations, Practices, and Protection Gaps." In *Producing and Negotiating Non-Citizenship: Precarious Legal Status in Canada*, edited by Luin Goldring and Patricia Landolt, 71–98.Toronto: University of Toronto Press.

Nakache, Delphine, and Paula J. Kinoshita. 2010. "The Canadian Temporary Foreign Worker Program: Do Short-Term Economic Needs Prevail over Human Rights Concerns?" IRPP Study 5. https://irpp.org/wp-content/uploads/assets/research/diversity-immigration-and-integration/new-research-article-3/IRPP-Study-no5.pdf.

National Post. 2007. "Where the Uninsured Go for Health Care." *National Post*, January 17, 2007, A12.

Ngai, Mae M. 2004. *Impossible Subjects: Illegal Aliens and the Making of Modern America*. Princeton, NJ: Princeton University Press.

Nicaragua Solidarity Network of Greater New York. 2011. "Argentine Junta's Last President Gets Life Sentence." *Weekly News Update on the Americas* 1076, April 17, 2011. http://weeklynewsupdate.blogspot.com/2011/04/wnu-1076-argentine-juntas-last.html.

Nicholls, Walter. 2013. *The DREAMers: How the Undocumented Youth Movement Transformed the Immigrant Rights Debate*. Stanford, CA: Stanford University Press.

No One Is Illegal – Toronto. 2015. *Often Asking, Always Telling: The Toronto Police Service and the Sanctuary City Policy*. Toronto: No One Is Illegal – Toronto.

Noble, Michael. 2009. *Lovely Spaces in Unknown Places: Creative City Building in Toronto's Inner Suburbs*. Toronto: Cities Centre, University of Toronto.

OHIP for All. 2016. "OHIP for All." https://ohip4all.home.blog.

Oikawa, Mona. 2000. "Cartographies of Violence: Women, Memory, and the Subjects of the Internment." *Canadian Journal of Law and Society* 15 (2): 39–68. https://doi.org/10.1017/s0829320100006360.

Olds, Kris, and Nigel Thrift. 2005. "Cultures on the Brink: Re-Engineering the Soul of Capitalism – on a Global Scale." In *Global Assemblages: Technology, Politics, and Ethics as Anthropological Problems*, edited by Aihwa Ong and Stephen J. Collier, 270–90. Malden, MA: Blackwell.

Oliver, Ranko Shiraki. 2007. "In the Twelve Years of NAFTA, the Treaty Gave to Me . . . What, Exactly?: An Assessment of Economic, Social, and Political Developments in Mexico since 1994 and Their Impact on Mexican Immigration into the United States." *Harvard Latino Law Review* 10: 53–133.

Ong, Aihwa. 2005. "Ecologies of Expertise: Assembling Flows, Managing Citizenship." In *Global Assemblages: Technology, Politics, and Ethics as Anthropological Problems*, edited by Aihwa Ong and Stephen J. Collier, 337–53. Malden, MA: Blackwell.

Ong, Aihwa, and Stephen J. Collier. 2005. "Global Assemblages, Anthropological Problems." In *Global Assemblages: Technology, Politics, and Ethics as Anthropological Problems*, edited by Aihwa Ong and Stephen J. Collier, 3–21. Malden, MA: Blackwell.

Orellana, Marjorie F., and Sarah Jean Johnson. 2012. "'Anchor Babies' and Dreams Deferred: Public Discourse about Immigrant Children and Implications for Civic and Educational Rights." *Encyclopaideia* 16 (33): 71–87.

Orr, Jackie. 2004. "The Militarization of Inner Space." *Critical Sociology* 30 (2): 451–81. https://doi.org/10.1163/156916304323072170.

Ortiz-Hernández, Luis, and Jose Arturo Granados-Cosme. 2006. "Violence against Bisexuals, Gays and Lesbians in Mexico City." *Journal of Homosexuality* 50 (4): 113–40. https://doi.org/10.1300/j082v50n04_06.

Outright Action International. 2004. "Mexico: Mexico City Amends Civil Code to Include Transgender Rights." June 15, 2004. https://www.outrightinternational.org/content/mexico-mexico-city-amends-civil-code-include-transgender-rights.

Oxman-Martinez, Jacqueline, et al. 2005. "Intersection of Canadian Policy Parameters Affecting Women with Precarious Immigration Status: A Baseline for

Understanding Barriers to Health." *Journal of Immigrant Health* 7 (4): 247–58. https://doi.org/10.1007/s10903-005-5122-2.

Paperny, Anna Mehler. 2018. "Canada Wants U.S. Cooperation in Turning Back Asylum Seekers." *Reuters*, April 30, 2018. https://www.reuters.com/article/us-canada-immigration-border/canada-wants-u-s-cooperation-in-turning-back-asylum-seekers-idUSKBN1I12AR.

Pastor, Manuel Jr., and Carol Wise. 1998. "Mexican-Style Neoliberalism: State Policy and Distributional Stress." In *The Post-NAFTA Political Economy: Mexico and the Western Hemisphere*, edited by Carol Wise, 41–81. University Park: Pennsylvania State University Press.

Pastrana, Daniela. 2016. "Los sin tierra mexicanos." *Pie de Pagina*, December 11, 2016. http://piedepagina.mx/Los-sin-tierra-mexicanos.php utm_content=buffer96901&utm_medium=social&utm_source=twitter.com&utm_campaign=buffer.

Pendleton Jiménez, Karleen. 2005. "Lengua Latina: Latina Canadians Shaping Identity and Community through Writing." PhD diss., York University.

Pérez Salazar, Juan Carlos. 2015. "Así ocurrió la peor matanza de inmigrantes en México." *BBC Mundo*, August 21, 2015. http://www.bbc.com/mundo/noticias/2014/08/140828_mexico_matanza_inmigrantes_centroamericanos_aniversario_jcps.

Pessar, Patricia, and Sarah J. Mahler. 2003. "Transnational Migration: Bringing Gender In." *International Migration Review* 37 (3): 812–46. https://doi.org/10.1111/j.1747-7379.2003.tb00159.x.

Portal for North America. 2009. "Canada's New Visa Policy." July 15, 2009. http://www.portalfornorthamerica.org/spotlight/2009/07/canada%E2%80%99s-new-visa-policy.

Portal Politico. 2017. "Artistas mexicanos lanzan en Canadá iniciativa intercultural." January 16, 2017. http://www.portalpolitico.tv/cultura/artistas-mexicanos-lanzan-en-canada-iniciativa-intercultural.

Pratt, Anna. 2005. *Securing Borders: Detention and Deportation in Canada*. Vancouver: UBC Press.

Pratt, Anna, and Sara K. Thompson. 2008. "Chivalry, 'Race' and Discretion at the Canadian Border." *British Journal of Criminology* 48 (5): 620–40. https://doi.org/10.1093/bjc/azn048.

Pratt, Anna, and Mariana Valverde. 2002. "From Deserving Victims to 'Masters of Confusion': Redefining Refugees in the 1990s." *Canadian Journal of Sociology* 27 (2): 135–61. https://doi.org/10.2307/3341708.

Preibisch, Kerry, and Evelyn Encalada Grez. 2010. "The Other Side of el Otro Lado: Mexican Migrant Women and Labor Flexibility in Canadian Agriculture." *Signs* 35 (2): 289–316. https://doi.org/10.1086/605483.

Preibisch, Kerry, and Luz Maria Hermoso Santamaria. 2006. "Engendering Labour Migration: The Case of Foreign Workers in Canadian Agriculture." In *Women, Migration and Citizenship: Making Local, National and Transnational Connections*, edited by Evangelia Tastsoglou and Alexandra Z. Dobrowolsky, 107–30. Burlington, VT: Ashgate.

Press, Jordan. 2011. "U.S. Believed New Canadian Visa Rules Would Stop Flow of Illegal Mexican Immigrants: Cable Says." *Vancouver Sun*, August 25, 2011.

Puar, Jasbir K. 2005. "Queer Times, Queer Assemblages." *Social Text* 23 (3–4): 121–40. https://doi.org/10.1215/01642472-23-3-4_84-85-121.

–. 2007. *Terrorist Assemblages: Homonationalism in Queer Times, Next Wave.* Durham, NC: Duke University Press.

Quan, Douglas. 2016. "'Ghost Consultants': How Fraudsters Con Canada's Immigration System – and Their Clients." *National Post*, January 14, 2016. http://news.nationalpost.com/news/canada/ghost-consultants-how-fraudsters-defraud-canadas-immigration-system-and-their-clients.

Queensway Carleton Hospital. 2015. "Hospital Fees for Patients Without Canadian Provincial or Federal Health Insurance." https://www.qch.on.ca/uploads/Finance/Fees%20for%20Cdns%20without%20insurance.pdf.

Razack, Sherene. 1998. "Policing the Borders of Nation: The Imperial Gaze in Gender Persecution Cases." In *Looking White People in the Eye: Gender, Race, and Culture in Courtrooms and Classrooms*, 88–129. Toronto: University of Toronto Press.

Recio, Graciela. 2002. "Drugs and Alcohol: US Prohibition and the Origins of the Drug Trade in Mexico, 1910–1930." *Journal of Latin American Studies* 34 (1): 21–42. https://doi.org/10.1017/s0022216x01006289.

Reeves, Madeleine. 2015. "Living from the Nerves: Deportability, Indeterminacy, and the 'Feel of Law' in Migrant Moscow." *Social Analysis* 59 (4): 119–36. https://doi.org/10.3167/sa.2015.590408.

Rehaag, Sean. 2008. "Troubling Patterns in Canadian Refugee Adjudication." *Ottawa Law Review* 39 (2): 335–65.

–. 2014. "2013 Refugee Claim Data and IRB Member Recognition Rates." Canadian Council for Refugees, April 14, 2014. http://ccrweb.ca/en/2013-refugee-claim-data.

–. 2017. "2016 Refugee Claim Data and IRB Member Recognition Rates." Canadian Council for Refugees, March 8, 2017. http://ccrweb.ca/en/2016-refugee-claim-data.

–. 2018. "2017 Refugee Claim Data and IRB Member Recognition Rates." Canadian Council for Refugees, March 26, 2018. http://ccrweb.ca/en/2017-refugee-claim-data.

Richard, Analiese, and Daromir Rudnyckyj. 2009. "Economies of Affect." *Journal of the Royal Anthropological Institute* 15: 57–77. https://doi.org/10.1111/j.1467-9655.2008.01530.x.

Rivera, Juan M., Scott Whiteford, and Manuel Chávez Márquez. 2009. *NAFTA and the Campesinos: The Impact of NAFTA on Small-Scale Agricultural Producers in Mexico and the Prospects for Change*. Scranton, PA: University of Scranton Press.

Robertson, Shanthi. 2018. "Migrant, Interrupted: The Temporalities of 'Staggered' Migration from Asia to Australia." *Current Sociology* 67 (2): 169–85. https://doi.org/10.1177/0011392118792920.

Robinson, Cedric J. 1983. *Black Marxism: The Making of the Black Radical Tradition*. Chapel Hill, NC: University of North Carolina Press.

Robinson, W.G. 1984. "Illegal Immigrants in Canada: Recent Developments." *International Migration Review* 18 (3): 474–85. https://doi.org/10.1177/019791838401800306.

Root, Jesse, Erika Gates-Gasse, John Shields, and Harald Bauder. 2014. "Discounting Immigrant Families: Neoliberalism and the Framing of Canadian Immigration Policy Change." RCIS Working Paper 2014/7, Ryerson Centre for Immigration and Settlement, Toronto. http://www.ryerson.ca/content/dam/rcis/RCIS-WP-Root-No2014-7.pdf.

Rose, Gillian. 2001. *Visual Methodologies*. London: Sage.

Ross, John. 2009. "Canadian Gold Mining Companies vs. Farmers, Ecologists and Indians: Undermining Mexico." *Counterpunch*, June 16, 2009. http://www.counterpunch.org/ross06162009.html.

Rotman, Maia, and Kristin Marshall. 2016. *"Unsafe" and on the Margins: Canada's Response to Mexico's Mistreatment of Sexual Minorities and People Living with HIV*. Toronto: International Human Rights Program (IHRP), Faculty of Law, University of Toronto.

Rousseau, Cécile, François Crépeau, Patricia Foxen, and France Houle. 2002. "The Complexity of Determining Refugeehood: A Multidisciplinary Analysis of the Decision-Making Process of the Canadian Immigration and Refugee Board." *Journal of Refugee Studies* 15 (1): 43–70. https://doi.org/10.1093/jrs/15.1.43.

Rousseau, Cécile, Youssef Oulhote, Mónica Ruiz-Casares, Janet Cleveland, and Christina Greenaway. 2017. "Encouraging Understanding or Increasing Prejudices: A Cross-Sectional Survey of Institutional Influence on Health Personnel Attitudes about Refugee Claimants' Access to Health Care." *PloS One* 12 (2): 1–14. https://doi.org/10.1371/journal.pone.0170910.

Ruiz-Casares, Mónica, et al. 2013. "Access to Health Care for Undocumented Migrant Children and Pregnant Women: The Paradox between Values and Attitudes of Health Care Professionals." *Maternal and Child Health Journal* 15 (1): 292–98. https://doi.org/10.1007/s10995-012-0973-3.

Rygiel, Kim. 2011. *Globalizing Citizenship*. Vancouver: UBC Press.

Saad, Samia. 2013. "The Cost of Invisibility: The Psychosocial Impact of Falling Out of Status." In *Producing and Negotiating Non-Citizenship: Precarious Legal Status in Canada*, edited by Luin Goldring and Patricia Landolt, 137–53. Toronto: University of Toronto Press.

Salter, Mark B. 2007. "Governmentalities of an Airport: Heterotopia and Confession." *International Political Sociology* 1 (1): 49–66. https://doi.org/10.1111/j.1749-5687.2007.00004.x.

Santa Ana, Otto. 2002. *Brown Tide Rising: Metaphors of Latinos in Contemporary American Public Discourse*. Austin: University of Texas Press.

Sassen, Saskia. 2010. "Incompleteness and the Possibility of Remaking Membership." Paper presented in the Centre for Diaspora and Transnational Studies Guest Lecture Series, University of Toronto, April 28, 2010.

Schwartz, Daniel. 2015. "Canada's Refugees by the Numbers: The Data." *CBC News*, October 4, 2015. http://www.cbc.ca/news/canada/canada-s-refugees-by-the-numbers-the-data-1.3240640#IRBgraph.

Scoffield, Heather. 2010. "Visa Clampdown Near for Hungarian Visitors." *Toronto Star*, January 9, 2010. http://www.thestar.com/news/canada/article/748501-visa-clampdown-near-for-hungarian-visitors.

Scott, Joan W. 1992. "'Experience.'" In *Feminists Theorize the Political*, edited by Judith Butler and Joan W. Scott, 22–40. New York: Routledge.

Scotti, Monique. 2017. "Number of Mexican Asylum Claims Spikes to Nearly 1,000 So Far This Year." *Global News*, October 3, 2017. https://globalnews.ca/news/3782274/number-of-mexican-asylum-claims-spikes-to-nearly-1000-so-far-this-year/.

Segura Loarte, Alejandro. 2007. "'Y Ahora ¿Quien Podrá Defendernos?': Maltratos a turistas y refugiados Mexicanos." *Toronto Hispano*, August 15, 2007. http://www.torontohispano.com/columnas/inmigracion/inmi27.shtml.

Seif, Hinda. 2014. "'Layers of Humanity': Interview with Undocuqueer Artivist Julio Salgado." *Latino Studies* 12 (2): 300–9. https://doi.org/10.1057/lst.2014.31.

Selley, Chris. 2017. "Should Canada Build a Wall?" *National Post*, February 18, 2017, A1.

Service Canada. 2004. "Agriculture Programs and Services: Overview." http://www.hrsdc.gc.ca/en/on/epb/agri/overview.shtml.

Sharma, Nandita. 2002. "Immigrant and Migrant Workers in Canada: Labour Movements, Racism and the Expansion of Globalization." *Canadian Woman Studies* 21 (4): 18–25.

–. 2011. "Canadian Multiculturalism and Its Nationalisms." In *Home and Native Land: Unsettling Multiculturalism: Lands, Labours, Bodies*, edited by May Chazan, Lisa Helps, Anna Stanley, and Sonali Thakkar, 85–101. Toronto: Between the Lines.

Showler, Peter. 2009. *Fast, Fair and Final: Reforming Canada's Refugee System*. Toronto: Maytree Foundation.

Sidhu, Navjeet. 2008. *The Right to Learn: Access to Public Education for Non-Status Immigrants*. Toronto: Community Social Planning Council of Toronto.

Silverman, Stephanie J. 2014. "In the Wake of Irregular Arrivals: Changes to the Canadian Immigration Detention System." *Refuge* 30 (2): 27–34. https://doi.org/10.22215/etd/2018-13376.

Simich, Laura, Fei Wu, and Sonja Nerad. 2007. "Status and Health Security: An Exploratory Study of Irregular Immigrants in Toronto." *Canadian Journal of Public Health* 98 (5): 369–73. https://doi.org/10.1007/bf03405421.

Simmons, Alan. 2010. *Immigration and Canada: Global and Transnational Perspectives*. Toronto: Canadian Scholars' Press.

Simpson, Jeffrey. 2010. "While Mexicans Fume, Canada's Reputation and Revenues Take a Hit." *Globe and Mail*, February 1, 2010. http://www.theglobeandmail.com/news/opinions/while-mexicans-fume-canadas-reputation-and-revenues-take-a-hit/article1452487/.

Sladkova, Jana. 2016. "Stratification of Undocumented Migrant Journeys: Honduran Case." *International Migration* 54 (1): 84–99. https://doi.org/10.1111/imig.12141.

Smith, Andrea. 2006. "Heteropatriarchy and the Three Pillars of White Supremacy: Rethinking Women of Color Organizing." In *Color of Violence: The Incite! Anthology*, 66–73. Cambridge, MA: South End Press.

Soennecken, Dagmar. 2013. "The Managerialization of Refugee Determinations in Canada." *Droit et société* 84 (2): 291–311. https://doi.org/10.3917/drs.084.0291.

Somerville, Siobhan B. 2005. "Sexual Aliens and the Racialized State: A Queer Reading of the 1952 U.S. Immigration and Nationality Act." In *Queer Migrations: Sexuality, U.S. Citizenship, and Border Crossings*, edited by Eithne Luibhéid and Lionel Cantú Jr., 75–91. Minneapolis: University of Minnesota Press.

Staeheli, Lynn A., et al. 2002. "Immigration, the Internet, and Spaces of Politics." *Political Geography* 21 (8): 989–1012. https://doi.org/10.1016/s0962-6298(02)00083-5.

Standing Committee on Citizenship and Immigration. 2009. "Temporary Foreign Workers and Nonstatus Workers." House of Commons, Ottawa. https://www.ourcommons.ca/DocumentViewer/en/40-2/CIMM/report-7/.

Stanley, Alison. 2014. *Free to Some: Examining the Landscape of Health Services for Uninsured Residents in Toronto*. Toronto: Toronto South Local Immigration Partnership and Canadian Centre for Victims of Torture. http://www.torontolip.com/Portals/0/Resources/Health/Free%20to%20Some%20-%20Examining%20the%20Landscape%20of%20Health%20Services%20for%20Uninsured%20Residents%20in%20Toronto.pdf.

Statistics Canada. 2009. *International Travel 2008*. Catalogue no. 66-201-x. Ottawa: Minister of Industry. https://www150.statcan.gc.ca/n1/en/pub/66-201-x/66-201-x2008000-eng.pdf?st=5RgMLykR.

–. 2013. *Immigration and Ethnocultural Diversity in Canada*. Catalogue no. 99-010-X2011001. Ottawa: Statistics Canada. https://www12.statcan.gc.ca/nhs-enm/2011/as-sa/99-010-x/99-010-x2011001-eng.pdf.

–. 2016. "Travellers to Canada by Country of Origin, Top 15 Countries of Origin (2015)." November 1, 2016. http://www.statcan.gc.ca/tables-tableaux/sum-som/l01/cst01/arts38e-eng.htm.

Steele Gray, Carolyn, Michaela Hynie, Linda Gardner, and Angela Robertson. 2010a. "Network of Uninsured Clients Study, Fact Sheet #1: Common Health Issues of the Undocumented and Uninsured." Women's College Hospital Network on Uninsured Clients, Toronto. http://www.womenscollegehospital.ca/assets/legacy/wch/pdfs/UNINSURED_FACT_SHEET_1_rev05-11-1.pdf.

–. 2010b. "Network of Uninsured Clients Study, Fact Sheet #2: Barriers to Accessing Healthcare." Women's College Hospital Network on Uninsured Clients, Toronto. http://www.womenscollegehospital.ca/assets/legacy/wch/pdfs/UNINSURED_FACT_SHEET_2_FNL.pdf.

–. 2010c. *Qualitative Research Project on Health-Care Access for the Uninsured*. Toronto: Women's College Hospital. http://www.womenscollegehospital.ca/assets/legacy/wch/pdfs/WCHNUC-Qualitative-Research-Project-on-Health-Care-Access-for-Uninsured-july-15-2010.pdf.

Strauss, Kendra, and Judy Fudge. 2013. "Temporary Work, Agencies and Unfree Labour: Insecurity in the New World of Work." In *Temporary Work, Agencies and Unfree Labour: Insecurity in the New World of Work*, edited by Judy Fudge and Kendra Strauss, 1–25. New York: Routledge.

Teelucksingh, Cheryl, and Grace-Edward Galabuzi. 2005. *Working Precariously: The Impact of Race and Immigrants' Status on Employment Opportunities and Outcomes in Canada*. Toronto: Canadian Race Relations Foundation.

Terra Networks. 2011. "La ONU pide a México que investigue asesinatos de periodistas." September 30, 2011. http://noticias.terra.com.pe/internacional/europa/la-onu-pide-a-mexico-que-investigue-asesinatos-de-periodistas,0c8dc10848ab-2310VgnVCM4000009bf154d0RCRD.html (accessed September 30, 2011).

Teves, Carolina. 2008. "Mexicanos, bajo la sombra de la imposición de visa de entrada al país." *Hispanos en Canada*. http://hispanosencanada.ca/portal/content/view/739/84/.

Thobani, Sunera. 2007. *Exalted Subjects: Studies in the Making of Race and Nation in Canada*. Toronto: University of Toronto Press.

Thompson, Elizabeth. 2009. "Made in Canada Fix for Job Crisis: Feds Prepared to Limit Immigration." *Toronto Sun*, February 11, 2009. http://www.torontosun.com/news/canada/2009/02/11/8345706-sun.html.

Toronto Board of Health. 2013. "Medically Uninsured Residents in Toronto." April 15, 2013. http://www.toronto.ca/legdocs/mmis/2013/hl/bgrd/background file-57588.pdf.

Toronto District School Board. 2007. "Summary of Decisions Regular Meeting May 16, 2007." http://www.tdsb.on.ca/wwwdocuments/students/pathways_for_success/docs/70516%20summ.pdf.

Toronto Paramedic Services. 2014. "Frequently Asked Questions." http://toronto paramedicservices.ca/frequently-asked-questions/.

Toronto Public Health and Access Alliance Multicultural Health and Community Services. 2011. *The Global City: Newcomer Health in Toronto*. https://www.toronto.ca/legdocs/mmis/2011/hl/bgrd/backgroundfile-42361.pdf.

Torpey, John C. 2000. *The Invention of the Passport: Surveillance, Citizenship, and the State*. Cambridge, UK: Cambridge University Press.

UNICEF. 2010. "At a Glance: Mexico." http://www.unicef.org/infobycountry/mexico_statistics.html (accessed May 25, 2010).

United Kingdom Foreign and Commonwealth Office. 2010. "Country Profile: Mexico." http://www.fco.gov.uk/en/travel-and-living-abroad/travel-advice-by-country/country-profile/north-central-america/mexico/?profile=all (accessed May 25, 2010).

United Way. 2011. *Vertical Poverty: Declining Income, Housing Quality and Community Life in Toronto's Inner Suburban High-Rise Apartments*. Toronto: United Way. https://www.unitedwaygt.org/document.doc?id=89.

Urquijo-Ruiz, Rita E. 2012. *Wild Tongues: Transnational Mexican Popular Culture*. Austin: University of Texas Press.

Valentine, Gill. 1998. "'Sticks and Stones May Break My Bones': A Personal Geography of Harassment." *Antipode* 30 (4): 305–32. https://doi.org/10.1111/1467-8330.00082.

Vancouver Sun. 2014. "How Tourists Acquire a Canadian Visitor's Visa." *Vancouver Sun*, September 4, 2014. http://www.vancouversun.com/tourists+acquire+Canadian+visitor+visa/10175667/story.html.

Van Houtum, Henk. 2010. "Human Blacklisting: The Global Apartheid of the EU's External Border Regime." *Environment and Planning D: Society and Space* 28 (6): 957–76. https://doi.org/10.1068/d1909.

Vasquez, L. 2009. "Visa para mexicanos: Se desvanecen las esperanzas de revertir la decisión." *El Correo Canadiense*, August 20, 2009. http://elcorreo.ca/2009/08/visa-para-mexicanos-se-desvanecen-las-esperanzas-de-revertir-la-decision/ (accessed May 9, 2011).

Vaughan-Williams, Nick. 2015. "'We Are *Not* Animals!' Humanitarian Border Security and Zoopolitical Spaces in EUrope." *Political Geography* 45: 1–10. https://doi.org/10.1016/j.polgeo.2014.09.009.

Verne, Jules. 2005. *Journey to the Center of the Earth*. Mineola, NY: Dover Publications. First published 1876 by George Routledge and Sons (London and New York).

Villegas, Francisco. 2006. "Challenging Educational Barriers: Undocumented Immigrant Student Advocates." MA thesis, San Jose State University.

–. 2013. "Getting to 'Don't Ask Don't Tell' at the Toronto District School Board: Mapping the Competing Discourses of Rights and Membership of Institutional Stakeholders." In *Producing and Negotiating Non-Citizenship: Precarious Legal Status in Canada*, edited by Luin Goldring and Patricia Landolt, 258–73. Toronto: University of Toronto Press.

–. 2016. "'Access without Fear!': Reconceptualizing 'Access' to Schooling for Undocumented Students in Toronto." *Critical Sociology* 43 (7–8): 1179–95. https://doi.org/10.1177/0896920516677352.

Villegas, Paloma E. 2013a. "Negotiating the Boundaries of Membership: Health Care Providers, Access to Social Goods and Immigration Status." In *Producing and Negotiating Non-Citizenship: Precarious Legal Status in Canada*, edited by Luin Goldring and Patricia Landolt, 221–37. Toronto: University of Toronto Press.

–. 2013b. "Migrant Illegalization and Transnational Precarities in Maya's Toronto." *Latin American Perspectives* 1 (1): 1–8.

–. 2014. "'I Can't Even Buy a Bed Because I Don't Know if I'll Have to Leave Tomorrow': Temporal Orientations among Mexican Precarious Status Migrants in Toronto." *Citizenship Studies* 18 (3–4): 277–91. https://doi.org/10.1080/13621025.2014.905269.

–. 2015a. "Fishing for Precarious Status Migrants: Surveillant Assemblages of Migrant Illegalization in Toronto, Canada." *Journal of Law and Society* 42 (2): 230–52. https://doi.org/10.1111/j.1467-6478.2015.00706.x.

–. 2015b. "Moments of Humiliation, Intimidation and Implied 'Illegality': Encounters with Immigration Officials at the Border and the Performance of Sovereignty." *Journal of Ethnic and Migration Studies* 41 (14): 2357–75. https://doi.org/10.1080/1369183x.2015.1057111.

–. 2016. "Desinformación sobre la Visa para Mexicanxs en Canadá: Un Llamado de Solidaridad ante un Pánico Moral." *Revista debate*, December 6, 2016. http://www.revistadebate.net/desinformacion-sobre-la-visa-para-mexicanxs-en-canada-un-llamado-de-solidaridad-ante-un-panico-moral/.

–. 2019a. "Bridging Borders: Teaching a Bridging Course with Precarious Status Students Transitioning to the University." In *Critical Schooling: Transformative Theory and Practice*, edited by Francisco J. Villegas and Janelle Brady, 245–68. New York: Springer.

–. 2019b. "'I Made Myself Small like a Cat and Ran Away': Workplace Sexual Harassment, Precarious Immigration Status and Legal Violence." *Journal of Gender Studies* 28 (6): 674–86. https://doi.org/10.1080/09589236.2019.1604326.

–. 2019c. "Mis Roots." In *The Reflexivity of Pain and Privilege: Auto-Ethnographic Collections of Mixed Identity*, edited by Ellis Hurd, 89–90. Rotterdam: Sense Publishers.

Vosko, Leah F. 2003. "Precarious Employment in Canada: Taking Stock, Taking Action." *Just Labour* 3: 1–5. https://doi.org/10.25071/1705-1436.163.

Vosko, Leah F., Valerie Preston, and Robert Latham, eds. 2014. *Liberating Temporariness? Migration, Work and Citizenship in the Age of Insecurity*. Montreal and Kingston: McGill-Queen's University Press.

Vukov, Tamara. 2003. "Imagining Communities through Immigration Policies: Governmental Regulation, Media Spectacles and the Affective Politics of National Borders." *International Journal of Cultural Studies* 6 (3): 335–53. https://doi.org/10.1177/13678779030063006.

Waldie, Paul, Alan Freeman, and Tara Perkins. 2007. "Windsor Braces for Refugee Tide." *Globe and Mail*, September 22, 2007, A1.

Walia, Harsha. 2013. *Undoing Border Imperialism*. Oakland, CA: AK Press.

White, Melissa Autumn. 2014. "Archives of Intimacy and Trauma: Queer Migration Documents as Technologies of Affect." *Radical History Review* 120: 75–93. https://doi.org/10.1215/01636545-2703733.

Whittington, Les. 2010. "Canadian Mining Firms Worst for Environment, Rights: Report." *Toronto Star*, October 19, 2010. http://www.thestar.com/news/canada/article/877438-canadian-mining-firms-worst-for-environment-rights-report.

Willen, Sarah S. 2007. "Toward a Critical Phenomenology of 'Illegality': State Power, Criminalization, and Abjectivity among Undocumented Migrant Workers in Tel Aviv, Israel." *International Migration* 45 (3): 8–38. https://doi.org/10.1111/j.1468-2435.2007.00409.x.

–. 2012. "Migration, 'Illegality,' and Health: Mapping Embodied Vulnerability and Debating Health-Related Deservingness." *Social Science and Medicine* 74: 805–11. https://doi.org/10.1016/j.socscimed.2011.10.041.

Wilson-Mitchell, Karline. 2013. "Midwifery Care for the Uninsured Migrating Family in Ontario." *Canadian Journal of Midwifery Research and Practice* 12 (2): 38–41.

Wilson, Ruth Marie, et al. 2011. *Working Rough, Living Poor: Employment and Income Insecurities Faced by Racialized Groups in the Black Creek Area and Their Impacts on Health*. Toronto: Access Alliance Multicultural Health and Community Services. https://accessalliance.ca/wp-content/uploads/2018/06/Access-Alliance_Working-Rough-Living-Poor-Final-Report-June-2011.pdf.

Woldemikael, Olivia. 2017. "A Crisis of Definition: Re-Humanising the Refugee." *Media Diversified*, July 7, 2017. https://mediadiversified.org/2017/07/07/a-crisis-of-definition-re-humanising-the-refugee/amp/.

Wood, Patricia K., and Liette Gilbert. 2005. "Multiculturalism in Canada: Accidental Discourse, Alternative Vision, Urban Practice." *International Journal of Urban and Regional Research* 29 (3): 679–91. https://doi.org/10.1111/j.1468-2427.2005.00612.x.

Workers' Action Centre. 2014. "New WAC Factsheet: Undocumented Workers Rights at Work." October 1, 2014. https://workersactioncentre.org/new-wac-factsheet-undocumented-workers-rights-at-work/.

Yuval-Davis, Nira. 2006. "Belonging and the Politics of Belonging." *Patterns of Prejudice* 40 (3): 197–214. https://doi.org/10.1080/00313220600769331.

Y.Z. v. Canada (Citizenship and Immigration). 2015. FC 892. https://decisions.fct-cf.gc.ca/fc-cf/decisions/en/item/110850/index.do.

Zlolniski, Christian. 2006. *Janitors, Street Vendors, and Activists: The Lives of Mexican Immigrants in Silicon Valley*. Berkeley: University of California Press.

Index

Printed and bound in Canada by Friesens
Set in Zurich, Univers, and Minion by Apex CoVantage, LLC
Copy editor: Dallas Harrison
Proofreader: Caitlin Gordon-Walker
Cover designer: John van der Woude